Easy X10 Projects for Creating a Smart Home

INDY-TECH ®

PUBLISHING

Easy X10 Projects for Creating a Smart Home

As this book is technical in nature, we recommend that a professional be consulted if you feel you have gone too far. Electronics involve electricity, which should be dealt with very carefully.

International Standard Book Number: 0-7906-1306-9

Chief Executive Officer:	Alan Symons
President:	Scott Weaver
Chief Operating Officer:	Richard White
Acquisitions Editor:	Brad Schepp
Editorial Assistant:	Dana Eaton
Copyeditor:	Hoffman Paulson Associates
Technical Editor:	Austin Instruments
Pagination Editor:	Robin Roberts
Cover Design:	Robin Roberts
Illustrations, Photos, & Drawings:	Provided by the authors, with proper permissions obtained.

Technica Pacifica Staff:	Mary Adair
	Sam Allen
	Yoko Kuramochi
	Christy Parry
	Jeff Richards
	Jacci Weller

Printed in the USA, at Ripon Community Printers, Ripon WI.

Easy X10 Projects for Creating a Smart Home

The Staff of Technica Pacifica

General Manager: Sam Allen

Writers:
Mary Adair
Sam Allen
Christy Parry
Jeff Richards

Photography:
Jeff Richards
Sam Allen
Christy Parry

Illustrations and Photoshop: Sam Allen

Design consultants:
Yoko Kuramochi
Jacci Weller

Technica Pacifica Staff Biographies

Mary Adair has a BA in history from Utah State University (1992). She has worked at Technica Pacifica for five years as a proofreader and writer. Before that, she taught English as a Second Language for two years.

Sam Allen has written scores of articles for Popular Electronics, Popular Mechanics, various computer magazines, and other technical publications. He is the author of over ten books. His skills include writing, Web site design, computer programming, and Photoshop. He graduated from Brigham Young University with a bachelor of science degree.

Yoko Kuramochi graduated from the Tokyo University of Agriculture in 1988. She was a translation coordinator for DHC Corporation and continued her study of landscape design in Tokyo for seven years before moving to the U.S. At that time, she started work as a Japanese language consultant to Technica Pacifica. Since moving to the Southwest., she has become an active proponent of xeriscape design. She also creates handmade gift cards and children's art/story books.

Christy Parry has worked for Technica Pacifica for over eight years as assistant manager, has written two courses for DHC's Japanese-to-English Technical Writing mini-course series, and has edited and proofread several others. In addition to teaching complex aspects of English grammar to Japanese students, she has worked as an English tutor for native English speakers at the local community college. She is a licensed insurance agent in the state of Utah and has extensive experience in writing and editing business documents.

Jeff Richards has worked as a newspaper journalist and photographer for the past fourteen years. A former junior high school English teacher, he has been a technical writer at Technica Pacifica in Moab since 1997. He is a graduate of the University of Utah (BA, English) and of Utah State University (BS, secondary education).

Jacci Weller has a BA from the University of California at Los Angeles in fine art (drawing and painting) and an MA from California State University at Long Beach in fine art (sculpture). Before she started working at Technica Pacifica in 1994, she worked as a public muralist in Los Angeles and taught design and drawing at Lane Community College in Oregon. In addition to working at Technica Pacifica, she continues her work as a studio artist.

Disclaimer

Electrical shock can cause severe damage and death. Before working on any electrical systems or components, turn off the circuit breaker and double check that the circuit you are working on is indeed off.

Always follow the printed installation guidelines that the manufacturer supplies when you install any electrical or X10 product.

Readers installing X10 products or other electrical devices must follow national and local electrical codes.

Always use caution when controlling appliances with X10 systems. For example, if you send an On command to a heating device, and the device is near something flammable, a fire could occur. Never use X10 to turn on a heating device that does not contain an internal auto shutoff such as a thermostat.

The author and publisher are not liable and assume no responsibility for injuries sustained during the installation of any electrical products, including X10 products, or damage caused during installation or use of any electrical products, including X10 products.

Table of Contents

Preface 13

What is it like to live in a smart home? We interview a family that has ten years of experience living in a home controlled by X10 devices. Find out what they like, what they don't like, and how different family members react to the technology.

Introduction 19

We give a brief description of X10 and how it works. We discuss the history of X10, where the industry is today, and what to expect in the future.

Chapter 1. Up and Running in Twenty Minutes 23

We walk you through the steps to add some basic home control features in less than twenty minutes without any wiring. This system uses modules that simply plug into existing outlets or screw into light sockets.

Buying the Parts 24
Mini-controller 25
Lamp Module 26
Screw-in Lamp Module 26
Local Control 27
Appliance Module 28
Installing the System 28
Dressing Up the Controllers 32
Magic Box Project 32

Chapter 2. Expanding and Automating Your System 35

Building on the basic system installed in Chapter 1, we give examples of ways to expand the system and show how to install a mini-timer that controls simple automated tasks, and a photocell controller.

Holiday Decorations 35
Fountains 36
Low-Voltage Outdoor Lighting...37
Fans, Air Conditioners, and Heaters..37
Audio...37
Maxi-controller...38
Automate the System 38
Mini-timer..39
Using the Mini-timer 39
Photocell Controller 41

Chapter 3. Wireless Control...........43

Add wireless remote control to your basic system. We describe how to choose and install wireless components that let you control any X10 module in your house from a handheld remote.

Base Transceiver..43
Keychain Remote...46
Handheld Remote 47
Universal Remote...48
Wireless Wall Switch..49
Wireless Motion Detector 51

Chapter 4. Hardwired Controls: Basics...........55

If you want to go beyond a basic system, you will need to replace some wall switches or outlets with X10 controllers. We show you how to install them with step-by-step directions.

General Instructions...55
Definitions 56
Removing the Original Switch or Outlet 57
Installing a New Module 60
Light Switches...61
Two-wire Switch Modules 62
Installing the Switch 63
Outlet Modules 64

Chapter 5. Hardwired Controls: Advanced 67

This chapter shows how to manage more complicated wiring procedures, such as installing fixture relay modules and transmit-only wall controllers. It also discusses installing three-way and four-way switches.

Neutral Wire 67
Transmit-Only Wall Controller 69
Fixture Relay Modules 70
Converting a Switch-Leg-Only Box to Hot and Neutral............................71
Feed-Through Outlet Modules 73
Three-Way Switches 74
Master/Companion Switches 75
Four-Way Switches 75

Chapter 6. High-End Modules...77

There are many modules on the market that have special capabilities. We describe these modules, tell you what you can do with them, and show you how to install them.

Advanced Features **77**
At-the-switch dimming 78
Soft Start 78
Resume Dim / Preset On-Level 78
Scene Lighting 78
Three-way Ready 78
AGC / Noise Reduction 79
Nondimming Switches 79
Electronic Addressing 79
Two-way X10..79
Installing High-End Modules **80**
Finding the Hot Wire 81
Switches that Require a Neutral Connection 82
Three-way Switches...83

Chapter 7. Low-Voltage Modules 89

This chapter discusses modules that control devices that use low voltage. We give you ideas on how you can use these modules and tell you how to install them.

Universal Relay Module 90
Powerflash Module 91
Multiple Relay Controller 92
Projects **92**
Sprinkler System Rain Delay 92
Gas Fireplace Log Remote 94
Remote Doorbell 94
Remote Thermostat 95
Code Translation 96
Using Switches with Low-Voltage Modules 96
Garage Door Control 97
Status Indicator Light 98
Close Only Switch 99
Speaker Mute 100
Box-Lid Switch 101

Chapter 8. Wireless Home Security 103

You can use X10 devices to increase the security and safety of your home. We show you how to add a security system that incorporates motion detectors, door/window sensors, and more.

Basic X10 Security **103**
Security Console 104
Handheld Security Remote 105
Keychain Remote 106
Installing a Basic X10 Security System **106**
Door/Window Sensors 108
Special Wiring for Multiple Window and Door Combinations 111
Glass-breakage detectors 112
Motion Detectors 113
Programming the Console to Make Calls 114
Outdoor Motion Sensor with Floodlights 115
More Sophisticated Systems **116**

Chapter 9. Infrared Interface..119

Devices that use infrared remote controls can be integrated into an X10 system by using IR interfaces. These units convert X10 commands to IR signals to control audio, video, and other home electronics.

Setting up the IR Interface **120**
Programming..**122**
Using the bright/dim Buttons 124
Programming Troubleshooting..125
Macros..125
Using Probes **126**
Do-It-Yourself IR Interface 128
X10 IR Mini-controller 129

Chapter 10. Computer Control...131

You can use your computer to program automated events. The computer control system adds more flexibility than a stand-alone timer module. We describe different types of systems and explain their pros and cons.

Choosing a Computer Power Line Interface Module **132**
Software..**133**
Module Selection 134
Timed Events 134
Macros..135
Logging 135
Basic Software Setup..135
Advanced Software 139

Chapter 11. Macros and Scenes...141

Using a computer or a stand-alone controller, you can program complex events involving several different devices. This allows you to set several devices to turn on, off or dim in response to a single button.

Macros **141**
Planning a Macro 141
Triggers 143
Time 143
Sunrise/Sunset 143
Change in Status of a Device 144
Conditionals 144
Code Translation 144
Scenes 145

Chapter 12. Controlling Your Home by Phone, Internet, or Voice 151

When you're away from home, you can use a telephone interface or a computer connected to the Internet to control X10 devices. We also discuss how to make your home talk to you and respond to voice commands.

Touch-Tone Controller **152**
Internet Control **154**
Controlling Heating and Cooling systems 154
Controlling Hot Tubs and Water Heaters 156
Voice Announcements and Voice control **156**
Computer-Generated Voice Announcements 157
Controlling X10 with Voice Recognition 158
Do-It-Yourself Voice Control Module 159

Chapter 13. Troubleshooting 161

X10 is simple and reliable, but there are times when something goes wrong. Usually, it is simple to fix. We'll guide you through the troubleshooting procedure and tell you some of the most common problems and how to fix them.

Problems **161**
Interference 161
Attenuation 161
Signal Conflict 163
Diagnosis **163**
Solutions **165**
Plug-in Noise Filter 165
Plug-in Coupler 165
Automatic Gain Control 166
Booster Repeater 166
Whole-house Blocking Coupler 167
Case Studies 167

Afterword: Example Home Theater System 171

Appendix A: X10 in Depth 175

This appendix discusses how X10 works and technical specifications.

X10 Operation **175**
Receiving modes 177
Three-phase X10 177
X10 Command Codes 177
X10 Minimum Specification 179
X10 RF Remote Frequency 179

Appendix B. Suppliers 181

Preface:
Living in a Smart Home

Interview with an X10 Homeowner

We've all seen news stories about celebrities' smart homes where computers and remote controls activate a myriad of amazing features. Usually, you get the impression that you must be a millionaire to have such a home. Most people don't realize that they can add many smart home features to their own home easily and affordably by using X10 devices.

What would it be like to have X10 in your home? To help you get an idea, let's have a peek inside the home of a family that has been using X10 for the past decade.

Arriving home from work in the early evening in a shady residential area, Rob pulls his car into the driveway. He reaches up near the visor and clicks a button on a small remote control. The home's porch light comes on (fig. P-1). Another click and the front room lights also turn on. Inside the front door, Rob reaches for a small box on a side table and pushes another button. Melodic background music fills the air.

When his wife Diane arrives home, she pushes a button on another remote control and the family room lights come on. As she sits on the couch in the family room, she reaches for the master remote, presses a button, and turns on the TV to watch the news (fig. P-2). The room feels a bit warm, so she presses another button on the remote and turns on the air conditioner. Later, after the room has cooled down, she'll be able to turn off the air conditioner with another couple of presses of the remote control.

Getting Started
"It all started when I just wanted to turn on a light in the house from my car," says Rob, holding the worn tan remote purchased nearly a decade ago (fig. P-3).

Fig. P-1: With an X10 keychain remote, you can turn on your porch light from inside your car.

Fig. P-2: A universal X10 remote.

Fig. P-3: This old keychain remote still works.

"I saw a kit on sale at the local Radio Shack that included everything I would need to control one light from a keychain remote. I didn't realize at the time I was starting a smart-home project, but once I started using X10, I just kept finding more applications." Nowadays, Rob has dozens of more sophisticated X10 products, including a variety of plug-in and screw-in modules, wireless controllers, and computer controls. Rob bought much of his original X10 equipment at the local Radio Shack electronics store, but lately he has also ordered modules and controllers over the Internet.

Although Rob has invested hundreds of dollars in X10 products over the past decade, his initial start-up cost was under $30. "You don't have to start with hundreds of dollars' worth of equipment," he notes. "You just start out with a couple of modules for the things you want to control, like your porch light or your front room light, and add a simple X10 control device to turn them off and on. You can always add more things later, as you need or can afford them. I started my system for less than $30, and today you can still start up for about the same amount, especially if you shop around."

He adds, "I really like the fact that with X10, everything is compatible. It doesn't matter what brand a device is, it will work with any other brand. I always shop around to get the best deal. Sometimes you can get modules for a third of their regular price by buying them in bundles of five or six."

Rob also notes that there are several X10 Web sites that offer introductory package deals. For example, one leading X10 company offers four different modules, a controller, and a remote for around the same price as three modules purchased separately.

Favorite Things
Rob says the convenience of being able to control everything with one remote is one of his favorite things about X10. "The master remote has buttons for TV, VCR, DVD, and X10. I just have to remember the unit code number," he notes. "The front room is unit code 2, so if I want to turn off the lights in the front room, I just push the 'X10' button, then '2,' and then 'channel down' for 'off.' If I want to dim the lights, I simply push 'volume down'."

There are several reasons that this family uses X10
It saves time. "I don't have to get up and turn off all the lights in the house. I just reach over and hit the **All Off** button when I go to bed at night," says Rob. "Anytime we have to get up and go in another room to turn something on or off, we think, 'Aha! We can use X10 for this'."

It saves energy. "Sometimes the kids leave the lights on in the family room or the front room, and if they were the last to leave the house, those lights would just stay on all day," notes Rob. "I programmed the system to turn off the lights in those two rooms every hour. If someone is in the room, they just turn the lights back on. If not, the lights stay off. You can also program your house so that things that consume energy are either off or turned down low during the day when everyone is gone. This makes a difference on the electric bills because the power company charges extra for electricity usage during peak energy rate hours. We try to keep our electricity consumption at a minimum during those hours, and X10 helps."

It adds to the home's atmosphere. X10 also controls the family's stereo system with speakers in multiple rooms piping in soothing music.

They keep their living room phone in a cleverly disguised box with a switch that automatically turns off the background music when the lid is lifted. "When the phone rings, I open the box and the music goes off," says Rob. The music system itself is housed in a hallway closet, with speakers hardwired to each of five rooms around the house. In each room, the speakers can be turned off or on individually via an X10 command.

If I'm in living room and want to listen to music but my wife is in the family room watching TV, I can mute the speakers in the family room so the music won't disturb her," Rob notes. "The music stays on in the living room where I can listen to it while reading a magazine or newspaper."

Fig. P-4: The fountain in the backyard is controlled by an X10 module. It can be programmed by computer to come on at preset times.

Even the fountain in the backyard is controlled by X10. It comes on automatically when someone walks by it and can also be turned on or off with a switch mounted on the wall by the patio (fig. P-4). "Our cat enjoys getting a drink from the fountain, so we have the computer turn on the fountain several times a day while we are gone to give the cat fresh water," says Rob.

It's fun to show off. "Sometimes it's just fun to impress your guests," Rob explains. "One evening we were talking to friends in the living room and it started to get dark. I have a controller in a small decorative box near my chair, so I nonchalantly opened the box and turned on the room lights. Our friends were duly impressed and their little girl exclaimed, 'I want a magic box like that in our house!' Since then, we call that controller our magic box" (fig. P-5).

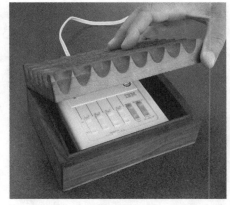

Fig. P-5: The family call the controller "our magic box"

The Whole Family Enjoys It

Jenny, at thirteen the youngest in the household, enjoys showing off the system to her friends when they come over. "They think it's cool and they usually wish they had something like it at home. It's funny, but I don't even think about X10 stuff at home because I've grown up using it. I notice it more when I go to my friends' homes and they don't have it. Their parents yell at them when they accidentally leave the lights or the TV on. Things like that turn off automatically at my house."

"We like it," says Gary, sixteen, the older of the family's two children. "We've had it for so long, we don't even think about it anymore. We use [the X10 system] just like other people use regular light switches."

Rob's wife Diane likes the fact that they can turn off the house lights, TV, and sound system after they have climbed into bed for the night. "We don't have to worry about getting up to turn off anything," Diane observes. "It's really nice not to have to get out of bed and turn off everything in the house." She smiles as she thinks back to the early days when Rob had just installed X10 switches. One evening, someone in another room hit the **All Off** button on a controller and every light in the house went off, plunging them into darkness. Diane remembers exclaiming, "Can't we just have regular light switches in this house?!" However, she says she has since retracted that comment many times. "I'd never go back now. I can't imagine having to go around the house turning off all the things the kids leave on, and I love being able to turn the air-conditioning on and off from bed" (fig. P-6).

Diane says that she probably uses the system more than anyone else. "I really like being able to listen to music no matter which room I am in," she says.

Another of Diane's favorite applications is "vacation mode," in which all the lights can be set to come on at certain times to mimic the typical patterns used when people are home. The computer or timer controllers have a security feature that will randomize the on/off times within a range around the set time, so that the lights don't come on and go off at exactly the same time every night (fig. P-7).

Diane also says that she enjoys being able to turn on all of the family's holiday decorations (particularly during the Christmas and Halloween seasons) with a single button (fig. P-8). "It doesn't really matter where you plug them in, any controller in the house will turn them all on or off," she says. Remembering the code numbers hasn't been a problem; the family uses a system of small stickers on each of the controllers to identify what each number controls.

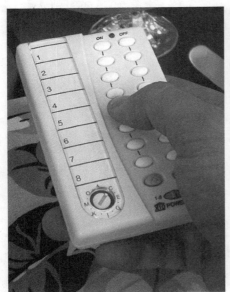

Fig. P-6: You don't have to go around the house turning off all the things the kids leave on when you have an X10 remote nearby.

Fig. P-7: To set the house to "vacation mode" the timer controller has a security feature that will randomize the on/off times within a range around the set time, so that the lights don't come on and go off at exactly the same time every night.

Fig. P-8: X10 makes controlling holiday decorations easy. You can control them with a single button on a remote control and You can program a timer or your computer to turn them on and off.

In the winter, Rob sets up an electric heater in the garage and plugs it into an appliance module. He has programmed the computer interface so that the heater comes on about thirty minutes before he's ready to leave for work. "It makes the car easier to start and takes the chill off the air in the car. It's more pleasant to start the drive in a car that is already warm inside." After Rob leaves for work, the computer turns the heater off.

X10 to the Rescue

Recently, Rob overheard one of his coworkers, a man named Jim, complaining that he had to go out every evening to plug in a heat lamp in his chicken coop and again every morning to unplug it. The coop, which houses a dozen chickens, is about sixty feet away from Jim's house. Rob recommended an appliance module to control the 350 watt infrared heat lamp and a photocell controller. Jim was able to set up the system in a matter of minutes. He plugged in the photocell controller and placed it on his bedroom windowsill where it could respond to the outdoor light. Now Jim's chicken coop heat lamp comes on every evening at dusk and turns off at dawn. "All Jim needs now is a way to feed and water his chickens automatically," says Rob with a grin.

X10 also came to the rescue of Rob's next-door neighbor, who routinely left his carport light on twenty-four hours a day. When Rob mentioned it to the neighbor, a retired man who lives alone, the man said he didn't mean to leave it on all the time; it was just difficult for him to reach the pull-chain fixture. Rob told the neighbor (who had never before heard of X10) about the technology, and the problem was soon solved. Rob helped his neighbor install a screw-in lamp module and a timer controller. The light now goes off around 10 o'clock each night. The neighbor has since added several devices to his own X10 system.

Expanding the System

Rob says the family started their X10 system small, and they have added to it over the years. "I like how interchangeable it is," he says. "You can start with just the basics and add on as needed, without needing electrical expertise or any extra wiring. You just plug in the module anywhere in the house, and you can put the controller anyplace else in the house."

Rob started with a simple remote light controller ten years ago, but after about five years, he decided to add computer control.

"Setting the computer control to perform certain macros [an assigned series of tasks] may sound difficult, but it's actually relatively easy," Rob notes. Most computer controls on the market are easy to program (fig. P-9). Not only that, most have a battery-powered memory-retention feature, so that if the power goes out, you won't lose your programming. Also, even if you shut down your computer, all programmed events will still occur. Once the date and geographic coordinates have been input, most computer controllers will also remember the year-round sunrise and sunset times for that particular location, enabling lights to be programmed on the basis of those times.

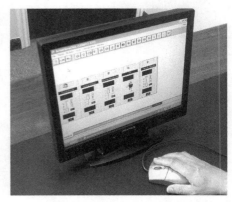

Fig. P-9: Using an X10 computer interface, you can program your computer to control up to 256 devices, including macros that control devices with a single command.

Cost and Reliability

Rob estimates that his total out-of-pocket cost over a nine-year period is still under $1,500, which translates to an investment of less than $150 per year. "The most I've ever spent at one time was when I added a computer interface," he recalls. " At that time, it cost about $150 with software, but nowadays you can get one for much less."

Even after nearly a decade of moderately heavy use, most of the family's original X10 equipment is still in use. "I'm still using the same controllers I started with nine years ago," says Rob. "I just use them in different ways. I've unplugged things and swapped them with different devices over the years. The nice thing about it is that any of the old modules can still be reprogrammed and reused any way you want."

Wish List for the Future

Rob says his next X10 project will be to create a macro for watching movies. "If we decide it's time to watch a movie, we can simply press a button and the family room will go into 'home theater' mode," he envisions. "The lights will dim, the drapes will close, the TV and DVD player will both turn on. The background music will turn off, and we'll be ready to sit down and watch the movie. Maybe I'll even set up the popcorn popper to start popping automatically."

There are still many other applications that they haven't tried. For example, they might add a home security system (with motion-activated lights and alarms, electric door locks, or cameras). Other X10 applications that Rob and his family may try include weather-based sprinkler system control, kitchen appliance control (dishwasher, slow cooker, coffeemaker, microwave oven, etc.), electric drapes or blinds, voice-activated control, and telephone-activated control.

"There really is so much that you can do. X10 products can be used to control virtually any electrical device," says Rob. "I find them easy to install, easy to control, and, best of all, affordable. The possibilities are endless. Some things, like voice activation, might not seem too useful or practical, but you never know, in a couple of years I might be talking to my house. And I'll bet it could talk back. Wouldn't it be nice if my house could remind me to wheel the garbage cans out to the curb on Monday nights?"

Introduction

Purchasing this book is the first step toward understanding everything you need to know about how X10 works and how to install X10 devices and modules in your home. In the first few chapters, we'll show you how to control lights and appliances with plug-in modules that don't require extra wiring. In later chapters, we'll introduce you to basic wiring techniques and show you how to wire more complicated X10 devices. We'll also teach you how to program your computer to control X10 devices and lights, and we'll talk about home security measures that use X10.

Let's start off with some basics about X10 technology. X10 is a type of power line control (PLC) protocol, which is a communications protocol that enables electronic devices to communicate over standard 120V house wiring. PLC systems use the existing house wiring to carry control signals. This allows you to set up a home control system quickly without having to add additional wiring.

How did X10 start? Pico Electronics, Ltd., a firm established in Glenrothes, Scotland, by a group of engineers, first developed this technology. In the early 1970s, the company mainly developed integrated circuits (ICs) for electronic calculators. The company gave each of their development projects a number (X-1 for experiment 1, X-2 for experiment 2, and so on). X-1 through X-8 all involved the development of calculator ICs.

When the price of calculator ICs fell, Pico Electronics looked for ways to branch out. For project X-9, the company, in partnership with BSR (British Sound Reproduction), developed the Accutrac, an automatic record changer. The Accutrac was controlled by a remote control that used ultrasonic signals. This feature of the Accutrac led to the company's next project, using remote control for appliances and lights: experiment 10, or X-10.

Engineers started working on X10 in 1975. In 1978, the first X10 products became available in the United States. Radio Shack was the first retailer to carry the products and is still a major retailer of X10 products. The earliest X10 systems simply had a command console, a lamp module, and an appliance module. Soon after, the company developed a wall switch module, and later, an X10 timer. The system was first called the BSR System X10 and later the X10 Powerhouse System.

In 1997, the original patent for X10 expired. As a result, several companies now manufacture X10-compatible products. Although the home automation industry has been fragmented for years, many companies are shifting toward providing integrated home network solutions that incorporate existing protocols like X10 along with newly developing technologies. This is helping X10 and home automation products in general move toward greater acceptance and mainstream use.

X10 products are easy to install, program, and use. X10 provides simple product solutions at relatively low cost, following established industry-wide standards. With many modules now costing less than $10 apiece, X10 is by far the cheapest option for home automation. High-end modules cost more but should come down in price, just as the regular modules have done.

Another advantage of X10 is that power outlets in existing homes are far more numerous than phone jacks, allowing users to start building their home networks anywhere in the house, without needing any extra wiring.

What can you control in your home with X10? The most useful application of X10 is the ability to control lights. You can use X10 for things as simple as turning on a single porch light at a certain time each night and off again at midnight, but you can also use it for more complicated lighting scenarios; for example, setting different lighting levels in one room all at the touch of a single button.

You can control how simple or how complicated a system is according to what you want. The real beauty of X10 is the ability to start with a simple system and then gradually expand it into a sophisticated control system as your needs change. A sophisticated system might incorporate the following: You could program the lights and devices in your smart home to adjust themselves constantly in response to certain events or other changes in the house. You could have motion sensors track a person's movements around the interior of the home, and you could have X10 regulate lights, temperature, and airflow accordingly. You could also set up your family room for instant "home theater mode." If a person sits down in a recliner in front of the television and presses the On button on the remote control for the DVD player, you could have X10 immediately dim the lights to a preset level and turn on both the DVD player and the TV.

The home automation market has grown steadily over the past couple of decades, but it has not yet reached true "mass market" status. However, there are already well over 100 million X10 modules in American homes, and the home automation market (already with nearly $2 billion in annual sales as of 2004) is poised to nearly double in size within the next few years as X10 becomes more mainstream. As it does so, the variety and versatility of available X10 products is also expected to increase. For example, many two-way modules are still relatively pricey now, but they should drop in price as they become easier and cheaper to make. Two-way X10 modules also allow for increased reliability, since they can provide confirmation that the action requested via an X10 signal did in fact take place. One of the major advantages of X10 is that its intercompatibility allows new products to be used alongside old ones. Once you buy an X10 module, you will be able to use it in any X10-based system in the future, even if you later add more-sophisticated controlling systems and other components. As homeowners expand their systems, the older one-way modules and newer two-way X10 modules will always be compatible with each other. Just as they have traditionally done in the past, X10 users will be able to keep finding new uses for their old modules.

Although X10 was originally designed as a one-way protocol only, the functionality and versatility of X10 modules have increased dramatically over the years. In the future, home appliances and other devices are expected to become "smarter," with the built-in ability to communicate with each other and perform certain tasks automatically, with little or no user intervention. For example, an entire home could be programmed to go from "unoccupied" to "occupied" mode, either via an automatic timer system or by a simple event trigger, such as clicking on the garage door opener when coming home from work.

A number of other home networking protocols have been developed in recent years. Such protocols will probably not replace X10, but rather expand on it. For example, there are systems in development that can link to and communicate with devices via several different means, including 120VAC power line, twisted-pair cable, coaxial cable, radio frequency, and infrared signals. Even though such integrated systems will have more advanced capabilities than a simple X10-only system, they will still use X10 signals to communicate with any X10 modules or devices that are connected via power lines. In other words, rather than being phased out by newer technological advances, X10 is being incorporated by them.

In addition, other networking protocols are fairly expensive, especially for the middle-class consumer. X10, with a proven track record dating back nearly thirty years, remains the least expensive and most versatile option available to the average do-it-yourself homeowner.

Earlier instances where competing technologies have battled for market dominance have shown that the product with the greatest installed base generally wins out in the end, as was the case in the classic VCR battle between VHS and Beta in the early 1980s. Among home automation products, the X10 protocol is the most prevalent, with an already strong foothold in millions of homes across the United States and in other areas of the world. Any new technologies designed to improve the capabilities of end-user home networks will almost certainly need to be able to communicate using the X10 protocol.

The personal computer is likely to emerge as the central control hub of the house, integrating entertainment media (movies, TV, music, etc.) with the universal control of household lights and appliances. A good example of how the older X10 technology is being incorporated into new methods of home control is newly developed software that transforms X10 signals to HTML and uploads them automatically onto a password-protected Web site, which the home owner can access from anywhere on the Internet. This is essentially taking home-computer control a major step further. Under such a setup, users are able to visit their home's own dedicated Web site and monitor and control virtually every electrical or electronic device in their homes, including heating and air conditioning, lights, appliances, sprinklers, and security systems. The possibilities truly are endless. Although controlling systems and software may change and evolve over time, the products at the very backbone of X10—the modules and controllers plugged into the home's electrical supply—are likely to remain a useful and integral part of nearly every home automation system.

You're now ready for the first steps toward acquiring home automation. In the first chapter, we'll discuss how you can be up and running with X10 in just twenty minutes.

Chapter 1

Up and Running in Twenty Minutes

In this chapter, we'll walk you through the steps to add basic home control features in less than twenty minutes without having to add any wiring. This system uses modules that simply plug into existing outlets or screw into light sockets. This chapter will also introduce the concepts used in more complex systems and provide installation procedures for the following modules: lamp module, appliance module, lamp-base module, and mini-controller (fig. 1-1).

One of the great things about X10 technology is its scalability. You can start with a small system and add to it at any time. All of the components you buy for the small system will still be useful in a larger one, so there is no duplication of effort if you expand later. Another benefit to starting with a small system is that you can use it in a home or apartment that you are renting, since you don't have to modify existing wiring. Then, when you move, you can take your home automation system with you.

How does X10 work? An X10 controller sends a low-voltage coded signal embedded in the AC sine wave (fig. 1-2).

X10 receivers perform a programmed action when they receive the coded signal. Typically the controller sends **On/Off** and **Dim/Bright** signals to modules that control light fixtures and appliances. Special-purpose receivers can be adapted to control almost any type of electronic device. Because this protocol is an industry standard, different companies offer compatible products (fig. 1-3).

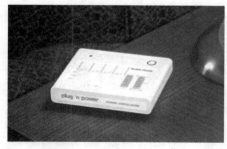

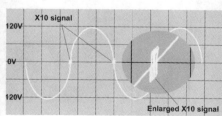

Fig. 1-1: Using mini-controllers and lamp and appliance modules, you can add home control features in less than twenty minutes without having to add any wiring.

Fig. 1-2: An X10 controller sends a low-voltage coded signal embedded in the AC sine wave.

Fig. 1-3: Because this protocol is an industry standard, several different companies offer compatible products; all the lamp moduless shown here are compatible with the X10 module.

23

In fact, there are several major manufacturers of X10 products, and these products are available under various brand names in stores around the country, including Radio Shack, Lowe's, and a few other stores that carry electric and electronic products. Many companies also sell X10 products via Internet Web sites (like www.smarthome.com and www.X10.com). For a complete list, please see the appendix.

In the X10 standard, there are sixteen house codes and sixteen unit codes. In this chapter, we'll discuss how to use codes 1–8. The next chapter discusses expanding this basic system to codes 9–16. More sophisticated systems require certain groupings of codes, so it's a good idea to follow the groupings discussed in this handbook. As you become familiar with the products available and the capabilities of the various types of equipment, you'll probably want to use different groupings, but for now, in this simple starter system, we'll group the codes on the basis of the capabilities of the mini-controllers (fig. 1-4). A mini-controller can control codes 1–8.

For a simple system, all of the modules use the same house code. Later we'll show you how to expand your system using different house codes. With the combination of house code and unit code, there are 256 different addresses available. Most modules are preset to house code A. Generally there is no reason to change the house code. However, if your lights seem to have a mind of their own after you install your system, it may be that one of your neighbors also has an X10 system on house code A. In that case, just switch to another house code. In chapter 13, we'll show you how to block signals from your neighbor's house, but this is only necessary if you plan to install a large system that uses multiple house codes.

X10 signals continue over the power lines until they reach a transformer. The power transformer blocks the X10 signal. Transformers are typically mounted on a power pole or in a large green box on the ground (fig. 1-5).

They typically deliver power to three to five houses. X10 equipment in any of the houses served by the same transformer can be controlled from any of the other houses as long as the house codes are set the same. This can actually be a useful property because it allows you to control modules in an unattached garage or home office. For example, you can control the light in the garage even if there is no physical connection with the house.

Buying the Parts

In this example project, we are going to add remote control capability to three rooms in a typical suburban house. To complete this project, you will need to buy three mini-controllers, five lamp modules, one appliance module, and one screw-in lamp module (fig. 1-6).

  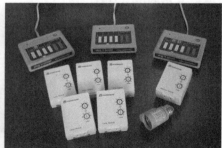

Fig. 1-4: As you plan your system, try to assign the unit codes logically. Here is a plan of the example house we are using. We will assign codes in the living room and dining room area to the 1-4 range and codes in other areas of the house to the 5-8 range.

Fig. 1-5: Power Lines and Transformers.

Fig. 1-6: Here are all the X10 products you will need to complete this project.

Several companies sell X10-compatible devices. Any device labeled X10-compatible will work in your system. Because all X10 modules are intercompatible, you can shop around for the best price. You should be able to buy the components for this starter system for around $100.

In this chapter we will cover only the basic, inexpensive types of modules. In later chapters we will introduce modules that have more advanced features. You should probably read the whole book before you buy the parts; you may decide to spend a little more initially to buy the more advanced modules.

There is probably a Radio Shack store within a few miles of your house. They sell their own line of X10 products called Plug 'n Power. A few times a year, they run a sale on Plug 'n Power modules, so watch their flyers. Most Radio Shack stores stock the basic modules. They can order the more specialized modules and have them for you in about a week. Large home centers may also stock the basic modules (fig. 1-7). If you don't see them in the electrical department, check in the home security department. For the best prices and selection, you can buy through several Internet Web sites that specialize in X10 products. Please see the appendix for a complete list of these sites.

Fig. 1-7: You can find X10 modules at large home centers and electronics stores. Look in the electrical or home security departments.

Mini-controller

The mini-controller is the remote control that sends commands to the receiver modules (fig. 1-8).

It plugs into any 120VAC outlet. It has six rocker switches and a rotary dial that sets the house code. The first four switches control modules set to individual codes. There is a slide switch below the rocker switches. With the slide switch in the first position, the four rocker switches control codes 1–4; if you change the slide switch to the second position, the rocker switches control codes 5–8. The fifth switch is the **Dim/Bright** control. To use this function, you first select the device to be controlled by pressing the **On** side of the rocker for the individual code; then press **Dim** or **Bright**. As long as you hold down the rocker, the light will get progressively brighter or dimmer. The sixth switch controls the **All On/All Off** function. When you press the **On** side of this switch, all lamp modules set to the same house code as the controller will turn on. Appliance modules will not turn on with this function. This is a safety feature because appliance modules may control devices that you wouldn't want to turn on unintentionally. Pushing the **Off** side of the switch turns off all modules with the same house code, including appliance modules. This is a nice feature to use as you leave the house. You can press the **All Off** button and turn off all the lights and appliances that you have under X10 control.

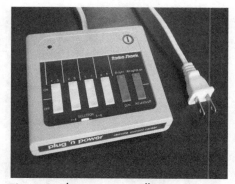

Fig. 1-8: The mini-controller is a remote control that sends commands to the receiver modules. The rotary dial in the upper right corner sets the house code. The first four switches control modules set to individual codes. The slide switch below the rocker switches changes the range from 1-4 to 5-8. The fifth switch is the **Dim/Bright** control. The sixth switch controls the **All On/Off**.

Lamp Module

The lamp module is a small box with a two-pin polarized plug and outlet built in (fig. 1-9). It is about the size of the plug-in transformers used on many electronic devices. There are two dials on the face of the module. One sets the house code, and the other sets the unit code. The module typically is rated at 300 watts. This means that you can control up to three 100-watt bulbs or any combination that adds up to 300 watts. Lamp modules respond to the **On/Off** and **Dim/Bright** commands and act as dimmer switches. They use an electronic type of switch that operates silently. Lamp modules can only be used with incandescent lights. The electronic switching will not work with fluorescent lights, low-voltage lights, electronic devices, or appliances. Severe damage to the module and the controlled device can occur if you attempt to use a lamp module with anything other than incandescent lights. To control these devices, use an appliance module.

Screw-in Lamp Module

The screw-in lamp module fits into a standard light socket and has a socket for a lightbulb. It is useful for converting built-in light fixtures that can't use the wall-plug-type lamp module. There are two types of screw-in lamp modules. The larger of the two has a house code and a unit code dial that can be manually set to the desired code (fig. 1-10).

This type will act as a dimmer in response to the **Dim/Bright** command from the controller. The smaller type of screw-in lamp module has no external controls (fig. 1-11).

To program it, you send three consecutive signals from the controller immediately after it is powered on for the first time. This programming is stored in nonvolatile memory, so even after a power outage, the programming remains. These modules do not have a dimmer function. Because there are no external controls, this unit is rated for outside use. These units are for use only with incandescent lights; even though a compact fluorescent bulb will screw into the unit, do not use it, or damage to the controller and the light may occur.

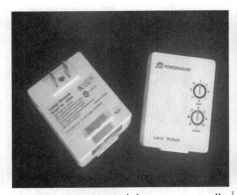

Fig. 1-9: Lamp modules are typically rated at 300 watts. They responded to the **On/Off, Dim/Bright,** and **All On/Off** commands. Lamp modules can only be used with incandescent lights.

Fig. 1-10: This screw-in lamp module fits into a standard light socket and has a socket for a lightbulb. It has a house code and a unit code dial that can be set to the desired code manually. This type will act as a dimmer in response to the **Dim/Bright** command from the controller.

Fig. 1-11: This type of screw-in lamp module has no external controls. To program it, you send three consecutive signals from the mini-controller immediately after it is powered on for the first time.

If the screw-in module is used in a fixture that is controlled by a wall switch, leave the wall switch in the on position so that you can control the light with an X10 command. You will still be able to turn the light off from the wall switch, but you won't be able to turn it on from the wall switch. To turn it on, you must use an X10 controller. If the wall switch is in the off position, the light cannot be controlled by X10.

 The large screw-in-type lamp module may not fit in some fixtures. Even if you think that it is screwed in, it may have bottomed out on the inside of the fixture before the base is fully screwed in. If that happens, the module will appear to be totally dead. Before you decide that the module is defective, test it in a fixture with more clearance (fig. 1-12).

Local Control

Some X10 modules have a feature called local control. This feature allows you to turn on a lamp or appliance with its original switch when the module is turned off. This means that if you are sitting next to a lamp, you don't need to use an X10 controller to turn it on; you can turn it on using the switch on the lamp. However, there is a small trick to this. The lamp switch will already be in the on position if the lamp was last turned off by X10 control. To turn on the lamp, you must first turn the switch off and then turn it back on. This is actually a pretty natural response; if a light doesn't turn on at first try, most people will flick the switch again.

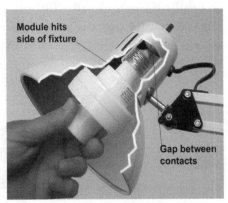

Fig. 1-12: A lamp module that has bottomed out inside the fixture before the base is fully screwed in.

You can also turn off a lamp with its built-in switch, but when you do this, you have disabled the X10 function until you manually switch the lamp back on. In other words, once you switch off a lamp with the built-in switch, you won't be able to turn it on by remote control.

The local control function is a bit confusing to many people. The following explanation may help make it clear. When an X10 module is in the **Off** mode, it sends a small current through the load (the lamp or appliance) to sense if there is a continuous circuit through the load. As long as the switch on the load is in the on position, this sensing current will continue to flow. When the circuit is broken by turning off the switch on the lamp or appliance (at the load), the sensing current stops flowing. This sets the module to a state that waits for the sensing current to flow again. When you turn on the switch at the load, the sensing current begins to flow, signaling the module to turn on. If there is another path for the sensing current—a second lamp, for example—turning off one switch won't stop the sensing current. In this case the local control won't be triggered. Local control only works on the load side of the module. If you have a module in a switched outlet, the wall switch won't trigger the local control.

Appliance Module

Appliance modules are wall-plug units that use a mechanical relay instead of electronic switching (fig. 1-13).

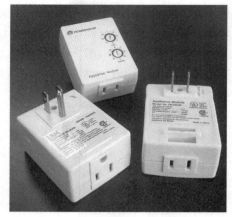

They come with either two-pin or three-pin plugs and outlets and are available in 120VAC and 240VAC with several different wattage ratings. The mechanical relay makes an audible click that sounds like a standard toggle-type light switch. These modules can control anything within their voltage and wattage rating, including fluorescent lights, low-voltage light transformers, electronic devices, heaters, fans, and small air conditioners. Appliance modules have no dimming function, and they do not respond to the **All On** command. However, they do respond to the **All Off** command.

Fig. 1-13: Appliance modules are available with both two-and three-pin plugs and outlets.

Appliance modules come in two- or three-pin models. If you have grounded three-pin outlets in your home, the three-pin modules will be more versatile. They will still work with two-pin devices and you have the option of using them with appliances with three-pin plugs.

Installing the System

Okay, enough explanations, let's start installing the system. This is really pretty simple, and I'll bet you can get it done in less than twenty minutes. First off, place the mini-controllers in convenient locations. In our layout, we'll put one on an end table in the living room between the couch and an easy chair. This table is also close to the front door, so you can reach the controller as you enter or leave the house. In the family room, we'll place one on the counter near the entrance from the kitchen.

The third one goes in the master bedroom on the nightstand (fig. 1-14).

The mini-controllers simply plug into any outlet. They draw hardly any current, so it's okay to use extension cords if they're needed. Unless you know that there will be a house-code conflict, just leave the controller house code set to **A**. In this system we will use unit codes 1–4 in the front of the house and unit codes 5–8 in the back of the house.

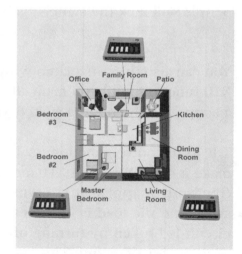

Fig. 1-14 Here is a plan of our example layout.

Most of the time you'll want the slide switch on the mini-controller set to the codes for the area it is in, but if, for example, you want to control the family room from the living room, just slide the switch to the 5–8 setting (fig. 1-15).

We won't be using all eight codes right now, but we've planned the code layout to allow for future expansion of the system. You don't have to use the codes we've chosen; you could group all four codes in the 1–4 range if you want.

Now, we'll tackle the living room lights. There are three table lamps in the room and no ceiling lights (fig. 1-16).

In this room, we'll use two lamp modules. Prepare the modules by setting the house code and unit code dials. Using a smallscrewdriver, rotate the unit code dial to position 2 (fig. 1-17).

Leave the house code on **A** unless you've changed the mini-controller to a different house code. You can use a multitap (a multitap is a device that allows you to plug more than one thing into single outlet) to connect more than one lamp to a module as long as you don't exceed the wattage rating, but you will lose the local control function (fig. 1-18) because current can flow through the other lamps that are still in the on position. If local control isn't important to you, you can save money by controlling several lights in the same area from a single module. If local control is important, you can retain this control by connecting a power strip with an on/off switch to the module and plugging your lamps into the power strip. To manually control all of the lights plugged into the power strip, just turn the power strip switch off and then on again. This will have the same effect as if you only had one lamp connected to the module.

Fig. 1-15: This slide switch on the mini-controller changes the rocker switches from the 1-4 range to the 5-8 range.

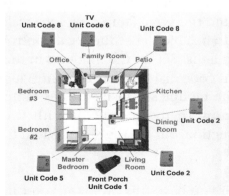

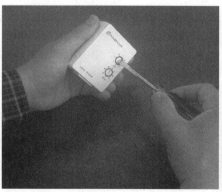

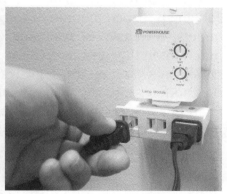

Fig. 1-16: This plan shows how we've assigned the unit codes in our example layout.

Fig. 1-17: Use a small screwdriver to rotate the unit code dial.

Fig. 1-18: You can use a multitap to connect more than one lamp to a module.

We'll use one module to power both of the lamps by the couch. Insert a three-way power tap into the outlet on the lamp module and plug the two cords from the lamps into the tap. Turn the switches on both lamps to the on position. If the lamps use three-way bulbs, turn the switch to the brightest setting. Don't worry if the lights don't turn on when you first turn on the switch.

Now, plug the remaining lamp into the other lamp module on the other side of the room. Make sure the switch on the lamp is in the on position. If either outlet is controlled by a wall switch, leave the wall switch in the on position.

 Tip–If possible, use an unswitched outlet, because whenever the wall switch is in the off position, the lights won't respond to X10 commands.

Okay, the living room is now done. That was easy, wasn't it? You can test the operation now. Press the **On** side of the second rocker switch on the mini-controller. All three lamps should turn on. When you press the **Off** side of the switch, all three should turn off. Turn the lights back on and press **Dim**; the lights should get progressively dimmer as you hold down the switch.

Be sure to press the On side of the switch for the light you want to dim or brighten before you press the dimmer switch. The dim function won't work if you just used the All On switch. In my family, we joke about dueling remotes because the dim function works with whichever switch was pressed last. Sometimes I'll turn on a light and wait a minute before I dim it. If someone else in the house has turned on a light in the meantime, that light will dim instead of mine. I usually hear one of the kids scream from the other room when that happens.

Because we used one module for the two lamps by the couch, we can't use the local control function with them. However, the local control function should work on the lamp on the other side of the room. To test it, turn off all the lights with the mini-controller. Now, go to the lamp and turn the lamp switch off and back on again. The light should turn on when you turn the switch back to on. This feature is useful when you only want one light on out of a group of lights that share a unit code. When you're done with the light, don't switch it off with the lamp switch or you won't be able to turn it on by remote control. Leave the lamp switch in the on position and turn off the light using the mini-controller.

Now let's move to the family room. In this room, we'll control a table lamp and a swag lamp. We'll also add an appliance module to turn the TV off. Both the table lamp and the swag lamp plug into wall outlets, so we can use wall-plug lamp modules. This time we want to be able to use the local control function on the table lamp, so we'll use a separate module for each light. Set up the modules in the same way we set up the living room lamp modules, but turn the unit code dial to **8** on each one. Plug the modules into the wall outlets and plug the lamp cords into the modules. Make sure the lamp switches are in the on position. The family room lights are now ready to control with the mini-controller. Test them as described earlier in the living room section, but set the slide switch to **5–8** and use the fourth rocker switch on the mini-controller.

Kids have a habit of leaving the room without turning off the TV. If you have this problem, you can add an appliance module to the TV. With this system you can turn off the TV from any mini-controller in the house without getting up and walking to the family room. There are a few caveats about using an appliance module with an electronic device like a TV.

Turning off the module is the equivalent of unplugging the device. If your TV loses its programming when it is unplugged, then you probably don't want to use this method. (In Chapter 9 we'll describe a method to use infrared remote signals to turn off this type of TV.) Also, if an electronic device is plugged into a surge protector, the surge protector may filter out the X10 signals. Some TVs and other electronic devices have built-in surge protectors; refer to chapter 13 for ways to get around this problem. Unless you have a really old TV, it probably has a remote control. Anytime you control a device that has a remote control, the appliance module will turn the device off, but you won't be able to turn the device on with the X10 controller. To turn the device on, you must first turn the appliance module on with the mini-controller and then use the remote to turn on the TV or other electronic device. If you also want to be able to turn the device on from an X10 controller, refer to Chapter 9.

Our TV has a nonvolatile memory that stores channel settings, so it can be controlled with a simple appliance module. It has a three-pin plug, so we'll use a 15-amp three-pin appliance module. Set up the module by using a screwdriver to turn the unit code dial to position 6. Unless you're using a different house code, leave the house code dial set to A. Unplug the TV from the wall socket and plug the TV cord into the appliance module. Now plug the module into the wall socket.

Now let's test the TV module. With the slide switch set to **5–8** on the mini-controller, press the **On** side of the second rocker switch to make sure the module is switched on. Now use the TV remote to turn on the TV. Next, press the **Off** side of the rocker switch on the mini-controller. You should hear first the module and then the TV click off. Wait a few seconds, and then press the **On** side of the rocker switch. You will hear the module click on, but the TV will remain off. Use the TV remote to turn on the TV again. If you get in the habit of pressing the **On** side of the switch a few seconds after you turn it off, the TV will always be ready to turn back on with the remote.

The next room in our example is the master bedroom. This room has a bedside lamp and one ceiling light controlled with a wall switch. The best way to control this room's ceiling light is to replace the wall switch with an X10 wall-switch module, which we'll discuss in Chapter 5. In this example, we'll add X10 control only to the bedside lamp.

Set the unit code on a lamp module by twisting the dials with a small screwdriver. In our system, the master bedroom is unit code **5**. Leave the house code on **A** unless you've changed to a different house code in your system. Use the mini-controller (again with the slide switch set to **5–8**) to test the operation of the module. Try turning the lamp on and off by pressing the first rocker switch, then test the dimming function.

Before you go to bed, you can turn on the bedroom light from one of the controllers in another room; that way you won't have to walk into a dark room. When you get into bed, you can turn off the light using the mini-controller on the nightstand.

Tip–You'll find that this nightstand controller becomes your favorite feature of the system. As you head for bed, you can leave the lights on in the other rooms, so you aren't stumbling along in the dark to get to the bedroom. After you've settled into bed, push the All Off button, and everything under X10 control will turn off.

For the final project of this basic system, we'll add a screw-in lamp module to the front porch light. We'll use the smaller, outdoor-rated module, which doesn't have external controls. Remove the bulb from the light fixture and screw the module into the fixture; then screw the bulb into the module. Here's an important note: These lamp modules are usually preprogrammed to house code **A** unit code **1**, so after you've replaced the bulb, you should be able to turn it on and off with a mini-controller without having to do anything else. Test the module by pressing the rocker switch on the mini-controller for unit code **1** (make sure the slide switch on this mini-controller is set to **1–4**). Leave the wall switch in the on position and control the light from the mini-controller.

If you want to use a different unit code or if your module did not come preprogrammed, you'll need to use a mini-controller to program it. Once the lamp module is installed and the wall switch turned on, press the **On** button on the mini-controller for the desired unit code three times at about one-second intervals. After the third time, the light should turn on. The module is now programmed to respond to the house code and unit code you selected. Even if the power goes off or if you unscrew the module from the light fixture, the module will remember its programming.

Dressing Up the Controllers

Now that your system is up and running, you may want to take a little more time to dress up the controllers. The controllers come with a set of stickers that you can use to label the switches. Put labels for codes 1–4 along the top row and codes 5–8 along the bottom row (fig. 1-19).

Magic Box Project

In his house, Rob has hidden the living room mini-controller in a small wooden box (fig. 1-20). If you would like to make a similar container, buy a carved wooden box at an import store. Before you can put the mini-controller in it, the box must be modified to provide a way to get the cord out of the box. You'll need a 1 in. diameter hole for the plug to pass through, but the box will look better if there isn't a large visible hole. Here are step-by-step directions for modifying the box to accommodate a mini-controller.

The large hole is cut in the bottom of the box where it won't show, and a smaller slot is cut in the back of the box for the cord to slide up into. Start by marking the location of the cord with the controller positioned in the box (fig. 1-21).

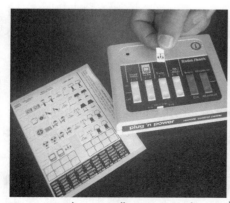
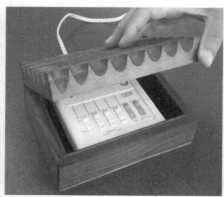

Fig. 1-19: The controllers come with a set of stickers that you can use to label the switches.

Fig. 1-20: This small wooden box purchased at the import store hides a mini-controller.

Fig. 1-21: Place the mini-controller in the box and mark the location of the cord.

Next drill a 1 in. diameter hole in the bottom (fig. 1-22).

The hole should be 3/4 in. away from the back edge of the box. Next drill a 1/4 in. hole in the back of the box, making sure that the 1/4 in. hole is lined up with the centerline of the 1 in. hole in the bottom.

Position the 1/4 in. hole so it just clears the bottom of the box (fig. 1-23).

Now use a handsaw to cut out a 1/8 in. wide slot that connects the two holes (fig. 1-24).

To install the controller in the box, push the controller plug through the large hole in the bottom. Next, thread the cord through the slot and up into the smaller hole in the back (fig. 1-25).

You now have all the information you need to start your own basic X10 system. In the next chapter, we'll show you how to expand on the basics.

Fig. 1-22: Drill a 1 in. diameter hole in the bottom 3/4 in. away from the back edge of the box.

Fig. 1-23: Next, drill a 1/4 in. hole in the back of the box. Line up the hole with the centerline of the 1 in. hole in the bottom.

Fig. 1-24: Use a handsaw to cut out a 1/8 in. wide slot that connects the two holes.

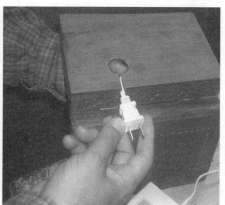

Fig. 1-25: Push the controller plug through the large hole in the bottom, then thread the cord through the slot and into the smaller hole in the back.

Chapter 2

Expanding and Automating Your System

After you've used your system for a while, you'll probably think of other things you want to do with X10 technology. In this chapter, we'll discuss controlling things like decorations, fountains, fans, heaters, and outdoor lighting. We'll also discuss ways to expand and automate your system with the following pieces of equipment: a maxi-controller, mini-timer controller, and photocell controller.

Holiday Decorations

Holiday decorations are a natural for remote control. Use an appliance module to control Christmas tree lights as well as other holiday lights and yard decorations (fig. 2-1). You can use several modules all set to the same unit code, so all of the decorations will go on or off at once. One of the best features is that when you hit the **All Off** button at night, all of the decorations will turn off.

In our example home, we have an electric fireplace log (fig. 2-2). It is a faux log with an orange lightbulb and a small motor that turns tinsel to make the "flames" flicker (fig. 2-3). Because the log has a motor, it requires an appliance module. With this type of module controlling the log, you can light up the fireplace from your easy chair. If you have a gas log, we'll show you how to control it in chapter 8.

Fig. 2-1: Holiday decorations are a natural for remote control.

Fig. 2-2: An electric fireplace log can light up at the touch of a remote control.

Fig. 2-3: Because this faux log uses a small motor you must use an appliance module. A lamp module cannot be used to control a motor.

> **Tip**
>
> The mini-timer described later in the chapter is a perfect companion for X10-controlled holiday decorations. In our example home, we have lighted holiday decorations in the front window for most holidays, including a jack-o'-lantern for Halloween and a lighted flag decoration for the Fourth of July. We use a mini-timer to turn them on at a certain time and off at 11:00 p.m.

Fountains

Indoor and outdoor fountains are popular decorations (fig. 2-4). To control an indoor fountain, simply add an appliance module. For outdoor applications, you will need to add a waterproof enclosure for the module. The box shown in figure 2-5 is meant for a sprinkler-system timer, but it is perfect for protecting an appliance module.

Any outdoor applications should be connected to a GFCI (ground fault circuit interrupter) outlet, a safety device that protects against shocks (fig. 2-6). Most newer homes already have them installed in outdoor outlets. If you don't have a GFCI outdoor outlet, you can buy a plug-in GFCI that will convert a regular outlet to a GFCI outlet. Another option is to have an electrician install one for you. Mount the waterproof box near the GFCI. Plug the cord from the box into the GFCI. Now you can plug an appliance module into the outlet inside the box. There is actually room inside the box for several modules; use a short extension cord to connect the modules to the outlet. You can plug in the cord from a submersible fountain pump or other outdoor decorations into the modules and then close the box. This type of box is also good for outdoor Christmas or other holiday lighting or for low-voltage outdoor lighting.

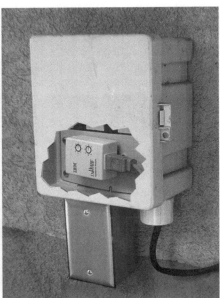

Fig. 2-4: This fountain in the backyard of our example house uses a submersible pump controlled with an appliance module.

Fig. 2-5: The box shown here is meant for a sprinkler system timer, but it is perfect for protecting an appliance module.

Fig. 2-6: Any module used outdoors should be connected to a GFCI outlet.

Low-Voltage Outdoor Lighting

Low-voltage outdoor lighting uses a transformer to reduce 120VAC to a lower voltage. There are both indoor and outdoor types of low-voltage lighting. The outdoor type is useful in landscaping (fig. 2-7). Low-voltage cables can be buried without any danger of a shock hazard. To control low-voltage lighting, plug the transformer into an appliance module. You can't use a lamp module for this application because the transformer is not dimmable.

Fans, Air Conditioners, and Heaters

It seems that you never notice that you're too hot or too cold until you are comfortably seated or lying in bed. Wouldn't it be great to be able to control a fan, air conditioner, or heater by remote control? Well, of course, you already know the answer: add an appliance module. Portable fans are low wattage devices, so any appliance module will work. For a heater or air conditioner, you will need to check the wattage rating. If you want to control a ceiling fan, refer to chapter 5. Most appliance modules are rated for 15 amps, which is the same rating as a standard home outlet. If the heater or air conditioner you want to control plugs into a standard outlet, it will work with a 15-amp appliance module. If the plug on the heater or air conditioner won't fit into a standard outlet, it may be a 20-amp or a 240VAC plug (fig. 2-8). You can get a special appliance module to handle it, but these are usually available only by special order.

Audio

Okay, you're in your easy chair, you've got the temperature just right and the lights are dim—how about some soft music? You can use an appliance module to switch audio equipment on or off. The same caveats we mentioned for the TV apply. If you want to control a sophisticated system that has volatile memory and infrared remote control, you would be better off following the instructions in Chapter 9. However, if you simply want to turn on the radio from your easy chair, an appliance module works great.

We have a reproduction 1940s radio that works well with an X10 controller (fig. 2-9). Leave the radio turned on and set to the station you like. Then switch it on and off using an X10 controller. You can control any audio equipment that has a switch that can be left in the on position.

Fig. 2-7: Low-voltage lighting can add dramatic nighttime effects to your landscaping. Connecting the transformer to an appliance module allows you to control the lighting by remote control or by programming on/off times with a timer.

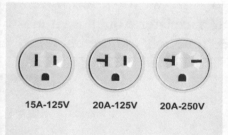

15A-125V   20A-125V   20A-250V

Fig. 2-8: If the heater or air conditioner you want to control plugs into a standard outlet, it will work with a 15A appliance module. If the plug on the heater or air conditioner won't go into a standard outlet, it may be a 20A or a 240VAC plug.

Fig. 2-9: If you want to turn on a radio from your easy chair, an appliance module works great. Use a radio with a manual on/off switch, like this modern reproduction of a 1940s radio in our example home. Leave the radio turned on and set to the station you like. Then switch it on and off from an X10 controller.

The amplifier shown in figure 2-10 is a good example. To control this amplifier, we leave the rocker switches on and use an appliance module to switch it on and off by remote control.

Maxi-controller

If you expand your system to the point that you need to use more than eight unit codes, you will need a maxi-controller (fig. 2-11). A maxi-controller is only slightly larger than a mini-controller, but it operates differently. Turning a unit on or off is a two-step process with the maxi-controller. First you press the numbered button for the desired unit, then you press the **On** or **Off** button. To dim or brighten a light, press the numbered button, and then press **Dim** or **Bright**. The maxi-controller has **All On** and **All Off** buttons just like the mini-controller. This controller also has a multiple-control function that allows you to pick several units to control at once. For example, if you wanted to dim the lights in the dining room and the living room simultaneously, you would first press the respective unit code buttons for the two rooms, then press the **Dim** button. The lights in both rooms will then dim.

Automate the System

So far your system is a remote control system, but it doesn't really automate your home. In this section, we'll show you how to set up a couple of controllers that do just that. There are two ways to control your home automatically with X10: you can either use a simple device called a mini-timer or you can use your home computer. In this chapter we discuss mini-timers; in chapter 10, we'll discuss computer automation. The computer interface and software required to automate your home have become affordable for most homeowners, so if you can imagine yourself wanting more sophisticated home automation, you can use your computer to achieve that and forgo mini-timers. The computer-controlled system will perform all of the functions that mini-timer controllers will, plus many more. However, if you would prefer a simple home automation system without using a computer, read on.

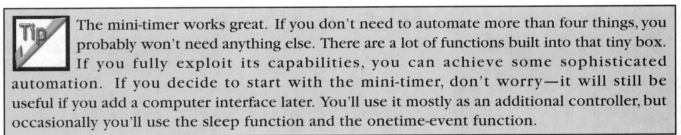

The mini-timer works great. If you don't need to automate more than four things, you probably won't need anything else. There are a lot of functions built into that tiny box. If you fully exploit its capabilities, you can achieve some sophisticated automation. If you decide to start with the mini-timer, don't worry—it will still be useful if you add a computer interface later. You'll use it mostly as an additional controller, but occasionally you'll use the sleep function and the onetime-event function.

Fig. 2-10: Audio equipment that has a manual switch like this amplifier can be controlled with an appliance module.

Fig. 2-11: The maxi-controller can control all sixteen unit codes.

Mini-timer

The mini-timer looks like a mini-controller grafted on top of a bedside alarm clock, and in fact that's about what it is (fig. 2-12). This controller works well as a nightstand controller. You have all of the functions available on the standard mini-controller plus an alarm clock and a timer that can control up to four unit codes. You can program the mini-timer to wake you in the morning and at the same time turn on the bedroom lights. You can switch off the alarm function but still keep the other functions running if you don't like to wake up to an electronic beep.

The alarm on the mini-timer has an interesting "snooze" feature. With the mini-timer, you don't have to fumble around to find the snooze button; you can hit any button at all while the alarm is sounding and get another ten minutes of sleep because it disables the **On** and **Off** functions of all other buttons. You can choose snooze as many times as you like.

On the opposite end of the spectrum, the mini-timer also has a handy sleep function. It lets you set one or two devices to turn off or on after a delay of fifteen to forty-five minutes. This can be useful if you tend to fall asleep reading with the light on.

The mini-timer also has a security feature that will give your home a lived-in look while you're away. With the **Security** function set, lights turn off and on at slightly different times each night.

Using the Mini-timer

You will need to plan ahead when you make the unit code assignments because you can only set timed events for codes in either the 1–4 or the 5–8 range, not both. That means that you can't have unit code **4** and **6** both controlled by the timer. Plan to have all of the timed devices in only one of the two ranges set by the slide switch. If you want to use the alarm beeper, be aware that it is tied to the first button, which means that the alarm will only work with unit code **1** or **5**. If you want the bedroom light to come on with the alarm, you will need to set the bedroom light to either code **1** or **5**.

You should also be aware that the programmed events are affected by the position of the slide switch that selects the range 1-4 or 5–8 (fig. 2-13). So, for example, if you program 5–8 as timed events and then change the slide switch to 1–4 to turn off the front porch light and forget to change it back to 5–8 before you go to sleep, the front porch light will come on in the morning instead of the bedroom light. However, the alarm beeper will still go off, so you won't be late for work—unless, of course, you use the snooze feature too many times.

Fig. 2-12: The mini-timer combines the feature of a bedside alarm clock with a mini-controller and allows you to program up to two **On** and **Off** times for each of four unit codes.

Fig. 2-13: The programmed events are affected by the positions of the slide switch that selects the range 1-4 or 5-8.

In our example home, we'll use the timer to control the bedroom lights (unit code **5**), holiday lighting (unit code **6**), and the air conditioner (unit code **7**). All of these codes are in the 5–8 range, so make sure the slide switch is set to **5–8**.

When you go to bed, you can set the bedroom light to turn off thirty minutes after you start reading; first press the **On** side of the first rocker switch (code unit **5**) and then immediately (within four seconds) press the **Sleep** button (fig. 2-14). Press the **Sleep** button once and the bedroom light will automatically turn off in fifteen minutes; press it twice and the light will turn off in thirty minutes. Each press of the button will give you an additional fifteen minutes of delay time.

If you want to wake up at 6:45 a.m. and have the bedroom lights turn on as the alarm sounds, just follow these steps. First, slide the program switch in the upper left-hand corner to **Prog Set** (fig. 2-15). Next, press one end of the **Time** switch to select 6:45 a.m. If you hold the switch down, it advances through the minutes rapidly; if you just press it up and down, it advances minute by minute. Make sure that you set it to **a.m.**, not **p.m.** The right side scrolls ahead through the minutes; the left side scrolls backward. Once you have **6:45 a.m.** lit up on the clock display, push the **On** side of the rocker switch for unit code **5**. Slide the upper left-hand corner switch back to **Run**, and you're set. Tomorrow morning, and every morning after that, the alarm clock and bedroom lights will come on at 6:45 a.m.

But wait! What if you just want to get up *tomorrow* at 6:45 a.m., but you don't want to get up this early every morning? Look to the right of the six rocker switches that control the units. You'll see a button that says **Once**. If you hit this button within four seconds of setting the time for unit code **5**, then your lights and alarm will turn on at 6:45 a.m. tomorrow morning only. They won't wake you up the day after that. What if you do want to get up every weekday morning at 6:45 a.m., but not on Saturday and Sunday? On Friday night, when you go to bed, simply slide the **Wake Up** switch to **Off** and slide the program switch to **Clock Set** (when the program switch is in the **Clock Set** position, it cancels the timer function). Just remember on Sunday night to move these switches back to the appropriate positions.

Remember the security function? You can program your bedroom lights to turn off at a slightly different time each night when you are away from home. Thieves may be on the lookout for lights that are obviously being turned on by timer; every night, these lights blink on at exactly the same time as the evening before. But the security function on the mini-timer picks random times within the hour to turn your lights on. To program your bedroom light to do this, first, slide the program button to **Prog Set**. Next, advance the time switch to the time you would like the light to come on, say, 9:30 p.m., and then depress the **On** rocker for code unit **5**.

Fig. 2-14: To set the sleep function, press the On or Off side of the appropriate rocker switch, and then immediately press the Sleep button. Each press of the Sleep button will give you an additional fifteen minutes of delay time.

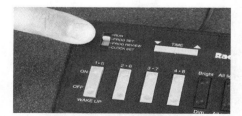

Fig. 2-15: Use this switch to set the timer to the appropriate mode. For normal operation it should be set to the **Run** position. To program the timers, set the switch to **Prog Set**.

To the right of the code unit rocker switches is a button marked **Security** (fig. 2-16). Simply press this button within four seconds of depressing the **On** rocker switch for the bedroom lights. The lights are now programmed to turn on that evening at 9:30; however, tomorrow, they may come on at 9:10, and the night after that, they might come on at 9:55. Now, to program the lights to turn off, go back to the time switch and advance the time to, say, 10:15 p.m. Press the **Off** rocker for code unit **5**, and once again, press the **Security** button within four seconds. The bedroom lights will now go off at 10:15 p.m. that evening. The next night, they might go off at 10:05, and the night after that, they might go off at 10:45. Any would-be thieves canvassing your neighborhood will assume that someone is at home.

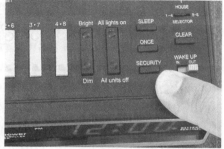

Fig. 2-16: Pressing this **Security** button during the timer programming sequence sets the timer to a random mode that will turn lights on and off at slightly different times each night.

> Don't worry if the display shows 18:88 while you're programming the mini-timer. You haven't crashed the system. This is just the signal that you have tried to enter more than two times for a single event. The mini-timer can store two ON and two OFF times for each of the four switches. If you inadvertently try to program a third time, you will get the 18:88 message. To clear the message, change the Mode switch to Prog Review then press the ON or OFF side of the rocker switch for each device to see what the programmed times are. When you find the incorrect one, remove it by pressing the Clear button. That should return the display to normal. If you can't find the problem, you can clear all the programming by unplugging the power cord and removing the backup battery. Of course, once you do this, you will need to reset the clock and reenter all of the programming.

If you'd like the air conditioner to cool the house down before you get home, you can set it to come on at 4:00 p.m. Do you ever have to get up in the middle of the night to turn the air conditioner off because it has gotten too cold? An X10 appliance module combined with a mini-timer can solve that problem.

Here are step-by-step instructions to turn on your air conditioner at 4:00 p.m. and then turn it off at 11:30 p.m. First, on your mini-timer, slide the program switch to **Prog Set**, then, with the **Time** rocker switch, advance the time to **4:00 p.m.** Remember that the air conditioner is code unit **7** (it should be plugged into an appliance module), so press the **On** end of the third rocker switch (3/7). Next, advance the time to **11:30 p.m.** and then press the **Off** end of the 3/7 switch. Now, slide the program switch to **Run**, and you're set! *IMPORTANT!* Always make sure that the **Unit Selector** switch is set correctly. If your programmed actions are for units 5–8, the **Unit Selector** switch must also be set for units 5–8. Also, remember that you can only program four unit codes with a mini-timer and that these units have to be set to either 1–4 or to 5–8; you can't mix and match automatic timed unit codes.

Photocell Controller

The photocell controller looks almost the same as a standard mini-controller, but it has a built-in photocell to detect changes in the light level (fig. 2-17). It will control up to four unit codes at sunset and sunrise. In our example home we use it to turn on the front porch light at sunset. To set up this controller, turn it over. You will find four switches on the bottom for controlling unit codes. Set the first one to the **On** position and set the remaining three to **Off**. Turn the unit right side up and set the slide switch to the **1–4** setting. Now the controller is set to turn on unit code **1** at sunset. Find a location near a window that won't be affected by other lights and plug in the controller. You may need to adjust the sensitivity control on the bottom of the unit to get it to respond at the appropriate light level. With this setup, the front porch light will turn on automatically at sunset and off at sunrise.

However, you can manually turn it off or on anytime using the unit code **1** button on a mini-controller or the **All Off** button. Even though the porch light turned on automatically at sunset, it will still switch off when you hit the **All Off** button as you go to bed. If you're not home to manually turn off the porch light, it will stay on until sunrise. If you want the light to turn off at a preset time, 11:00 p.m. for example, you can use the mini-timer. You could let the sundowner controller automatically turn the light on at sunset and then have the mini-timer turn it off at a preset time.

Fig. 2-17: The photocell controller has a built-in photocell to detect changes in the light level and sends an **On** signal at sunset and an **Off** signal at sunrise.

You now have X10 set up throughout your home. Wouldn't it be cool to control your lights and appliances with a hand-held remote control? The next chapter discusses the different remote control options that are available with an X10 system.

Wireless Control

It's time for dinner. The kids are away tonight at after-school activities; when you sit down at the table, you decide a romantic dinner would be nice. You'd like to dim the lights in the dining room and the living room, start some music, and turn off that annoying TV in the family room that the kids left on. You can do all this without leaving the table when you have a wireless handheld remote (fig. 3-1).

With a basic system installed in your home, you can add wireless remote control components that will enable you to control your home from a remote in your car or from other handheld remotes. If you have purchased a new car recently, it may already be equipped with a built-in X10 remote. Some cars come with a universal remote built into the mirror or visor. These remotes can be programmed to operate garage-door openers, electric gates, and X10 modules.

To use wireless remotes, you will need to add a base transceiver that receives radio frequency (RF) signals and converts them into power line signals that the X10 modules will recognize. In this chapter, we'll describe how to choose and install wireless components that let you control any X10 module in your house from a wireless remote.

Base Transceiver

The base transceiver is the heart of the wireless system (fig. 3-2). It is slightly larger than a lamp module and has an antenna to receive the RF signals. Installation is simple: just plug the base transceiver into a 120VAC outlet.

Most base transceivers have an appliance module built in, which allows you to use the base transceiver to control one of the devices in your system. However, if you use the base transceiver as an appliance module, its location is dictated by the location of the device you want to control. This may not be the best location for over-all wireless coverage of your home. In this chapter, we are assuming that you already have several modules in your home and want to add wireless control to all of them. In this case, it is better to ignore the appliance-module feature of the base transceiver. Position the base transceiver in the best location for overall coverage and use a separate module to control other devices.

Fig. 3-1: With a handheld remote, you can dim the lights in the dining room and the living room, start some music, and turn off the TV in the family room, all without leaving the table.

Fig. 3-2: The base transceiver is the heart of the wireless system. Installation is simple: just plug the base transceiver into a 120VAC outlet.

The RF remotes have a range of about 100 feet if there is a clear line of sight from the remote to the base transceiver. Most of the time, the base transceiver will work fine no matter where you put it. You should be aware, however, that there are various forms of interference that can combine to create dead spots in your home where the wireless remotes cannot communicate with the transceiver. Walls, electrical fields, and metal objects will reduce the range, so you should locate the base transceiver somewhere that will minimize the number of obstructions in the way of the signal. The RF signal will travel through walls, but each wall the signal must pass through reduces the range. Electrical fields around computers, microwave ovens, and other electronic devices can interfere with the signal if the base transceiver is located near one of these things. Large metal objects like refrigerators, file cabinets, shelves, and metal doors can block the signal (fig. 3-3). Foil-backed insulation in the walls may also block the signal. If your home has metal siding or foil-backed insulation in the exterior walls, the remotes may work fine inside the house but they might not work in the driveway or out in the yard.

If you have trouble with dead spots, use an outlet in a central location away from electronic devices and metal objects. An outlet in a central hallway is usually a good spot (fig. 3-4).

One of the best spots we've found is in the attic of the house (fig. 3-5). You may find an electrical outlet in the attic used for an attic ventilation fan. The attic location gives you good coverage of both the inside and outside of your home, so the remote in your car or on the back patio will work as well as the one in your bedroom.

Once you have decided on the location, you can set up the base transceiver and plug it in. Extend the antenna to its full length and adjust it so that it doesn't touch anything. If there is something else plugged into the same outlet, route the cord away from the antenna. There is a house code dial on the face of the transceiver; be sure to set it to the house code that your system is using.

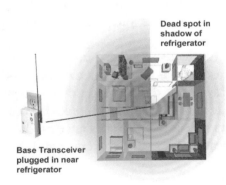

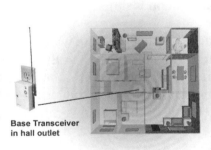

Fig. 3-3: Wireless remotes have a range of about a hundred feet if there is a clear line of sight from the remote to the base transceiver. Walls, electrical fields, and metal objects will reduce the range. In this example, a refrigerator is blocking the signal from part of the family room.

Fig. 3-4: To eliminate dead spots, find an outlet in a central location away from electronic devices and metal objects. An outlet in a central hallway is a good spot.

Fig. 3-5: One of the best spots we've found is in the attic of the house. The attic location gives you good coverage of both the inside and the outside of your home, so the remote in your car or on the back patio will work as well as one in your bedroom.

The base transceiver will only receive and transmit signals for the chosen house code. If you are using the internal appliance module on the base transceiver, the dial also sets the house code that the module will respond to. Usually the internal appliance module is preset to unit code **1** with no other options available, although sometimes it can be switched to unit code **9**. Usually, you should have only one base transceiver per house code, but you can add additional base transceivers if you set them to different house codes. This is a valuable feature if you have a complex system that uses more than one house code.

Most base transceivers only receive the 16 unit codes associated with one house code. If you have a complex system that uses more than one house code, spend a little extra on the base transceiver and get one that will receive all 256 possible codes.

If you are considering installing an X10 security system, read chapter 8 before you buy a base transceiver. The security console includes a base transceiver that communicates with the security sensors and remotes. Depending on the complexity of the system, you may choose to use an additional base transceiver set to a different house code for other home-automation functions.

You can have as many wireless remotes in your system as you like, but you should use only one base transceiver per house code in your home. If you use multiple base transceivers, they can interfere with each other. If you have a large house, some areas may be out of range of the base transceiver. In that case you can add RF repeaters to extend the range (fig. 3-6). An RF repeater receives a signal from a wireless remote and retransmits the signal. The process introduces a slight delay between the time you press the button and the time the light turns on. This might be a little disconcerting until you get used to it; otherwise, the repeater system works well.

You can use several RF repeaters in your home if you need them. The repeaters have a dial that looks like a house code. This dial doesn't actually change the house code; it sets the RF repeater to a special code that the other repeaters will recognize. The coverage areas of the RF repeaters may overlap (fig. 3-7). Each repeater in the system should be set to a different code so that the repeaters can differentiate between a signal from a wireless remote and another repeater. Because each repeater uses a different code, the repeaters can chain together to send a signal through several repeaters on its way to the base transceiver without causing interference. For example, a repeater set to **C** will repeat signals from a repeater set to **B** or **D**, but it won't repeat signals from repeaters set to **A**. The more repeaters in the chain, the longer the delay will be. If a signal has to be transmitted by four or more repeaters, the delay will be very noticeable. If you need several repeaters, it is best to locate the base transceiver in the center of the chain; that way the signal will never need to go through all of the repeaters.

Fig. 3-6: RF repeaters extend the range of remotes that are too far from the base transceiver.

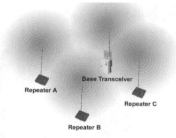

Fig. 3-7: The coverage areas of the various RF repeaters may overlap. Each repeater in the system should be set to a different code so that the repeaters can differentiate between a signal from a wireless remote and a different repeater. It is best to locate the base transceiver in the center of the repeaters.

Keychain Remote

Now that the base transceiver is installed, let's set up your first wireless remote. We'll use a keychain remote to turn on the porch light and living room lights from the car. As noted earlier, some new cars come with a universal remote built into the mirror or visor. These remotes can be programmed to send an X10 signal to a vehicle interface that is similar to the base transceiver. If you have one of these systems, you won't need a keychain remote; you can simply use the built-in remote.

The keychain remote can control two sequential unit codes. Remember how we chose unit code **1** for the porch light and unit code **2** for the living room in our example house? Because these two codes are sequential, you can use the keychain remote to turn on first the porch light and then the living room lights from the car, thereby avoiding walking into a dark house.

There are two types of keychain remotes: one uses manual addressing and the other uses electronic addressing (fig. 3-8). The default setting for both types of keychain remotes is house code **A**, unit codes **1** and **2**. If you have followed our recommendations for house and unit codes in chapter 1, the keychain remote should work without any additional programming. Let's try it out with your car in the driveway. From the car, when you press the number one **On** button, the porch light should come on. The second pair of buttons on the remote should control the living room lights. On some keychain remotes, there are two additional buttons at the bottom that control the dimmer. If the lights are controlled by modules that respond to **Dim/Bright** commands, you should be able to dim them using these buttons.

If you have changed the house code or if you are using the remote to control a different unit code, you will need to program the remote. The manual-addressing type uses switches inside the battery compartment to set the house code and the first unit code. With this type, the first unit code must be either **1** or **5**; the second code will automatically be set to **2** or **6**. To program a manual-addressing remote, first open the battery compartment and remove the batteries. Use a small screwdriver to turn the house code dial to the code you want (fig. 3-9). Then slide the unit code slide switch to either the **1,2** position or the **5,6** position. With the switch in the **1,2** position, the first button on the face of the remote will control unit code **1** and the second button will control unit code **2**. If you change the slide switch to the **5,6** position, the first button will control unit code **5** and the second button will control unit code **6**.

With the electronic-addressing type of keychain remote, you use the **On** and **Off** buttons to program the codes (fig. 3-10). This type of remote can be programmed to control any two sequential unit codes. To change the house code, press and hold the top **On** button. The red LED at the top of the unit will blink once. Continue to hold the button down, and three seconds later the LED will start blinking. Count the number of blinks.

Fig. 3-8: There are two types of keychain remotes. Both are small enough to fit in the palm of your hand. They are handy to keep on your keychain or in the glove box of your car to turn on house lights when you get home after dark.

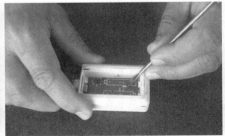

Fig. 3-9: To program the manual-programming type, open the battery compartment and remove the batteries. Use a small screwdriver to turn the house code dial to the code you want, then slide the unit code switch to the desired range.

Fig. 3-10: The elctronic programming type is programmed using the control buttons.

This tells you the current house code setting. If the remote is set to the default, the LED should blink once indicating house code **A**. If the house code has been changed, the number of blinks will tell you what the setting is. One blink equals house code **A**, two blinks **B**, and so forth—up to sixteen blinks for house code **P**. To change the house code, after the LED has stopped blinking, release the top **On** button, then press and release the button the appropriate number of times (one for **A**, two for **B**, three for **C**, etc.). The LED will blink each time you press the button; if it doesn't blink, you probably didn't press the switch hard enough and your count will be off. You may need to start over at this point if you think that your count is inaccurate. When you reach the final blink, press and hold down the **On** button for three seconds. The LED should begin blinking. Count the blinks to confirm that the house code has been set correctly. If the number of blinks is the same as the number of times you pressed the button, the house code is set correctly. If the LED lights up continuously for one second, there is an error in the programming, and the house code will remain unchanged. If the number of blinks is incorrect or if the LED lights up continuously for one second, start the programming process over again.

The process for setting the unit code on the remote is similar to setting the house code, only you press the top **Off** button. Press and hold the **Off** button until it begins blinking. The number of blinks indicates the current unit code setting for button number one. The second button is always the next higher unit code; for example, if the current unit code for button number one is **3**, then button number two will be set to **4**. Now release the **Off** button and then press it the number of times corresponding to the desired unit code for the first button. The second button will automatically be set to the next higher unit code. When you press the **Off** button for the last time, hold it down for three seconds. The LED will blink the number of the unit code to confirm the setting. If the LED lights continuously for one second, there is an error in the programming sequence.

Once you have a working remote, you can check for dead spots in the wireless coverage. Walk around your home with the remote and test it in different locations. If you discover a dead spot, try repositioning the base transceiver. If that doesn't work, you may need to add an RF repeater. Position the repeater about halfway between the base transceiver and the dead spot. That way the RF repeater will be in range of the base transceiver and the wireless remote. If you put the repeater too close to the dead spot, it may not have enough range to send the signal back to the base transceiver. You may need to do some experimenting with the position to get the repeater to work correctly.

Handheld Remote
The handheld remote can control all sixteen unit codes and send **Dim/Bright** commands. It has eight unit switches and a slide switch at the bottom that changes the unit code range to either 1–8 or 9–16. The **Dim/Bright** control is just above the slide switch at the bottom of the unit. This handheld remote runs on four AAA batteries. The only programming required is to turn the house code dial to the proper letter for your system (fig. 3-11). This is a very handy remote because of its ability to control all sixteen unit codes. The only thing it lacks is an **All On/All Off** button.

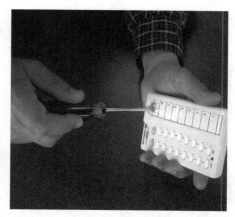

Fig. 3-11: To program this handheld remote turn the house code dial to the proper letter for your system.

Universal Remote

After dinner, you settle down on the couch to watch TV, but the TV won't turn on because you turned off the TV module from the dinner table. Don't worry! You won't need to get up again if you have a universal remote next to the couch. It looks and functions just like any TV universal remote. It can of course control the TV, DVD player, and other accessories, but it also controls anything you have connected to X10 modules. All you need to do is press the **X10** button on the remote, then press the unit number on the keypad (in our system the TV is unit code **8**) then press the **Channel +** button, which doubles as the X10 **On** button. You'll hear the appliance module that controls the TV click on. Now you can press the **TV** button on the universal remote and control the TV as usual. While you're at it, you can turn off the dining room light, dim the family room lights to the best level for TV viewing, or light the artificial fireplace log, all using the same remote that you use to control your TV.

There are many universal remotes available; we'll talk about two of the less expensive models. You'll find variations on these remotes sold under several brand names. One is a universal preprogrammed remote and the other is a universal learning remote (fig. 3-12).

To control X10 devices with these remotes, first press the X10 **Mode** button (fig. 3-13); this switches the remote from an infrared (IR) remote that controls audiovisual (A/V) devices to an RF remote that communicates with the X10 base transceiver. The default house code is **A**, so you won't need any additional programming to use the remote unless you've changed to a different house code.

The remote will control all sixteen unit codes and send **Dim/Bright** and **All On/All Off** commands. Both the universal preprogrammed remote and the universal learning remote come with a preinstalled database of codes for TVs, VCRs, DVDs, and other electronic devices. The only functional difference between these two remotes is that the universal learning remote also has the ability to learn new codes for devices that aren't listed in its database. The preinstalled database has hundreds of codes for TVs, VCRs, DVDs, and other electronic devices. To set up the remote to control one of the devices listed in the database, first press the **Set Up** key, followed by the **Mode** key that you want to program. Then, enter the three-digit code for the selected device.

The universal learning remote is useful if you have a device that is not listed in the database; this remote can "learn" the commands from the device's original remote. Simply point the two remotes at each other with about a one-inch gap between them. After you press **Set Up** and the appropriate **Mode** button, press **Learn** (fig. 3-14). Next, press the key you want to program and then press the corresponding key on the original remote. If the red LED on the learning remote turns off, the remote has learned the command. You can repeat the process for each of the keys on the remote.

Fig. 3-12: You'll find variations on these two remotes sold under several brand names. The one at the top of the photo is a universal preprogrammed remote and the other is a universal learning remote.

Fig. 3-13: To control X10 devices with these remotes, press the X10 **Mode** button.

Fig. 3-14: Use the **Learn** button to assign commands from the original remote control to buttons on the universal learning remote.

Reflected light can confuse the learning remote during the programming process. You can help eliminate the problem by closing the curtains in the room and placing the two remotes on a dark-colored towel.

To use the remote for X10 control, first press the X10 **Mode** button, then enter the unit code on the number keypad. You don't need to enter an initial zero for single-digit numbers. After you've entered the unit code, press the function key you want. The keys serve dual purposes on the remote, but they are all clearly labeled. Here is a list of the dual function keys:

A/V	X10
Channel+	On
Channel-	Off
Volume+	Bright
Volume-	Dim
Power	All On
Mute	ALL Off

If you need to change to a different house code, you can reprogram either of the universal remotes. First press the X10 **Mode** button; then press and hold the **Setup** button until the red LED lights up and stays on. Now press the number on the numeric keypad that corresponds to the desired house code (**1** for **A**, **2** for **B**, **3** for **C**, etc.). After you have entered the house code number, press the **Enter** key. If the red LED turns off, the programming has been completed correctly.

 The universal remotes we've described here are inexpensive remotes that can control A/V units and X10, but they are certainly not the only ones available. If you want to get really high-tech, you can buy touch-screen remotes that cost over $100.

Wireless Wall Switch

Do you have a room where the light switch is in the wrong spot? Maybe you've got a room with no wall switch, just a pull chain fixture. These are both perfect places to use a wireless X10 wall switch. A wireless wall switch attaches to the wall with double-sided tape or screws. You can have wall switches anywhere you want with no wiring involved. These switches use batteries that last at least a year, so you will only need to replace them annually.

There are two types of wireless wall switches available (fig. 3-15). Both are about the size and appearance of a standard wall-switch cover plate. They both will work with a standard base transceiver, so once you've installed a base transceiver in your home, you can add as many wireless wall switches as you like.

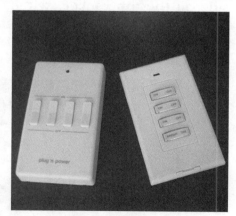

Fig. 3-15: Wireless wall switches allow you to add a wall switch anywhere without additional wiring. They simply stick on to the wall with double-sided tape. They transmit X10 signals to a base transceiver.

The manual-addressing type of wireless wall switch uses switches inside the battery compartment to set the unit code and house code. The rotary switch sets the house code, and the slide switch sets the unit code range (fig. 3-16). This switch can control four sequential unit codes in four ranges. The slide switch is labeled with the numbers 1, 5, 9, and 13. These numbers refer to the first unit code in the range. With this type of switch, you need to plan the unit code layout carefully so that the four unit codes you want will all be in the same range. For example, you can't control unit codes 6, 7, 8, and 9 with one switch because 9 is outside the range 5–8.

The electronic-addressing type of wireless wall switch can control three consecutive unit codes. Unlike the manual-addressing type, it is not limited to specific ranges. This means that you can set switch number one to any unit code, and the other two switches will be set to the next two unit codes. The fourth button on the switch is the dimming control.

The default setting for this switch is house code **A** and unit codes **1, 2,** and **3**. To change the house code, press and hold the **On** side on the top rocker switch (fig. 3-17). The red LED at the top of the unit should blink once. Continue to hold down the **On** side on the top rocker switch, and three seconds later the LED will start blinking to show you what the current house code setting is. One blink equals house code **A**, two blinks is **B**, and so forth, up to sixteen blinks for house code **P**. After the LED has stopped blinking, release the switch, then press and release the **On** side on the top rocker switch the appropriate number of times for your chosen house code (one for **A**, two for **B**, three for **C**, etc.)

The LED will blink each time you press the button. On the last press, hold the switch down for three seconds. The LED should begin blinking. Count the blinks to confirm that the house code has been set correctly. If the number of blinks equals the house code, the switch is set correctly. If the LED lights up continuously for one second, there is an error in the programming. The house code will remain unchanged, and you will need to repeat the process.

To set the unit code, press the **Off** side on the top rocker switch until the LED begins blinking. The number of blinks indicates the current unit code setting for button number one. The second and third switches are automatically set to the next two higher unit codes. Release the **Off** side on the top rocker switch, and then press it the number of times corresponding to the desired unit code for the first button. When you press the switch for the last time, hold it down for three seconds. The LED will blink the number of the unit code to confirm the setting. If the LED lights continuously for one second, there is an error in the programming sequence.

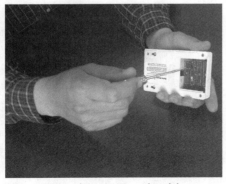

Fig. 3-16: The mannual-addressing wireless wall switch uses switches inside the battery compartment to set the unit code and house code.

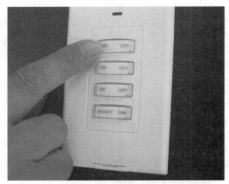

Fig. 3-17: Use the **On** and **Off** buttons to change the house and unit codes on an electronic-addressing wireless wall switch.

These switches have removable clear covers on the switch rockers. You can place labels under this clear cover. To remove the cover, press on one side of the rocker while you lift the other side with your fingernail (fig. 3-18). After you've inserted the label, press the cover back into place.

Our example home has a pull-chain light fixture in the garage. It's in a difficult location to get to, and you always trip over the lawnmower in the dark as you try to find the pull chain. It would be much more convenient to have a wall switch next to the door, so let's add a wireless wall switch here. First we'll need to make the light X10 controllable. To do that, simply add a screw-in lamp module, as we described in chapter 1. Next, we'll program the switch. We've grouped the garage light with two outdoor lights in the backyard, so we'll set the first switch to unit code **9** for the garage, and then we'll be able to control the patio and low-voltage outdoor lighting with the other two switches. Now remove the backing from the double-sided tape and attach the switch to the wall in the spot where your hand naturally reaches for a switch. The standard height of a wall switch in residential construction is 48 inches from the floor to the bottom of the box. Unless you have a good reason to change this, you should probably use this standard when you install wireless wall switches.

The patio light switch is inside the house. It would be convenient if we could also turn on the patio lights from the patio. We'll use another wireless switch to control the patio light, low-voltage lighting, and the submersible pump for the outdoor fountain. In this case, the best way to add X10 control to the patio light is to replace the switch inside the house with a hardwired X10 switch. Refer to chapter 5 for detailed instructions. Another option is to simply use a screw-in lamp module for the patio light.

These wireless switches are not weatherproof, so it's better to locate the switch under the patio roof. We'll put ours on a post that is well protected from the weather (fig. 3-19). When we program this switch, we'll set the first switch to unit code **10**. This means that we can't control the garage light (unit code 9) with this switch, but we will still be able to control the patio (unit code 10) and low-voltage outdoor lighting (unit code 11), and we'll pick up the fountain on the third switch at unit code 12. This also means that we can now control unit codes 10 and 11 with either the garage switch or the patio switch.

Wireless Motion Detector

A wireless motion detector will turn on an X10 module when it detects motion. You could use this to turn on a light when you enter a dark room. In our example house we have one in the kitchen to turn on a small light over the sink so you can get a drink in the middle of the night without fumbling for the light switch. We have another one in the back yard to turn on the fountain whenever someone walks by.

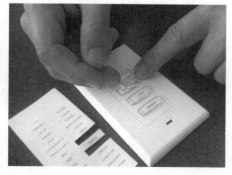

Fig. 3-18: You can place labels under the clear cover of the rocker switches.

Fig. 3-19: We put this switch on a post that is covered by the patio roof. it controls the patio light, low-voltage landscape lights, and the outdoor fountain.

Wireless motion detectors are available in both manual-addressing and electronic-addressing models (fig. 3-20). Some of them have an "off" timer that turns the device off after a programmed number of minutes.

The manual-addressing model is programmed with code wheels inside the battery compartment (fig. 3-21).

The electronic-addressing model is programmed by pushing buttons located inside the battery compartment (fig. 3-22).

 The procedure is similar to the programming described for the keychain remote, but the motion detector has some additional features to program. You can choose between twenty-four-hour motion sensing and motion sensing only after dark. The off timer is also programmable from 1 minute up to 256 minutes in nine steps that double the time on each step.

You'll need to think carefully about how you will use these motion detectors because they can have some unexpected results. First off, they have a photocell that activates the next higher unit code at dusk and turns it off at dawn. This can be a useful feature if that next unit code happens to be an outdoor light, but if you haven't planned the unit codes that way, you may find the kitchen lights turning themselves on at dusk. If you don't want to use the **On at Dusk/Off at Dawn** feature you may need to leave the next higher unit code unused. This can prove problematic when you try to group unit codes for other purposes, such as wireless wall switches.

The other thing to think about is the off timer. Once the motion sensor detects motion, it starts a timer that will send an off signal after the programmed number of minutes. This timer starts even if the unit was already switched on manually. This feature can lead to the unit turning off unexpectedly.

Fig. 3-20: Wireless motion detector.

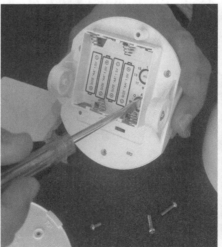

Fig. 3-21: To program the manual-addressing motion detector. Twist the code wheels with a screwdriver.

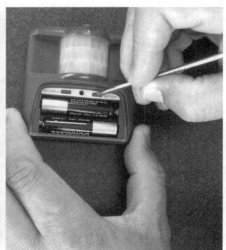

Fig. 3-22: Pushing buttons inside the battery compartment.

Let's use the backyard fountain as an example. We have a mini-timer set to turn on the fountain for one hour in the evening so that we can watch it through the window during dinner. We also have a motion sensor that will turn on the fountain whenever someone steps out onto the patio. If someone walks out on the patio a few minutes after the mini-timer has turned the fountain on, the fountain will turn off ten minutes later, even though we would expect it to stay on for the full hour (as set on the mini-timer). In the case of the fountain, this isn't a big problem, but if the motion sensor were controlling something more vital, an unexpected shutdown could be a problem.

One of the best ways to use these motion sensors is as a trigger for a macro. We'll discuss macros in chapter 11. If you use the motion sensor to trigger a macro, you can avoid some of the problems described in this section by carefully programming the macro.

You are now using plug-in modules to control your plug-in lights, but you think you would like to have your ceiling lights, which are controlled by wall switches, under X10 control. Chapter 4 will show you how to do this.

Chapter 4

Hardwired Controls: Basics

To truly achieve whole-house control, you must go beyond a basic system that uses only plug-in modules; you will need to add hardwired X10 controllers. To control built-in lighting, you can replace the wall switch with an X10 wall-switch module that will control a light from its original switch position as well as by remote control. For a really clean-looking installation, you can eliminate plug-in modules by installing outlet modules that look almost like standard outlets (fig. 4-1).

In this chapter, we'll show you how to install basic hardwired modules with step-by-step directions. If you would feel confident replacing a light switch or an outlet on your own, you can probably do most of the work in this chapter yourself. If you don't feel qualified to do minor electrical work, you can still do the planning, purchase the parts, and then call in a qualified electrician to do the actual installation.

General Instructions

These general instructions cover the basics of installing the switches and other devices discussed in chapters 4, 5, and 6. However, be sure to refer to the specific instructions for each type of switch or device before attempting installation. Also, before you do any work on the wiring in your home, be sure to turn off the power to the circuit at the circuit breaker box (fig. 4-2). If you still have an old-fashioned fuse box in your home, whenever we say to turn off the circuit breaker, you should remove the fuse.

 The instructions in this book assume that your home was originally wired by a qualified electrician in accordance with the National Electrical Code (NEC). If you find differences between your house wiring and the wiring we describe, you should ask a qualified electrician for advice.

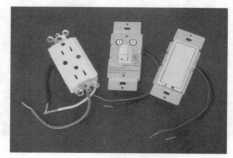

Fig. 4-1: Hardwired X10 modules replace standard wall switches and outlets. They give you X10 control over built-in fixtures in your home.

Fig. 4-2: Turn off the power to the circuit at the circuit breaker box before you do any work on the wiring in your home.

Definitions

In 120VAC electrical systems, two wires supply the current. One is called the hot wire; the other is the neutral wire (Fig. 4-3). The **neutral** wire is connected to ground at the service entrance. Although we don't recommend it, theoretically you could touch the neutral wire and something grounded (like a water pipe) without getting a shock.

To comply with the electrical code, the neutral wire should always be color-coded white. The **hot** wire is the one connected to the circuit breaker. If you touch the hot wire and something grounded, you will definitely get a shock. The color code for a hot wire is usually black, but it can be any color other than white, green, or bare. Green or bare is reserved for the ground wire. The **ground** wire is a safety precaution. It normally doesn't carry any current, but in case of a malfunction it provides an alternate path to neutral in the circuit breaker box. It should never be used as a substitute for the neutral wire. In most residential wiring, two or more insulated wires are grouped together in a **cable** that has a protective outer sheath. The most common type of cable contains one black (hot) wire, one white (neutral) wire, and one green or bare (ground) wire (fig. 4-4).

A **wiring device** is a component that doesn't consume power. For example, switches and outlets deliver power but don't consume it (fig. 4-5).

Something that consumes power, like a light or motor, is called a **load** (fig. 4-6).

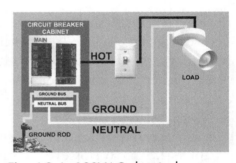

Fig. 4-3: In 120VAC electrical systems, the **hot** wire connects to the circuit breakers. The ground wire connects to a ground rod.

Fig. 4-4 The most common type of **cable** contains one black (hot) wire, one white (neutral) wire, and one green or bare (ground) wire.

Fig. 4-5 Switches and outlets deliver power but don't consume it.

Fig. 4-6 Something that consumes power, like a light or motor, is called a **load.**

A wiring device is mounted in a **box** that can be made of metal or plastic (fig. 4-7).

The box provides a mounting for the device within the wall and protection for the wire connections. Short wires used to connect a wiring device are called **pigtails**; they can also be called **leads** (fig. 4-8).

Removing the original switch or outlet
After you are sure the power is off, remove the cover plate (fig. 4-9).

Then remove the two screws that secure the old device in place (fig. 4-10).

Pull the device out of the box far enough to gain access to the wire connections (fig. 4-11).

Fig. 4-7: Mounting Box.

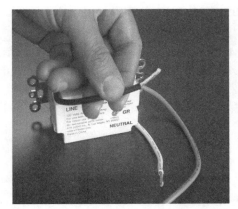

Fig. 4-8.

Fig. 4-9: Remove the cover plate.

Fig. 4-10: Remove the screws.

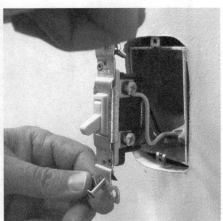

Fig. 4-11: Pull the device out of the box.

Before you remove any wires, write descriptive labels on strips of tape and apply them to the wires (fig. 4-12). Use any descriptive term that will make it clear to you where the wires were originally attached. For example, outlets have brass-colored screws on one side and silver-colored screws on the other. You could label the wires according to the color of the screw they were attached to.

The wires may be connected to the device in two ways: they may be wrapped around a screw terminal, or they may be back-wired (fig. 4-13).

Back-wired devices have holes in the back that grab the wires with a one-way action when the bare ends of the wire arepushed into the hole. You may even find a combination of both met

ods used on the same device. Sometimes an electrician will use the terminals as junction points for several wires (fig. 4-14). If you find this, be sure to mark the wires with strips of tape so you know which wires go together. If the device has wires attached to both screw terminals and back-wire terminals, group the wires that are in the back-wire holes with the wires on the screw terminal closest to the back-wire hole

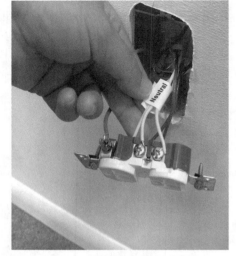

To remove the wires from the screw terminals, simply loosen the screws (fig. 4-15) and pull the wires off.

Fig. 4-12: Attach descriptive labels.

Fig. 4-13: Back-wired devices.

Fig. 4-14: In this photo, the black wires connected to the two screw terminals and the nearest back-wire hole are all electrically connected.

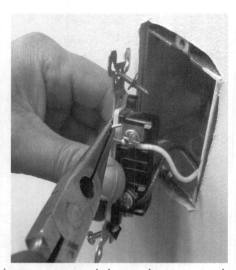

Fig. 4-15: Simply loosen the screws and pull the wires off.

After you remove the wires, straighten out the bend in the wire with pliers to get it ready to attach to the new module (fig. 4-16).

The easiest way to disconnect back-wired devices is to clip the wires off close to the back of the switch (fig. 4-17).

Most of the time, this is the best option, but if the wires are already very short and you need to preserve as much length as possible, you can try to release the wires from the one-way grabbing mechanism. There is usually a slot near the wire hole where you can insert the blade of a small screwdriver. Simply push in on the screwdriver and then pull out the wire (fig. 4-18).

There may be a green-colored screw attached directly to the metal frame of the device. This is the ground terminal. If there is a wire attached to this terminal, mark it so you can attach it to the new module (fig. 4-19).

Fig. 4-16: Straighten out the bend in the wire.

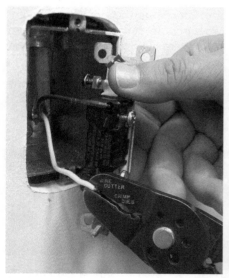

Fig. 4-17: Clip the wires off close to the back of the switch.

Fig. 4-18: Insert a screwdriver in a slot near the wire hole, push in on the screwdriver and then pull out the wire.

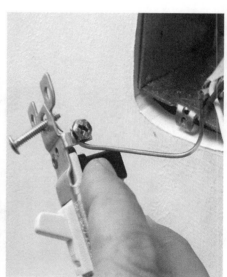

Fig. 4-19: The ground terminal.

Installing a new module

If you clipped the wire off, you will need to strip the ends to remove the insulation from about 1/2 in. of the end of the wire. Use a wire stripper to do this. Place the wire in the appropriate notch on the stripper (12 gauge [ga.] for most homes, 14 ga. for older homes), close the jaws of the stripper, and pull off the insulation (fig. 4-20).

The new modules use pigtails (short wires) instead of terminals to connect to the existing wiring. Use wire nuts to connect the pigtails to the wires. Wire nuts are color-coded for size (fig. 4-21).

The modules come with orange wire nuts, which can connect two wires. To connect three wires, use yellow wire nuts. For more than three wires, use red wire nuts. Place the wires to be connected side by side and screw one of the wire nuts included with the module over the ends of the wires until it feels tight (fig. 4-22).

The wire nut should completely cover the bare portion of the wire. If it doesn't, remove the wire nut and clip the wires a little shorter, then reinstall the wire nut (fig. 4-23).

Make sure there are not any small "whiskers" of wire extending out from the wire nut (fig. 4-24).

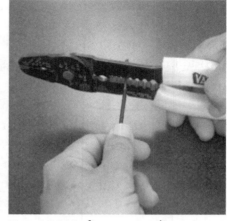

Fig. 4-20: Before you make any connections, all of the wires must have bare copper exposed at the end. If you clipped the wire off, you will need to strip the ends to remove the insulation from about 1/2 in. of the end of the wire. Use a wire stripper to do this. Place the wire in the appropriate notch on the stripper, close the jaws of the stripper, and pull off the insulation.

Fig. 4-21: Wire nuts are color-coded for size. Orange wire nuts (right) can connect two wires. To connect three wires, use yellow wire nuts (center). For more than three wires, use red wire nuts (left).

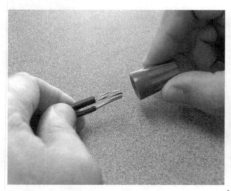

Fig. 4-22: Place the wires to be connected side by side and screw a wire nut over the ends of the wires until it feels tight.

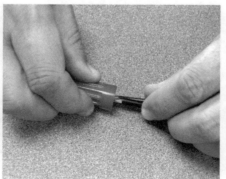

Fig. 4-23: The wire nut should completely cover the bare portion of the wire. If it doesn't, remove the wire nut and clip the wires a little shorter, then reinstall the wire nut.

Fig. 4-24: Make sure there are not any small "whiskers" of wire extending out from the wire nut. If the strands of wire touch metal, they may cause a short circuit.

If the original device was used as a junction point for several wires, you will probably need larger wire nuts. Place all of the wires that were grouped together on the original device side by side in a bundle and place one of the module pigtails in the bundle also. Screw the larger wire nut onto the bundle. Pull each wire individually to make sure that all of the wires are firmly attached (fig. 4-25).

Once all of the wire connections have been made, you can insert the module into the wall box. Carefully bend the wires back into the box (fig. 4-26).

Most newer homes will have fairly deep boxes, but older homes may have shallow boxes that will barely fit the new module. Position the wire nuts to the sides of the box to leave as much room as possible for the module. When you can get the module to fit in the box without pinching any wires, install the two screws that hold the module in place (fig. 4-27).

Light Switches

Now that you understand basic installation procedures, you're ready to start installing modules. The best way to control built-in lighting is to replace the old wall switch with an X10 wall switch module (fig. 4-28).

This gives you the ability to control a light from its original switch position as well as by remote control. Some switch modules have a small button that fits in the hole of a standard switch cover. Others have a large rocker switch and require a special cover plate (fig. 4-29).

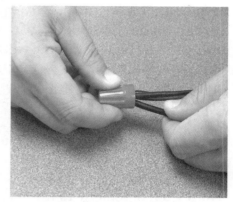
Fig. 4-25: Make sure that all of the wires are firmly attached.

Fig. 4-26: When you bend the wires back into the box, position the wire nuts to the sides to leave as much room as possible for the module.

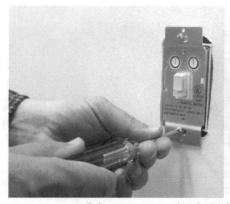
Fig. 4-27: Install the two screws that hold the module in place.

Fig. 4-28: An X10 wall switch module.

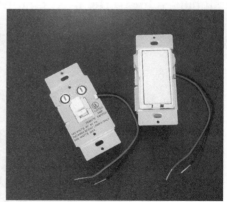
Fig. 4-29: Direct replacements for a standard toggle switch. This type of module has the same function as the lamp module, but it is directly wired into the wall.

There are also switch modules that look like traditional toggle switches. Wall switch modules are available in several different models with a variety of features. Heavy-duty switches are made to be more durable, and high-end models have a range of options that make them better suited for special applications. There are models that offer local dimming and others that can control fluorescent lights, ceiling fans, or low-voltage lighting. We'll discuss some of the additional features available on high-end switch modules in chapter 6. Some high-end switch modules require a neutral connection not found on standard switches. We'll cover installation procedures for these switches in the next chapter. In this chapter, we will focus on the most basic type of switch module.

Two-Wire Switch Modules

The switch module with the small push button shown on the left in fig. 4-29 is a direct replacement for a standard toggle switch. This type of module has the same function as the lamp module we described in previous chapters, but it is directly wired into the wall. It has a push button to control the light locally. The push button will turn the light on and off, but it won't dim the light. However, you can still dim the light by remote control—using a mini-controller or mini-timer, for example. The switch shown on the right has a larger push button, but electrically it is still a direct replacement for a standard toggle switch. It incorporates some high-end features like soft start and resume dim that we will discuss in chapter 6. A small slide switch below the push button on both types of switches disables the switch, so you can change lightbulbs without the light being turned on unexpectedly by someone using another controller elsewhere in the house (fig. 4-30).

 Tip Even though the switch with the large paddle looks like a rocker switch, it is really just a large push button. In a true rocker switch, you push the top to turn it on and the bottom to turn it off (fig. 4-31). Most of the high-end switches covered in chapter 6 are true rocker switches.

This type of switch receives X10 signals and controls a light, but it doesn't send X10 signals. This means that if you have several lights in a room controlled by separate switches set to the same unit code, they will all respond to a signal sent by an X10 controller, but when you switch on one of the wall switches, only the light connected to that switch will respond. Pushing the button on the wall switch doesn't send an X10 signal to other switches. If you want a switch that does send X10 signals, refer to the next chapter.

Fig. 4-30: A small slide switch below the push button disables the switch so you can change lightbulbs safely.

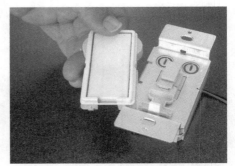

Fig. 4-31: Even though the switch with the large paddle looks like a rocker switch, it is really just a large push button. As you can see when the paddle is removed, the switch is essentially the same as the small button switch. In a true rocker switch, you push the top to turn it on and the bottom to turn it off.

In the past, these small-button switches gained a reputation for poor durability because of a design flaw in the mechanical portion of the switch. The switch relied on a metal contact attached to the plastic push button by a glob of melted plastic. When the head of this plastic rivet broke off, the metal contact would fall out of place, rendering the switch inoperable (fig. 4-32). Newer versions of this type of switch have corrected this problem by using an improved switch mechanism mounted on the circuit board. Now the plastic push button presses the switch on the circuit board instead of a metal contact. This has solved the reliability problem (fig. 4-33). Still, these are light-duty switches; so don't expect them to stand up to heavy-duty use. Because these switches are very inexpensive, they are a good choice for those on a limited budget. Usually when you are using X10 control on a light, you will use the wall switch less often than before, so a light-duty switch will often last a long time. We have ten-year-old switches of this type still operating in our example home. Even so, if you have a switch location that will be switched manually many times a day, you should opt for the heavy-duty type.

Installing the Switch

Whatever style of switch module you choose, as long as it only has two wires (not including the ground), the installation procedure is basically the same. Start by turning off the power at the circuit breaker. Even if you don't value your own safety, these switches contain electronic circuits that can be damaged if they are wired "hot."

Before you buy the new switch modules, turn off the power and remove the switch plate in your house. Look at the wires connected to the old switch. There may be a green-colored screw attached directly to the metal frame of the switch. This is the ground terminal. If there is a wire attached to this terminal, it must be attached to the green or bare pigtail or terminal on the switch module. Some switch modules don't have a ground pigtail or terminal. If the original switch has a ground wire connected to it, don't replace it with a module that doesn't have a ground connection without first consulting with your local building inspector.

Follow the general directions given above to remove the old switch (fig. 4-34). Most of the time, there will be only two wires attached to the switch. If the switch has three terminals, it is a three-way switch; in this case, you should follow the installation directions in the next chapter. If the switch terminals are junction points for several wires, be sure to mark the wires with strips of tape so you know which wires go together.

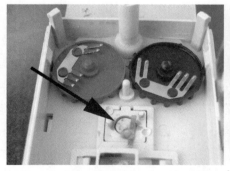

Fig. 4-32 Older switches had a design flaw in the mechanical portion of the switch. The switch relied on a metal contact attached to the plastic push button by a plastic rivet. As you can see in this photo, the rivet could break off, allowing the metal contact to fall out of place.

Fig. 4-33 Newer versions of this type of switch have corrected this problem by using an improved switch mechanism mounted on the circuit board. Now the plastic push button presses the switch on the circuit board instead of a metal contact. This has solved the reliability problem.

Fig. 4-34 Remove the old switch following the general directions given earlier in the chapter.

The new switch module usually has one blue and one black pigtail. The two wires that connect to a switch are interchangeable, so in this application, if both of the original wires are black it doesn't matter which color pigtail goes where. If only one of the original wires is black, connect the black pigtail to it for the sake of uniformity. Take one of the wires that connected to the old switch and one of the pigtails from the new switch and place them side by side. Screw one of the wire nuts included with the switch module over the ends of the two wires until it feels tight (fig. 4-35). If the original switch was used as a junction for several wires, place one of the switch module pigtails in the bundle of wires that were grouped together and connect them with a larger wire nut. After screwing the wire nut on firmly, pull on each wire individually to make sure that all of the wires are firmly attached.

Once all of the wire connections have been made, you can insert the switch module into the wall box. Use a screwdriver to set the house code and unit code dials (fig. 4-36).

Next, replace the cover plate (fig. 4-37), and then turn on the circuit breaker and test the switch.

Outlet Modules

If you don't like the look of plug-in modules, you can install outlet modules that look almost the same as a standard outlet. They are available in 120VAC 15 amp (A), 120VAC 20A, and 220VAC 20A models. They operate like an appliance module and don't have a dimming function. The most common type is a 120VAC 15A split receptacle. A split receptacle has one outlet that is X10 controlled and one unswitched outlet that is always on (fig. 4-38).

Fig. 4-35: Use wire nuts to connect the pigtails of the new module to the wires that connected to the old switch.

A duplex module is also available that has both outlets under X10 control. Some outlet modules also have a feed-through lead that can be used to control other outlets in the circuit. We will cover feed-through modules in the next chapter.

Fig. 4-36: Use a screwdriver to set the house code and unit code dials.

Fig. 4-37: Replace the cover plate and test the switch.

Fig. 4-38: A split receptacle has one outlet that is X10 controlled and one unswitched outlet that is always on.

The outlet module works like the appliance module described in chapter 2. You will hear a click as the internal relay switches on or off. There is no dimming feature on this module. This is for safety reasons, because you could inadvertently plug in something like a vacuum cleaner that can be damaged by dimming. This module should respond to the **All Off** command, but it won't respond to the **All On** command.

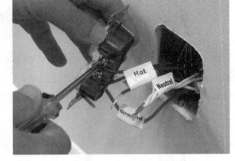

To install an outlet module, follow the general directions given earlier to remove the outlet (fig. 4-39). Then attach the pigtails on the new outlet to the existing wires with wire nuts.

Fig. 4-39: Follow the general directions given earlier to remove the outlet.

The new outlet will have one white pigtail, one black, and one ground. Be sure to connect the white pigtail to the white neutral wires in the box (fig. 4-40).

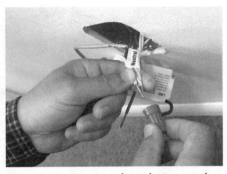

Connect the green or bare wire from the original outlet to the ground pigtail on the new module (fig. 4-41).

The black pigtail should be connected to the hot wires in the box (fig. 4-42). Usually the hot wires will be black, but they could be red, blue, or any color other than white, green, or bare. If the originaloutlet was wired correctly, the hot wires will be connected to the brass-colored screws or the back-wire holes labeled "Hot."

Fig. 4-40: Connect the white pigtail to the white neutral wires in the box.

When you have made all of the wire connections, bend the wires back into the box and secure the module in place with the two mounting screws (fig. 4-43), then install the cover plate (fig. 4-44).

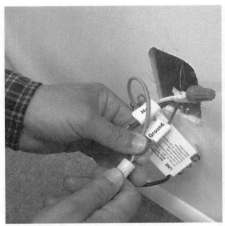

Fig. 4-41: Connect the green or bare wire from the original outlet to the ground pigtail on the new module.

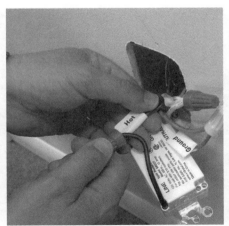

Fig. 4-42: The black pigtail should be connected to the hot wires in the box.

Fig. 4-43: Secure the module in place with the two mounting screws.

The house code and unit code dials are on the front of the outlet, so you can adjust them without removing the cover plate (fig. 4-45).

Now you can turn on the circuit breaker and test the outlet. Plug in a lamp to test the operation of the module. The unswitched outlet should always have power. After you plug a lamp into the switched outlet, try turning it off and on by X10 remote control.

You now have the basic knowledge necessary to replace your old standard switches with X10 wall switches. The next chapter focuses on installing more complicated devices, such as transmit-only wall controllers, fixture relay modules, and three-way switches.

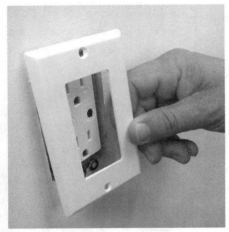

Fig. 4-44: Install the cover plate.

Fig. 4-45: The house code and unit code dials are on the front of the outlet, so you can adjust them without removing the cover plate.

Chapter 5

Hardwired Controls: Advanced

You're now used to using your mini-controller to turn off all your lights; however, you think it might be nice to have a wall switch by the front door that turns off these lights. On your way out of the house in the morning, you could simply hit the **All Off** button on the switch by the door, and all your lights and appliances would turn off (fig. 5-1).

If you want to control multiple unit codes from a single switch location, you can use transmit-only wall controllers, which are similar to mini-controllers, except that they're mounted on the wall. They look like wall switches, but they only send X10 signals; they don't control the flow of power to a fixture. They can be placed in any electrical box, even if there is no direct connection to the fixtures you want to control.

Fig. 5-1: On your way out of the house in the morning, you can hit the **All Off** button on the transmit-only wall controller by the door, and all of your lights and appliances will turn off.

Here's another possibility. You might have several lights in a room all controlled by a single switch, but you'd like to be able to create "scenes" with each light set to a different dim level. By adding a fixture relay module inside the ceiling box for each light, you can control each light individually. Fixture relay modules are also available in nondimming models that can control small motors. You could use a nondimming module to separate the light and fan functions in a ceiling fan currently controlled by a single wall switch. In this chapter, we will describe how to install transmit-only wall switches, fixture relay modules, feed-through outlet modules, and three-way and four-way switches.

In telling you how to make connections, we will use the following designations to describe the cables that are found in an electrical box. The cable that delivers power to the box is the **line**. The line can also be called the source. A cable that connects a switch to a light fixture is called a **switch leg.**

Neutral Wire

The switch modules we described in chapter 4 are direct replacements for the original two-terminal switch. To install the switch module, you simply remove the original wires from the switch and connect the two pigtails from the switch module to them. However, some high-end switch modules require a connection to the neutral wire. In this chapter and the next, we will describe how to install them.

A light switch makes or breaks the connection between the hot wire and the center contact of the light socket. The screwshell of the light socket is connected to the neutral wire.

 The National Electrical Code (NEC) requires that the neutral wire never be switched. If you find that a switch is installed incorrectly, have a qualified electrician correct the problem before you install X10 switches.

In residential wiring, there are two ways to wire a switch box. In one method, two cables enter the box (fig. 5-2). One, called the line, brings the power from the circuit breaker box. The other cable is the switch leg. It connects the switch to the light fixture. Each of these cables has three wires—one black, one white, and one ground (green or bare). In this arrangement, the white neutral wires of the two cables are connected with a wire nut and not connected to the switch.

The two black wires are connected to the two terminals on the switch. If you find a bundle of white wires connected with a wire nut but not connected to the switch inside the wall box, you have a neutral present in the box (fig. 5-3). If you have a neutral in the switch wall box, you can install any type of X10 module.

Unfortunately for X10 users, many switch boxes in residential construction use a second method of wiring. In this case only one cable, the switch leg, connects to the switch in the wall box (fig. 5-4). The black wire is connected to one terminal on the switch, and the white wire is connected to the other switch terminal. Even though there is a white wire in the box, there is no neutral present. This is an exception to the rule that white wires must always be neutral. When wires from just one cable are attached to the switch, both the black and the white wires in the cable can be hot.

In this situation, the switch leg cable in the switch box on the wall connects to the light fixture box in the ceiling. The line (the cable that delivers power) also enters the light fixture box, and the white neutral wire from the line connects to the light fixture. The hot side of the line connects to one wire in the switch leg cable and the other wire in the switch leg connects to the center contact of the light fixture.

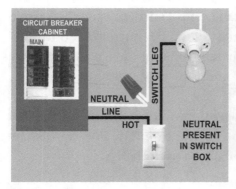

Fig. 5-2: There is a neutral present in the box when the white neutral wires of two cables are connected with a wire nut and not connected to the switch and the two black wires are connected to the two terminals on the switch.

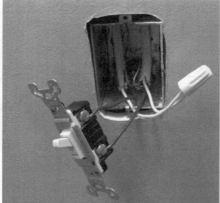

Fig. 5-3: If you find a bundle of white wires connected with a wire nut but not connected to the switch inside the wall box, there is a neutral present in the box.

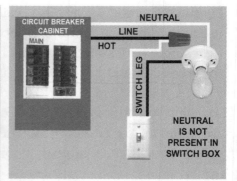

Fig. 5-4: There is no neutral in the switch box when one cable connects to the switch in the wall box with the black wire connected to one terminal on the switch and the white wire connected to the other switch terminal.

If you don't have a neutral present in the wall switch box, you can still use X10 modules, but your choices are limited. Some of the high-end switches with special functions cannot be installed in a box without a neutral. In most cases, running a neutral to the box is not worth the cost—an electrician would need to fish a new cable through the wall to the box. However, there is one method that you can use to rewire a wall switch box so that a neutral will be present. It involves using transmit-only wall controllers and fixture relay modules

Before you buy any switches, turn off the circuit breaker and open up the switch box you intend to use. If you don't see a bundle of white wires connected with a wire nut, you shouldn't buy switches that require a neutral connection.

Transmit-Only Wall Controller

Transmit-only wall controllers look like wall switches, but they don't actually switch the power to the light fixture. They only send X10 signals. They allow you flexibility in designing your system because they can be placed in any electrical box that has a hot and a neutral wire. They are available in single-address models that look just like regular switches and in multiple-address models that can control several different, but sequential, X10 addresses. It's like having a mini-controller mounted in a switch box (fig. 5-5). Some wall controllers have four buttons; the first three are sequential unit codes. That is, if the code switches are set to, say, A1, the address of the first button will be A1, the second will be A2, and the third, A3. The fourth button can be an **All Off** button, but some types use the fourth button for **Dim/Bright** functions.

Installation is fairly simple, but you must have a neutral wire in the box. Connect the white pigtail to the white neutral wires in the box and connect the hot pigtail from the controller to the hot lead in the box (fig. 5-6).

Once you've installed the switch, you need to set the house and unit codes. The code dials are under the keypad. Pull out on the bottom of the keypad to unplug it from its socket (fig. 5-7).

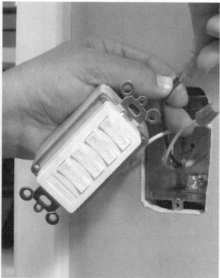
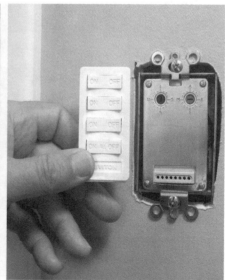

Fig. 5-5: A transmit-only controller is like a mini-controller mounted in a switch box.

Fig. 5-6: Connect the white pigtail to the white neutral wires in the box and connect the hot pigtail from the controller to the hot lead from the line.

Fig. 5-7: The code dials are under the keypad.

Use a small screwdriver to set the codes (fig. 5-8), then replace the keypad.

 Tip An outlet box always has a neutral wire. You can replace an outlet with a transmit-only controller. Most outlets are too low on the wall to be a convenient location for a controller, but outlets in kitchens and near counters are often at switch height.

Fixture Relay Modules

Fixture relay modules are switch modules that can be installed inside a fixture box (fig. 5-9). They are available in dimming and nondimming models. The dimming model can only be used with incandescent lights; the nondimming model can control fluorescent lights and small motors. Fixture relay modules are useful when you want individual control over fixtures that are presently controlled by a single switch.

For example, you may have several lights in a room that are all controlled by a single wall switch. If you replace the wall switch with an X10 module, you will be able to control all the lights remotely, but they will all respond together. If you want to create different "scenes" for the room where some lights are dim and others bright, you need to be able to control each fixture individually. Fixture relay modules allow you to do this.

 Tip Set the house code and unit code dials before you install the module. Once the module is inside the box, it may be difficult to reach the code wheels (fig. 5-10).

To install a fixture relay module, you must have enough room inside the fixture box to mount the module. After turning off the power, remove the fixture and look in the box before you start the installation to determine if there is enough room (fig. 5-11). You may need to remove unused cable clamps to make more room.

Fig. 5-8: Use a small screwdriver to set the house and unit code dials.

Fig. 5-9: Fixture relay modules are available in dimming and nondimming models.

Fig. 5-10: After the installation, it may be difficult to reach the code wheels, so it's a good idea to set the house code and unit code dials before hand.

Fig. 5-11: Remove the light fixture and determine if there is enough room.

Begin the wiring by disconnecting the hot wire from the fixture and connecting it to the black pigtail. Connect the blue pigtail to the black lead from the fixture. Remove the wire nut from the bundle of white neutral wires in the box and add the white pigtail from the module to the bundle. Reinstall the wire nut (fig. 5-12).

Now mount the module inside the box. Use double-sided tape to secure it (fig. 5-13).

Place the module inside the box and press it in place until the tape adheres (fig. 5-14).

Each light that you want to control separately needs its own fixture relay module, and the fixture relay module must also be set to a different unit code than the other lights. If there is already a switch controlling the fixture, you can leave the standard switch in place. However, a better method is to convert the wiring to accept a transmit-only wall controller, as described below.

Converting a Switch-Leg-Only Box to Hot and Neutral
As we discussed earlier in the chapter, some switch boxes do not have a neutral wire. This usually limits your options to only basic switch functions; however, here is a method that will allow you to install a high-end transmit-only wall controller. For this project, you will need a fixture relay module and a transmit-only wall controller.

With the power to the circuit off, remove the original switch (fig. 5-15).

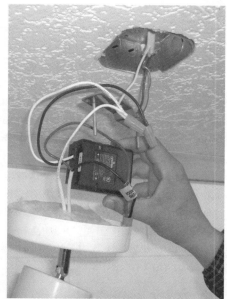

Fig. 5-12: To wire in the module, disconnect the hot wire from the fixture and connect it to the black pigtail. Connect the blue pigtail to the black lead from the fixture. Remove the wire nut from the bundle of white neutral wires in the box and add the white pigtail from the module to the bundle. Reinstall the wire nut.

Fig. 5-13: Remove the backing from the double-sided tape that comes with the module to expose the adhesive used to secure the module to the inside of the box.

Fig. 5-14: After you have made the wire connections, place the module inside the box and press it in place until the tape adheres. Then you can reattach the light fixture.

Fig. 5-15: To prepare to convert the wall switch to a transmit-only controller, turn off the power and remove the original switch.

Next, climb up and remove the light fixture in the ceiling, exposing the fixture box (fig. 5-16). Inside the fixture box, find the switch leg cable. It will contain a black wire and a white wire. One of these wires will be connected to the black wire of the fixture. The other wire in the switch leg cable will be connected to the hot wire of the line cable. Remove the wire nuts that connect the switch leg and disconnect the switch leg wires. Now connect the fixture relay module. Set the house and unit code dial on the fixture relay module before you install it. Bundle the black wire from the fixture relay module with the hot wire of the line and the black wire from the switch leg, and connect them with a wire nut. Next, connect the blue wire from the fixture relay module and the black wire of the fixture together with a wire nut.

Now remove the wire nut from the bundle of white neutral wires in the box, add the white wire from the switch leg and the white wire from the fixture relay module, and connect the wires with a larger wire nut (fig. 5-17). Now you can close the fixture box and reattach the light.

Now the black wire in the switch box on the wall is hot and the white wire is neutral. As a precaution, for future reference add a note inside the switch box that says, *"Attention: White wire is neutral, NOT switch leg—DO NOT replace switch with standard type."* This will alert anyone working on the switch in the future that they cannot use a standard switch in this box. Connecting the hot and neutral wires to a standard switch will create a short circuit when the switch is on. This will at least trip off the circuit breaker and may also damage the wiring or create a fire hazard.

 In homes built after the 1999 edition of the NEC became effective, the exposed part of a white wire in a switch leg should be covered with a black sleeve, tape, or paint to identify it as a hot wire. In this case, you must remove the black covering to identify the wire as a neutral.

You can now install the transmit-only wall controller. A transmit-only wall controller has only two pigtails; connect the white or gray pigtail to the neutral wire and the other to the hot wire. Now you can secure the controller in place with screws and install the cover plate (fig. 5-18).

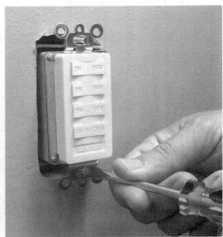

Fig. 5-16: Remove the light fixture, exposing the fixture box.

Fig. 5-17: Connect the black wire from the fixture relay module to the hot wire of the line and the black wire from the switch. Next, connect the blue wire from the fixture relay module and the black wire of the fixture. Finally, connect the white wire from the fixture relay module with the white neutral wires in the box.

Fig. 5-18: Now the black wire in the switch box on the wall is hot and the white wire is neutral. Screw the controller in place and install the cover plate.

After you turn on the circuit breaker, the light fixture should respond to X10 commands and the wall switch will transmit commands. One caution about this setup: there is no manual switch on the light fixture, so you should make sure you turn off the circuit breaker whenever you change lightbulbs.

Feed-Through Outlet Modules

Some outlet modules have a feed-through lead to connect to "downstream" outlets. When you use the feed-through leads, the module also controls all outlets or lights further down the circuit (fig. 5-19).

To use the feed-through feature, you will need to determine which of the hot wires in the box feeds the other outlets. To do this, turn off the circuit breaker and pull the existing outlet out of the box. Remove one of the hot wires from the outlet and cap it with a small wire nut (fig. 5-20). Now, reinstall the outlet and turn the power back on. Use a plug-in light to test each outlet. Outlets that no longer work are fed by the one you are working on. If the outlet you are working on still works, the wire you disconnected is the feed wire to the other outlets. If the outlet is dead, then the wire you disconnected is the line.

Turn the circuit breaker off again and remove the original outlet. Be sure to mark the line and feed wires so you can identify them later (fig. 5-21).

Fig. 5-19: This outlet module has a feed-through lead to connect to "downstream" outlets, so the module also can control all outlets or lights further down the circuit.

Install the new outlet module as described in chapter 4 except only the hot wire from the line should be attached to the black "LINE" pigtail (fig. 5-22).

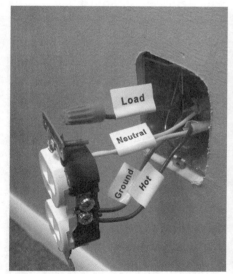

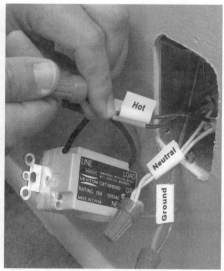

Fig. 5-20: To determine which of the hot wires in the box feeds the other outlets, turn off the circuit breaker and pull the existing outlet out of the box. Remove one of the hot wires from the outlet and cap it with a small wire nut.

Fig. 5-21: Be sure to mark the wires so you can identify them when you install the new outlet module.

Fig. 5-22: Attach the hot wire from the line to the black "Line" pigtail.

The hot wire marked as the one that feeds the other outlets should be attached to the blue "LOAD" pigtail (fig. 5-23).

Three-Way Switches
If you are replacing three-way switches, you will need to use a master and a companion module (fig. 5-24). A standard three-way-switch installation allows you to control a light from two different locations; for example, you may have three-way switches at the top and bottom of a staircase.

Figure. 5-25 shows how a standard three-way switch is wired. When you replace three-way switches with X10 switch modules, you install a master switch module in one location and a companion at the second location. The master does all the power switching.

The companion only sends signals to the master. Figure 5-26 shows the wiring diagram for a typical master/companion setup.

The installation procedure is much the same as described in chapter 4 for standard switches, but in this case the color-coding of the pigtails is critical. Before you disconnect the original switch, you will need to determine the function of each of the wires attached to the switch. A three-way switch has three terminals. One of the terminals will be a different color and placed in a position obviously different from the other two. For example, two terminals may be together on one end of the switch with the third alone on the other end. The two terminals that are together are called the "traveler" terminals. The one that is a different color and by itself is the common terminal (fig. 5-27).

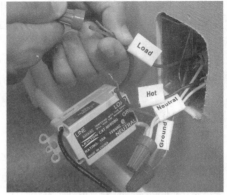
Fig. 5-23: Connect the hot wire that feeds the other outlets to the blue "Load" pigtail.

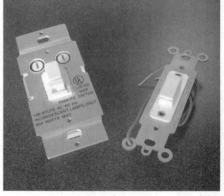
Fig. 5-24: Master and companion modules will replace standard three-way switches.

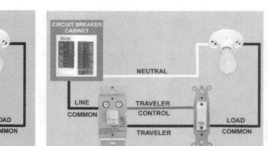
Fig. 5-25: A standard three-way-switch installation allows you to control a light from two different locations; for example, you may have three-way switches at the top and bottom of a staircase. This illustration shows how a standard three-way switch is wired.

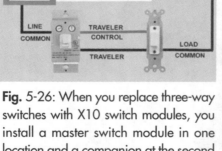
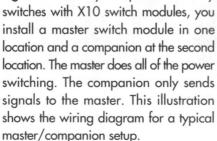
Fig. 5-26: When you replace three-way switches with X10 switch modules, you install a master switch module in one location and a companion at the second location. The master does all of the power switching. The companion only sends signals to the master. This illustration shows the wiring diagram for a typical master/companion setup.

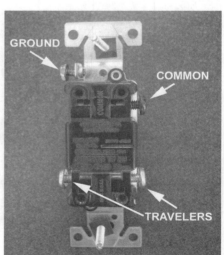
Fig. 5-27: Before you disconnect the original switch, label each of the wires attached to it.

There may be a fourth terminal colored green and attached directly to the metal frame of the switch. This is the ground terminal. If there is a wire attached to this terminal, attach it to the ground pigtail or terminal on the switch module. If the switch module doesn't have a green or bare wire or terminal, don't use it to replace a switch that has a ground wire attached. Buy a switch module that has a ground connection. Mark the wires with strips of tape to indicate their functions. Then remove the old switches following the procedures in chapter 4.

Master/Companion Switches

Master/companion switches are not too difficult to install because you can place the master in either wall box and there's no neutral connection. Refer to the directions that come with your switch for the correct color-coding. In this example, we will use blue for switch leg, red for control, and black for hot. The control pigtail attaches to a traveler wire and carries the signal from the companion switch to the master switch. First install the master switch. (This is the larger of the two switches.) Connect the blue switch leg pigtail to the wire that was attached to the common terminal of the original switch. Next, connect the red control pigtail to one of the traveler wires. Make a note of the color of this wire so you can find it in the other wall box. Now connect the black pigtail to the remaining traveler wire (fig. 5-28). This completes the wiring for the master switch. You can now bend the wires back into the box and attach the switch with its screws. Set the house code and unit code dials before you install the cover plate.

The companion switch has two blue pigtails and one red pigtail. Make sure that you connect the red pigtail to the same wire that you connected the red pigtail from the master switch to. Connect one of the blue pigtails to the wire that was connected to the common terminal on the original switch. The other blue pigtail connects to the remaining traveler wire (fig. 5-29).

After you have secured both switches in their boxes and replaced the cover plates, turn the circuit breaker back on and test the switches. You should be able to control the light from both the companion and the master switch and by remote control from an X10 controller.

Four-Way Switches

When there are three or more switches controlling the same light fixture, the switches in the middle of the circuit will be four-way switches. You might find a four-way switch in a stairwell that serves three floors. The switches on the first and third floor would be three-way switches and the switch on the second floor would be a four-way switch. The same type of X10 companion switch used in a three-way system will also replace a four-way switch, but the wiring is slightly different.

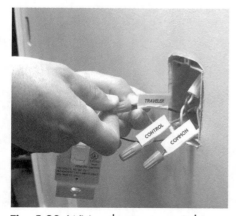

Fig. 5-28: Wiring the master switch.

Fig. 5-29: Wiring the companion switch.

When you remove the old switches, you will be able to identify the four-way switch because it will have four terminals. In the boxes with three-way switches, install a master and companion switch following the instructions given above. Now, move to the box with the four-way switch. There will be two sets of traveler wires connected to the four-way switch and there will be no common wires.

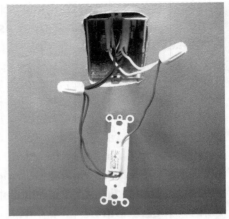

The X10 companion switch has two blue pigtails and one red pigtail. Bundle the two blue pigtails together and connect them to the two black travelers. Bundle together the two remaining traveler wires with the red pigtail and connect them with a wire nut (fig. 5-30).

Fig. 5-30: When you replace a four-way switch with an X10 companion switch, bundle the two blue pigtails together and connect them to the two black travelers. Bundle together the two remaining traveler wires with the red pigtail and connect them with a wire nut.

You now have some fairly advanced installation techniques under your belt. In the next chapter, we'll discuss installing high-end modules.

Chapter 6

High-End Modules

As you enter your bedroom, you reach beside the door and tap a large rocker switch; the ceiling light turns on dimly at first, then quickly brightens to full intensity (fig. 6-1). When you settle into bed, you reach over to the nightstand and press the **All Off** button on the mini-timer. The ceiling light in your bedroom and any lights you left on when coming to bed turn off with a gentle fade. The next morning, at the time you set on the mini-timer, the ceiling light in your bedroom gradually brightens like a sunrise, waking you up.

To achieve the type of control described above, you must go beyond the capabilities of basic modules and invest in high-end modules. High-end X10 modules come with a variety of advanced features. In this chapter, we'll describe the available features, so you can choose the ones you need. These features are available in both plug-in and hardwired modules (fig. 6-2).

High-end features can be a mixed blessing. As with any high-tech product, more features bring increased complexity, which can sometimes be frustrating. You should consider how you are going to use these types of modules before you invest in extra features. Just because a module is the most expensive doesn't mean it is the best for your application. The standard modules are fairly simple to set up and operate and usually don't give any unexpected results. The modules with advanced features can sometimes be tricky to program, and if you program them incorrectly, they may produce unexpected results.

This is not to say that high-end modules are lacking in advantages over the standard modules. One attractive feature in particular of most high-end modules is their advanced dimming and brightening capabilities.

Advanced Features
When you go shopping for high-end modules, you will be faced with a variety of features to choose from. Most modules will have several of the following features.

Fig. 6-1: This type of switch module offers advanced features such as soft start, which turns on the light dimly at first, then quickly brightens it to full intensity.

Fig. 6-2: High-end X10 modules are available in both hardwired modules (left) and plug-in modules (right).

77

At-the-Switch Dimming

Basic switch modules can be dimmed by remote control only. The button on the switch only turns the light on or off. If you want to be able to control the dimming from the wall switch, buy the type that has at-the-switch dimming capability. These dimmers allow the user to control the light's brightness either with the wall switch or with commands from an X10 controller. Some feature true rocker action; pressing and holding the rocker switch up brightens the light, while pressing and holding the switch down dims it.

Soft Start

This feature enables lights to come on gradually over a period of time and fade off in reverse fashion. With some modules you can adjust the length of time it takes to fade on or off. In a "home theater" mode, for example, the lights can be made to fade off over a period of thirty seconds, simulating a real movie theater. Have you ever noticed that lightbulbs seem to burn out most often right as you turn them on? This is due to a large inrush of current before the filament heats up. As the filament gets older, it weakens until eventually it can't take the stress caused by the inrushing current. Soft start can make bulbs last longer because it minimizes the stress on the filament. When the switch first turns on, only a small current is allowed to flow to the light, permitting the filament to heat up gradually.

Resume Dim / Preset On-Level

Modules with the "resume dim" feature can turn the lights back on to the same brightness/dimness level they were on at the time they were turned off. Alternatively, the lights can be made to come on at a designated brightness every time. For example, if you normally need only a 60-watt bulb in a room but would like to occasionally have it brighter, you can use a 100-watt bulb and have it come on at 60 percent brightness every time with the "preset on-level" feature. The light can then be brightened manually if needed.

Scene Lighting

This feature allows you to control multiple lights and circuits simultaneously using a single X10 command. For example, you might have different "scenes" for eating dinner, watching a movie, hosting a patio party, or soaking in the hot tub. Although it's also possible to set up scenes with a computer interface, modules with built-in scene capability make scene setup and control possible without using a computer. We'll discuss scene lighting in depth in chapter 11.

Three-Way Ready

We introduced you to three-way switches in chapter 5. Commonly found in hallways and stairwells, three-way switches are used where two wall switches control the same light. Some high-end switch modules can be used as either a standard switch or a three-way master switch. These three-way-ready switches have an additional control wire that is only used when the switch is set up as a three-way master.

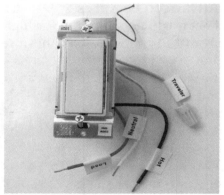

When it is used as a standard switch, this wire is capped off with a wire nut (fig.6-3). By using one three-way-ready master switch and one or more companion switches, you can replace three-way or four-way wall switches.

Fig. 6-3: A three-way-ready switch has an additional control wire that is capped off with a wire nut. When it is used as a standard switch.

AGC / Noise Reduction

AGC, or automatic gain control, strives to maintain a constant level of performance regardless of variations in the strength of the signal or interference. Computers and many other modern electronic components generate "electronic noise" that can transfer to the power lines in your home. This noise can interfere with the X10 signal. Modules with AGC reduce the amount of gain on the front end of the receiver, thereby reducing the amount of noise in the signal. We'll talk more about interference problems in Chapter 13.

Nondimming Switches

The ability to dim lights is one of the most convenient aspects of X10 switches; however, for some applications a dimming switch is not appropriate. For example, if the switch controls a motor or electronic device, dimming can damage the device. In these cases, you should use a nondimming switch A nondimming switch is basically like an appliance module. It uses a relay to switch the current. It's important to note that while some X10 dimmers are rated for ceiling fans, you should use only specially rated dimmers with these devices or use a nondimming switch. Low-voltage lighting and fluorescent lights also should not be dimmed with a standard dimmer.

Fig. 6-4: The high-end module on the left uses a small button to activate the programming mode and an LED to indicate the programming status. It sends signals to the module from an X10 controller like a maxi-controller. For comparison, a basic module that uses two dials to set the house code and unit code.

Electronic Addressing

Basic modules use two dials to manually set the house code and unit code. Some high-end modules don't have manual dials; instead they are programmed electronically (fig. 6-4).

We've discussed electronic addressing in previous chapters. The exact programming proceedure varies with each type of module, but basically you use an X10 controller, such as a mini- or maxi-controller, to send a sequence of signals to the module. The programming is stored in nonvolatile memory, so the device should keep its programming even after a power outage. Electronic addressing is the wave of the future, and more and more modules do without the standard code wheels used to select house and unit codes. Electronic addressing gives you more programming options, but it can prove confusing until you get used to it. For example, if you miss a step in the programming sequence, there's no visible way to discover what went wrong, so you simply have to repeat all the steps. This can be a little frustrating sometimes, but if you're careful, you shouldn't have any problems.

Two-Way X10

One of the newest developments in X10 technology is two-way X10. In two-way X10, modules not only receive commands from a controller but also acknowledge those commands by sending a verification signal back to the controller. In other words, two-way modules are capable of both transmitting and receiving X10 commands. Thus, if you have a two-way-compatible controller, you could have a visual verification of an X10 command. For example, there are keypad modules available that will let you know whether a light is on or off without your having to go and physically check it.

Two-way X10 can also be used to trigger a different set of actions or responses depending on the current state or status of the light or appliance that is plugged into it. In an action called "polling," a controller sends a signal to a two-way module to determine its state. The responses provided by the polled device can then be used to trigger other devices or events, effectively creating a macro (or multistep procedure). For this reason, two-way X10 modules are commonly used in conjunction with a computer controller (chapter 10 addresses computer controllers in detail).

Here's an example of how a two-way X10 module can be useful. Suppose a home has an automatic sprinkler system that starts its cycle every night at about 11:00 p.m. The homeowner sometimes entertains guests in the backyard. If the party lasts past the designated time, people in the backyard are likely to get a surprise soaking. Solution: place the outdoor patio lights under the control of a two-way X10 switch. Install a universal relay X10 module (see chapter 7) in the wire that leads to the sprinkler valves (the timer will still run normally, but the sprinklers themselves will be disabled any time that the module is off). Then, configure the computer controller to check whether the outdoor patio lights are on each night just before the sprinkler timer is scheduled to start the sprinklers. The computer controller sends a status request command and polls the patio lights. The two-way module responds, telling the controller whether the lights are on or off. If the computer controller is told that the patio lights are on, the controller will send an X10 command that disables the sprinkler valves. Once the patio lights are turned off, the valve module is switched on again, the sprinklers are automatically enabled, and the watering of the lawn immediately resumes at the point where the timer cycle happens to be. This situation clearly requires a two-way module, since it's possible that the patio lights were switched on or off locally. In other words, in this situation, the computer controller needs to know whether the patio lights are *actually* on, as opposed to whether they have merely received an **On** command via an X10 controller.

A two-way X10 controller can also be used to send notification if a lamp or device plugged into it fails to come on for some reason. For example, a lightbulb may be burned out or not screwed in properly, or the device may have been switched off locally. In such cases, you'll know that something is wrong right away, and you can immediately go to inspect the problem instead of finding out about it later at an inconvenient time.

 When you program a two-way module, you have the choice of having local control enabled or disabled. Unless you really need the local control function, it is best to disable it. With local control enabled, all of the lights on the same address will turn off if a bulb burns out because a quirk in the local control programming interprets a burned-out bulb as a local control Off command.

Although two-way X10 can be valuable in complicated home automation systems, many functions could be performed with a bit of creativity using regular (and cheaper) one-way modules. Remember that just because a two-way X10 module may be the most expensive one available, it isn't necessarily the best solution for your particular application. Situations requiring two-way X10 tend to be limited, so users should carefully consider whether two-way X10 modules are absolutely necessary before purchasing them. Also, two-way X10 has a tendency to weaken signals, so a booster may be needed, especially if you are using multiple two-way modules within the same system.

Installing High-End Modules

The features described above are available in both plug-in and hard-wired modules. You install the plug-in type just like standard modules. Just plug them in and plug in the cord from the device you want to control (fig. 6-5). To install the hardwired type, you should follow the same general directions that we gave in earlier chapters. Remember that some high-end switches require a neutral connection.

Fig. 6-5: A high-end plug-in module.

Finding the Hot Wire

Some high-end switches require that you identify the hot wire (also called the line). Finding the hot wire usually involves turning on the circuit breaker after you have removed the wires from the original switch. This poses a shock hazard and should only be done by someone qualified. However, we'll describe an alternate method here that doesn't involve working on energized lines; this method will show you how to identify the switch leg instead of the line. Once you know which wire is the switch leg, you know that the other wire is hot.

 This method will only work if your home has been wired in accordance with the National Electrical Code and good electrical practice. If you can't identify the switch leg with this method, your home may have been wired incorrectly. Consult a qualified electrician before proceeding.

To find the switch leg, you will need a continuity tester (fig. 6-6). This is a simple device with a battery and either a light or a beeper connected to test leads or a probe. If you touch the two leads together, the light or beeper will come on, signaling a continuous circuit.

You will also need a length of additional test wire long enough to reach from the wall box to the light fixture. After you have removed the old switch and with the power still turned off at the circuit breaker, use a wire nut to connect the additional wire to the common lead in one of the wall boxes. Connect one test lead from the continuity tester to the other end of this wire (fig. 6-7).

Now remove the lightbulbs from the fixture. Insert the other test lead or probe into the fixture until it touches the center contact of the socket (fig. 6-8). If the continuity tester lights or beeps, you have found the switch leg. If it doesn't show continuity, you are connected to the line, and the other wire should be the switch leg.

 Be sure to remove all the bulbs from the light fixture. If you leave a bulb in place, there is a chance that you will get a false reading through an alternate circuit formed by light bulb filaments to neutral and back to the hot wire.

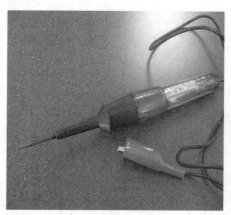

Fig. 6-6: The continuity tester shown here uses a light in the handle to signal continuity.

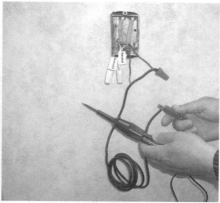

Fig. 6-7: Connect one test lead from the continuity tester to the other end of the wire.

Fig. 6-8: With the lightbulbs removed from the fixture, insert the test probe in the fixture until it touches the center contact of the socket. If the continuity tester lights, you have found the switch leg.

Switches That Require a Neutral Connection

We told you about the neutral wire in chapter 5. Normally, a standard switch doesn't require a neutral connection; however, some high-end switches will require such a connection. Be sure to check inside the switch box before you buy a high-end switch. If no neutral wire is present in the box (see chapter 5), don't buy a switch that requires a neutral connection.

If you do have a neutral connection, you should follow the general directions we've given in earlier chapters for most of the steps to install these switches. You may need to identify the hot wire. Follow the directions given above to find the switch leg with a continuity tester. Label this wire **Load.** The other wire that was attached to the original switch will be the hot wire (fig. 6-9).

The switch will have a black pigtail marked **Hot**. Connect the **Hot** pigtail to the hot wire that you identified earlier (fig. 6-10).

Next connect the red pigtail marked **Load** to the wire from the original switch that you identified as the load (fig. 6-11).

Remove the wire nut from the bundle of white wires in the box, add the white **Neutral** pigtail to the bundle and replace the wire nut (fig. 6-12).

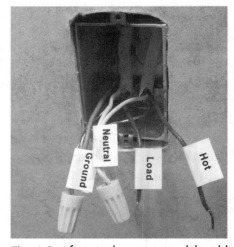

Fig. 6-9: After you have removed the old switch, find the switch leg with a continuity tester. Label this wire Load. The other wire that was attached to the original switch will be the hot wire.

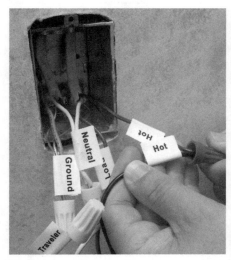

Fig. 6-10: Connect the Hot pigtail to the hot wire.

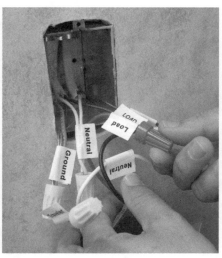

Fig. 6-11: Connect the red pigtail marked Load to the wire from the original switch, identified as load.

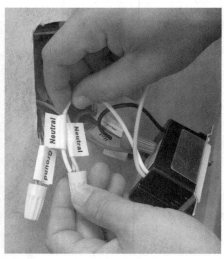

Fig. 6-12: Connect the white Neutral pigtail to the bundle of other white wires in the box.

Attach the **Ground** lead to the other ground wires in the box (fig. 6-13). Many high-end switches double as a master switch for a three-way setup.

If you are installing one of these three-way-ready switches in a single-switch installation, use a small wire nut to cap off the control pigtail on the switch (fig. 6-14). This pigtail is not used in a single-switch application. The wire nut will prevent the bare end of the pigtail from accidentally touching something and causing a short circuit.

Three-Way Switches

With three-way switches, two switches control the same light. On one switch, the common terminal is connected to the line (the wire that brings power into the box), and in the second box the common terminal of that switch is connected to the load wire (the wire that sends power to the light). Some high-end switches require that you identify which switch is connected to the hot wire and install the companion switch in this box. Refer to the directions that come with your switches to see if this is the case. This type usually will also require a neutral connection (fig. 6-15).

If your switches don't require that you identify the hot wire, the installation will be similar to that described in chapter 5.

To find the correct box for each switch, after you have removed the old switches and with the power still turned off at the circuit breaker, use a wire nut to connect the additional wire to the common lead in one of the wall boxes. Connect one test lead from the continuity tester to the other end of this wire (fig. 6-16).

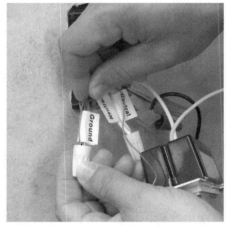

Fig. 6-13: Attach the Ground lead to the other ground wires in the box.

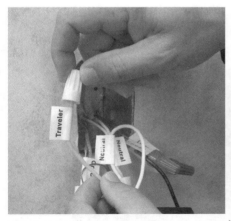

Fig. 6-14: Use a small wire nut to cap off the control pigtail on the switch.

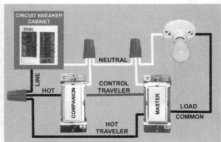

Fig. 6-15: This diagram shows how high-end three-way switches that require a neutral connection are wired.

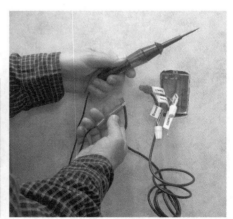

Fig. 6-16: Use the continuity tester method described above to identify the switch leg. Use a wire nut to connect a length of additional wire to the common lead in one of the wall boxes. Connect one test lead from the continuity tester to the other end of this wire.

Now, remove the lightbulbs from the fixture. Insert the other test lead into the fixture until it touches the center contact of the socket. If the continuity tester lights or beeps, you have found the load wire. If it doesn't show continuity, you are connected to the line, and the common wire in the other box should be the load wire. Disconnect your additional test wire, and then connect the test wire to the common wire in the other box and repeat the test just to make sure. Once you have determined which wire is the load wire and, by the process of elimination, which is the line, proceed with the directions below.

In this example, we will use the following pigtail color code:

Black	Hot (Line)
Yellow	Traveler (Control)
Red	Load (Switch leg)
White	Neutral
Bare	Ground

Check the instructions that come with your switch to confirm the color-coding. Begin by installing the companion switch in the wall box that you identified as having the line. Bundle the common wire with the black **(Hot)** pigtail and the black traveler wire and connect them with a wire nut (fig. 6-17).

Connect the yellow (control) pigtail to the remaining **traveler** wire. The yellow wire may be marked Traveler (fig. 6-18).

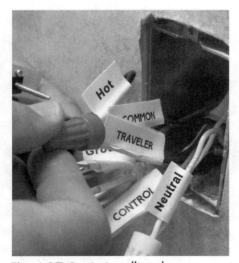

Fig. 6-17: Begin installing the companion switch by connecting the common wire with the black (hot) pigtail and the black traveler wire and connect them with a wire nut.

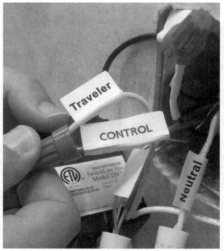

Fig. 6-18: Connect the yellow (control) pigtail to the remaining traveler wire. The yellow wire may be marked Traveler

Find the bundle of white neutral wires in the box and remove the wire nut. Add the white pigtail from the switch module to thebundle and replace the wire nut (fig. 6-19).

Finally, connect the bare ground pigtail to the green or bare ground wire from the original switch (fig. 6-20). Now the companion switch can be secured in the box and the cover plate replaced.

If you are replacing a four-way switch, bundle the two black traveler wires with the black (hot) pigtail and connect them with a wire nut. Bundle the two remaining traveler wires with the yellow (control) pigtail and connect them with a wire nut. Find the bundle of white neutral wires in the box and remove the wire nut.

Add the white pigtail from the switch to the bundle and replace the wire nut. Finally, connect the bare ground pigtail to the green or bare ground wire from the original switch (fig. 6-21).

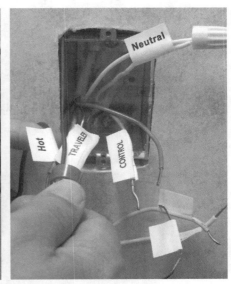

Fig. 6-19: Connect the white pigtail from the switch module to the bundle of white neutral wires in the box.

Fig. 6-20: Connect the bare ground pigtail to the green or bare ground wire from the original switch.

Fig. 6-21: Four-way switch replacement.

Next, install the master switch. Connect the common wire from the original switch to the red **(Load)** pigtail (fig. 6-22).

The black traveler connects to the black **(Hot)** pigtail (fig. 6-23).

The yellow **(Traveler)** pigtail connects to the remaining traveler (fig. 6-24).

Connect the white pigtail to the neutral wires in the box(fig. 6-25).

Fig. 6-22: To begin installing the master switch module, connect the common wire from the original switch to the red (Load) pigtail.

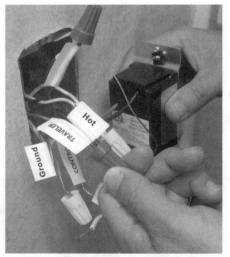

Fig. 6-23: The black traveler connects to the black (Hot) pigtail.

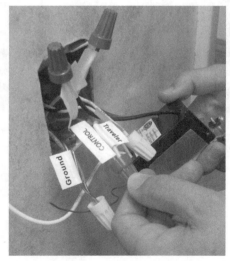

Fig. 6-24: The yellow (Traveler) pigtail connects to the remaining traveler.

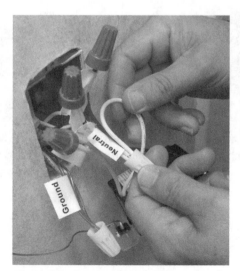

Fig. 6-25: Connect the white pigtail to the neutral wires in the box

Connect the bare pigtail to the original ground wire (fig. 6-26). After securing the switch in the box and installing the cover, turn the circuit breaker on and test the switches. If one of the switches doesn't control the light properly, you may have installed theswitches in the wrong locations. Turn off the circuit breaker and reinstall the switches in the opposite boxes.

You are now familiar with most of the extra features available with high-end modules and with some of the more complicated installation procedures. The next chapter will introduce you to the controls needed for low-voltage devices.

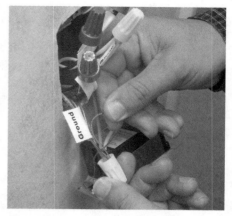

Fig. 6-26: To complete the wiring of the master switch module, connect the bare pigtail to the original ground wire.

Chapter 7

Low-Voltage Modules

You're enjoying listening to music—it's cranked up—and the phone rings. You pick up the receiver, but the music drowns out the words of your caller. Unfortunately, the remote control for the stereo is across the room, so you have to yell into the phone, "Just a minute! I have to turn down the music!" You stumble across the room and lunge for the remote, knocking it off the table in the process. Finally, you're able to turn the music down and get back to your caller, but when you pick up the telephone again, you find that he has already hung up. You think, "I wish I had a way to mute the stereo automatically when I answer the phone."

By now you are familiar with X10 products, so you know that a simple plug-in appliance module won't work for this problem. Low-voltage modules, combined with a microswitch, are the answer. At the end of this chapter, we'll show you how to install the modules and switches you need to mute your stereo system instantly with X10. The family in our example home has a phone inside a decorative box. A microswitch inside the box is depressed when the lid is closed. But when someone lifts the lid to use the phone, the switch activates a Powerflash module, which sends a signal to mute the sound system (fig. 7-1).

In this chapter we'll show you how to use two types of low-voltage modules: the universal relay module and the Powerflash module (fig. 7-2). Low-voltage modules have limited applications, and many homeowners might not have a specific problem that this type of module will solve. But if you, like many others who have become addicted to X10 solutions, like to experiment with gadgets, then it's important for you to know more about the low-voltage modules available and to have an understanding of how they work and what they do. In this chapter, we'll show you how to control things that you can't control with a standard module.

Fig. 7-1 When someone lifts the lid of this box to use the phone, a microswitch inside the lid activates a Powerflash module, which sends a signal to mute the sound system.

Fig. 7-2: In this chapter, we'll show you how to use two types of low-voltage modules, the universal relay module and the Powerflash module.

Because you need to run two-conductor low-voltage cable (like speaker wire) from the low-voltage module to the device you want to control, it is a good idea to plug in the module near the device that you're controlling (fig. 7-3).

Universal Relay Module

Many devices use a low-voltage control circuit to activate a function. Even though the device itself may plug into a standard 120VAC outlet, an internal transformer drops the control voltage to less than 30V. Simply switching the 120VAC supply off or on will not activate this type of device, so a standard module won't work. You must use a module that can control a low voltage. One of the more useful low-voltage modules is the universal relay module, the Swiss army knife of X10 modules (fig. 7-4).

A relay is a magnetically controlled switch composed of an electromagnetic coil and a set of switch contacts. When the coil is energized, it creates a magnetic field that pulls the switch contacts closed, completing the control circuit. A relay is used to isolate high and low voltages. With a universal relay module, the module plugs into a standard outlet and uses 120VAC to energize the coil. Because the relay switch contacts are isolated from the voltage, the relay can control any voltage up to 30V.

The universal relay module has two slide switches that set it to several different functions, so you can use it in numerous applications. The first switch sets the module to either momentary or continuous (fig. 7-5). In the momentary mode, the relay contacts close for about two seconds when the module receives an **On** command. This mode is used to signal a low-voltage device to perform an action; for example, the action of electronically pressing a push button. With the switch in the continuous position, the contacts close when the module receives an **On** command, and they stay closed until the module receives an **Off** command. The contacts also open in response to the **All Off** command, but they do not close with the **All On** command. This mode is used to turn on or off a low-voltage device like a sprinkler valve.

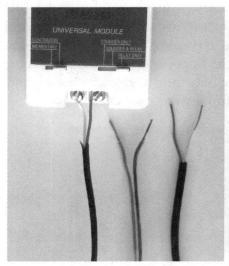

Fig. 7.3: Use two-conductor low-voltage cable like speaker or thermostat wire to connect the low-voltage module to the device you want to control. Try to keep the run short by plugging in the module close to the controlled device.

Fig. 7.4: The universal relay module can be called the Swiss army knife of X10 modules because of its versatility.

Fig. 7.5: This switch sets the universal relay module to either momentary or continuous mode.

The second slide switch lets you choose between a sounder and the relay (fig. 7-6). The sounder beeps when it receives an X10 **On** command. You can choose from sounder only, sounder and relay, and relay only.

Powerflash Module

What if you want to use a low-voltage device to trigger an X10 signal? That is the job of the Powerflash module. The Powerflash is the reverse of the universal relay module. When it receives a signal on its low-voltage terminals, it sends an X10 signal to something else. It signals a device to turn on, turn off, or flash (fig. 7-7).

Like the universal relay module, the Powerflash has slide switches that can set it to several function modes. The first switch selects the type of trigger input. In the A position, the module will be triggered when it detects 6V to 18V. In the B position, the module will be triggered by a switch connected to the terminals (fig. 7-8). The second slide switch detemines what kind of X10 signal the module will send when it is triggered. When the switch is set to position one, the module will send an **All On** command. You could use this to automatically turn on all the lights in the house when you open the front door. The second switch position sends **All On** and **All Off** commands repeatedly, causing all the lights on the house code to flash.

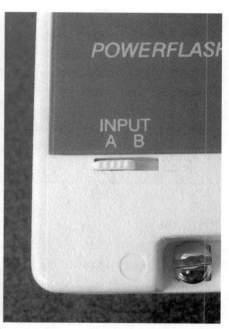

Fig. 7.6: This switch on the universal relay module lets you choose between the sounder and the relay. The sounder beeps when it receives an X10 On command. You can choose from sounder only, sounder and relay, or relay only.

Fig. 7.7: When the Powerflash module receives a signal on its low-voltage terminal, it sends an X10 signal to something else. It signals a device to turn on, turn off, or flash.

Fig. 7.8: This switch on the Powerflash module selects the type of trigger input.

The third position is the most useful. It sends a single unit code **On** command when the module senses a voltage or the switch contacts are closed, and it sends an **Off** command when the voltage stops or the switch contacts open (fig. 7-9).

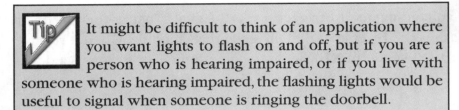

> **Tip** It might be difficult to think of an application where you want lights to flash on and off, but if you are a person who is hearing impaired, or if you live with someone who is hearing impaired, the flashing lights would be useful to signal when someone is ringing the doorbell.

Multiple Relay Controller

If you come up with an application that requires several relay modules, you can purchase a relay module that contains more than one relay. You can buy relay controllers with four, eight, or sixteen individual relays housed in a single enclosure, which can save you money. A four-relay controller costs about the same as three universal relay modules. And a sixteen-relay controller costs about the same as eight universal relay modules.

Fig. 7.9: The second slide switch on the Powerflash module determines what kind of X10 signal the module will send when it is triggered. When the switch is set to the first position, the module will send an All On command. The second switch position sends All On and All Off commands repeatedly, causing all the lights in the house to flash. The third position sends a single unit code On command when the module senses a voltage or the switch contacts are closed, and it sends an Off command when the voltage stops or the switch contacts open.

> **Tip** Catalogs often recommend a multiple relay controller as a way to control your sprinkler system. You can use a separate relay for each zone and control the sprinkling times with a computer interface. However, we think that in most cases it is better to keep the existing sprinkler timer and add a disabling feature with a relay module, as we describe below.

Projects

As you expand your X10 system, you will eventually find an application where you will need a universal relay module or a Powerflash module. We'll show you a few examples here to give you an idea of the kinds of things these modules can do, but don't limit your thinking about these modules; they can be real problem solvers in many different applications.

Sprinkler System Rain Delay

If you have an automatic sprinkler system, you want to be able to shut it off during rainy weather. The problem is that the timer is often outside in an inconvenient location. Shutting the system off involves removing the cover to the box while you're outside standing in the rain. To avoid this inconvenience, you can use a universal relay module to add a remote control to the sprinkler timer, which will allow you to shut off the system from the comfort of your home. Sprinkler valves usually operate on 24VAC, which is within the rating for the relay contacts.

To install the universal relay, use two-conductor cable to connect the module to the timer. Strip the ends of the wires and connect the two wires in the cable to the two screw terminals on the module. Run the cable to the timer. Now, open up thesprinkler timer box and find the screw terminals that the wires from the valves connect to (fig. 7-10).

To control all zones, disconnect the wire attached to the terminal marked "common" or "COM" from the timer and connect it to one of the wires from the module with a wire nut. Now connect the other wire from the module to the common terminal on the timer (fig. 7-11).

If you want to control only one zone, disconnect the wire for that zone from the timer and connect it to one of the wires from the module with a wire nut. Then connect the other wire from the module to that zone terminal on the timer (fig. 7-12). This is the way we connected the module described in chapter 6. When the two-way switch module for the backyard lights is on, it signals the computer interface to disable the backyard sprinklers. The universal relay module is connected to the wire for the backyard zone. This allows the other zones to operate normally.

Set the house and unit code dials on the module, set the slide switches to **Continuous** and **Relay Only,** and plug in the module. Now you can disable the sprinklers from any X10 controller with an **Off** command. When you turn the module back on, the timer will resume its normal schedule.

Once you disable the sprinklers, they will stay off until you turn them back on. If you would rather have a one-day cancel mode, use a mini-timer or computer controller to turn on the sprinkler module every day at a set time. Note: this should be sometime after the sprinklers are scheduled to turn off. This way, you cancel watering for one day by turning off the module anytime before the next time that the sprinklers are scheduled to turn on. After the sprinklers are scheduled to turn off, the timer will reset the module to on. The sprinklers will then run as scheduled the following day.

 Tip: Because the module responds to the All Off command, it's best to set it to a house code different from the other modules. Otherwise, every time you use the All Off command to turn off the lights at night, you will disable your sprinkler system.

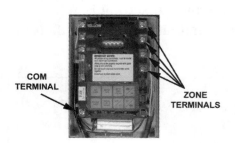

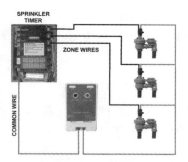

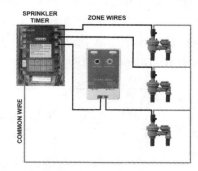

Fig. 7.10: In a sprinkler timer, there will be separate terminals for each zone and one terminal marked Com that connects to all zones.

Fig. 7.11: Disconnect the wire attached to the terminal marked common or Com from the timer and connect it to one of the wires from the module with a wire nut. Then connect the other wire from the module to the common terminal on the timer.

Fig. 7.12: To control only one zone, disconnect the wire for that zone from the timer and connect it to one of the wires from the module with a wire nut. Then connect the other wire from the module to that zone terminal on the timer.

In Chapter 12, we'll show you how you can set this up so that you can even be away from home and send the commands by telephone. So if you're at work when it starts to rain, you can call home and turn off the sprinklers.

Gas Fireplace Log Remote

In chapter 2, we talked about controlling an electric fireplace log with X10. Now we'll show you how to control some types of gas logs. If your gas log has a low-voltage thermostat, you can add a universal relay module to add remote control. Before you begin, you should have a qualified gas technician examine your system to make sure it will be safe to use a universal relay module. Also, you need to be aware that gas valves should not be cycled on and off rapidly. Make sure there is no way that the module could receive multiple rapid signals.

To install the module, find an outlet close to the thermostat to plug in a universal relay module and run a two conductor cable from the module location to the thermostat. Strip the ends of the wires in the two-conductor cable and connect one of the wires in the cable to one of the screw terminals on the module. Connect the other wire to the other terminal. Now move to the thermostat. Disconnect one wire from the thermostat and connect it to one of the wires from the module with a wire nut. Then connect the other wire from the module to the terminal on the thermostat from which you removed the wire (fig. 7-13).

Fig. 7.13: To control a gas log that has a low-voltage thermostat, use a universal relay module. Run a two-conductor cable from the module location to the thermostat. Disconnect one wire from the thermostat and connect it to one of the wires from the module with a wire nut. Then connect the other wire from the module to the terminal on the the rmostat from which you removed the wire.

Next, set the house and unit code dials on the module to the desired address. Set the slide switches to **Continuous** and **Relay Only** and plug the module in. Set the fireplace log thermostat to the desired room temperature.

With the universal relay module turned on, the thermostat will operate normally. However, when you turn off the module, the log will go off no matter what the thermostat setting is. When you turn the module back on, the log will light, as long as the room temperature is lower than the thermostat setting.

 If you already have an infrared remote control for your gas log, you can control it with an X10 IR interface. Please refer to chapter 9.

Remote Doorbell

Is there someplace in your house where you just can't quite hear the doorbell? You can use a Powerflash module along with a universal relay module to add a remote doorbell sounder. You could also use this setup to turn on a porch light or trigger a macro that turns on a porch light when someone rings the doorbell. Anything set to the same house code and unit code as the Powerflash module will be activated when the doorbell rings.

Begin by connecting the Powerflash module to the doorbell (fig. 7-14). Most doorbells operate on 16V, so the voltage-sensing feature of the Powerflash module will work. Connect a two-conductor cable to the two terminals on the Powerflash module. Connect the other end of the cable to the terminals on the doorbell chime.

Leave the original wires in place. If the chime has separate connections for the front door and the back door, you will need to choose one of them to connect to the Powerflash module. Usually there will be three terminals on the chime marked **Trans, Front,** and **Back.** Connect one wire to the **Trans** terminal and the other to either the **Front** or the **Back** terminal (fig. 7-15). Before you plug in the module, set the house and unit code dials and set the slide switches to **Input A** (voltage detect) and **Mode 3** (single unit code).

Now install a universal relay module in the room where you want to have the extension chime. You could set the universal relay module to the sounder-only position for this, but the sound is really aggravating, so it's really better to use the relay function to control a separate doorbell chime.

Connect the wires on the new chime and transformer that would normally go to the doorbell button to the two terminals of the universal relay module (fig. 7-16). To finish the installation, set the house and unit code dials on the module to the same settings as the Powerflash module and set the slide switches to **Momentary** and **Relay Only**, then plug in the universal relay module.

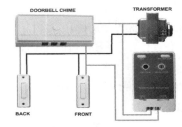

Fig. 7.14: This diagram shows how to connect a Powerflash module to a doorbell.

Remote Thermostat

In chapter 2, we talked about controlling a window air conditioner with an X10 controller. If you have an air conditioner controlled with an appliance module, you can add a remote thermostat using a Powerflash module. Buy a standard wall-mount air-conditioning thermostat. Mount it on a wall away from the direct airflow from the air conditioner. Connect the two air-conditioner terminals inside the thermostat to the two terminals on the Powerflash module (fig. 7-17). Set the house code and unit code dials on the Powerflash module to the same settings as the air conditioner. Set the slide switches on the module to **Input B** (switch contact) and **Mode 3** (single unit code). Now set the thermostat to the desired room temperature. The air conditioner should start if the room temperature is above that setting and run until the room is cooled to the set temperature. You still can also control the air conditioner from any other X10 controller.

Fig. 7.15: To connect a Powerflash module to a doorbell, leave the original wires in place, connect the other end of the cable to the terminals. Usually there will be three terminals on the chime marked **Trans, Front,** and **Back.**

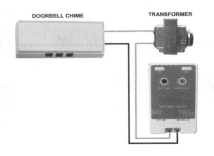

Fig. 7.16: This diagram shows how to connect a remote doorbell chime to a universal relay module.

Fig. 7.17: Connect the two air-conditioner terminals inside a standard wall-mount air-conditioning thermostat to the two terminals on the Powerflash module.

Code Translation

Sometimes you want to use one unit code to activate another unit code. This is called code translation. You can easily program a computer interface to perform code translation, and modules that are "scene capable" can be programmed to multiple unit codes; however, if you aren't using a computer interface or scene-capable modules, you can use a universal relay module in connection with a Powerflash module to perform code translation.

For example, you could use code translation if you wanted a table lamp to always come on when the general room lighting is turned on, but you also wanted to be able to control the table lamp separately. To begin, let's say that the general room lighting is unit code 2 and the table lamp is unit code 6. With code translation, when you press the unit code 2 button on a controller, the general room lights and the table lamp will both respond. When you press the unit code 6 button, only the table lamp will respond.

To set up the modules, connect the terminals on the Powerflash module to the terminals on the universal relay module with a piece of two-conductor cable. Plug the two modules intoside-by-side outlets (fig. 7-18). The outlets can be anywhere in the house; they don't need to be near the

devices you are controlling. Set the universal module to the correct house code and unit code. In this example, we will set it to unit code 2. Set the slide switches to **Continuous** and **Relay Only.** Set the Powerflash module to the correct house code and unit code. In this case, it is unit code 6. Set the slide switches on the Powerflash module to **Input B** (switch contact) and **Mode 3** (single unit code). Now when you send a unit code 2 signal, the universal relay module will respond, causing the Powerflash module to send a unit code 6 signal. This means that whenever you turn on unit code 2, unit code 6 will also turn on; however, the reverse is not true. When you turn on unit code 6, unit code 2 will not turn on.

Fig. 7.18: Connect the terminals on the Powerflash module to the terminals on the universal relay module with a piece of two- conductor cable, and plug the two modules into side-by-side outlets.

Using Switches with Low-Voltage Modules

Applications for low-voltage modules often require the use of external switches. Practically any type of switch will work with low-voltage modules, but two of the most useful are the microswitch and the magnetic switch.

Switch contacts on microswitches and magnetic switches are described as either normally open (**NO**) or normally closed (**NC**). With normally open contacts, the switch is **off** in its normal state. With normally closed contacts, the switch is **on** in its normal state. Single-throw switches offer you only one way. They have two terminals, and you must choose either **NO** or **NC** when you buy them. The most versatile for our purposes are double-throw switches, which allow you to choose either the **NC** or the **NO** function at the time of installation. Spring-loaded Double-throw switches have three terminals: a common (**Com**) terminal, a **NO** terminal, and an **NC** terminal. When you connect the switch, you always connect one wire to the **Com** terminal, and you choose between the **NC** and **NO** terminals, depending on what you want the switch to do.

The microswitch is a small spring-loaded lever switch. Some models have a roller on the lever (fig. 7-19). The switch has three terminals marked **Com**, **NO**, and **NC**. With nothing pressing on the lever, the **Com** and **NC** terminals will be connected inside the switch, and with the lever pressed the **Com** and **NO** terminals will be connected.

One wire from the Powerflash module connects to the **Com** terminal. You choose the other terminal depending on what you want the switch to signal. With nothing pressing on the lever, the C and NC terminals will be connected inside the switch, and with the lever pressed the C and NO terminals will be connected.

Magnetic switches are commonly used in alarm systems to indicate when a door or window has been opened. We'll cover alarms and other security applications in chapter 8. In this chapter, we'll tell you how they can be used with a Powerflash module. A magnetic switch consists of two parts: the switch, which mounts on a stationary surface; and the magnet, which mounts on a movable surface (fig. 7-20). For example, the switch can be mounted on a doorjamb and the magnet on the door. The big advantage of amagnetic switch is that there doesn't need to be any physical contact between the switch and the moving part. As long as the magnet is near the switch, it will be activated.

Garage Door Control

Many X10 catalogs recommend using a universal relay module to add X10 remote control to your garage door, so we've included installation instructions for this application in this chapter. With one of these relays wired to your garage door, you would be able to open and close it from inside your home. This could be handy when you're getting ready for bed and wonder if you left the door open. You could simply close the door with an X10 command. However, there are safety considerations regarding opening and closing a garage door when you can't see it. Most newer garage door openers include safety features that raise the door if it bumps against anything before it is totally closed, but it is still possible that a person could be hurt or property damaged by a closing garage door. Another consideration is security. If your garage door opener can be controlled by X10, it's possible that a thief armed with an X10 remote controller could open your garage and gain access to your home. For these reasons, you should consider carefully whether or not you want to be able to control your garage door using X10.

Fig. 7.19: This microswitch has a roller on the lever.

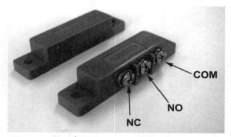

Fig. 7.20: Shown is a magnetic switch. Notice that this switch has three terminals marked Com, NO, and NC. This means you can choose the function of the switch at the time of installation. Other types only have two terminals and you must choose between NO and NC at the time of purchase.

Most garage door openers have a push button inside the garage to open and close the door. This button is similar to a doorbell button and operates on low voltage. Pushing the button opens the door if it's closed and closes the door if it's open. You can simply connect a universal relay module to the two wires that go to the push button to perform the same function by remote control (fig. 7-21). However, unless you can see the door, you won't know whether you are opening or closing it.

> Most garages with door openers have an outlet wired in the ceiling that the door opener's motor plugs into. You can minimize the amount of wire you will have to run by plugging the universal relay module into this convenient outlet (fig. 7-22).

Status Indicator Light

You can use a Powerflash module to provide a statusindication at a remote location in situations like this. Use a microswitch or a magnetic switch connected to a Powerflash module to send a signal to a device in another location to indicate the status. For example, on a garage door you could mount a magnetic switch at the bottom of the door behind the track (fig. 7-23).

When the magnet mounted on the door lines up with the switch, the Powerflash module will send a signal (fig. 7-24). The type of signal depends on how you connect the switch. If you use the **Com** and **NO** terminals, the Powerflash module will send an **On** command when the magnet is near the switch, indicating that the door is closed, and will send an **Off** command when the magnet is moved away from the switch. If you use the **Com** and **NC** terminals, the Powerflash module will send an **Off** command when the magnet is near the switch and an **On** command when the magnet is moved away from the switch. After choosing either **NO** or **NC**, set the slide switches on the Powerflash module to **Input B** (switch contact) and **Mode 3** (single unit code).

Fig. 7.21: If you connect a universal relay module to the two wires that go to the garage door opener push button, sending an On command opens the door if it's closed and closes the door if it's open.

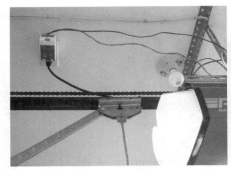

Fig. 7.22: The outlet on the ceiling for the garage door opener is a good place to plug in the universal relay module.

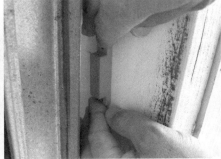

Fig. 7.23: The next two projects use magnetic switches to sense the position of the garage door. Mount the switches on the wood frame behind the track. Attach the magnet to the edge of the garage door so that it will line up with the switch when the door is closed.

Fig. 7.24: This diagram shows how to wire a Powerflash module to provide status indication. Use a microswitch or a magnetic switch connected to a Powerflash module.

At the remote location where you want to monitor the status, set an appliance module to the same house and unit code as the Powerflash module. Plug a light into the appliance module. When the Powerflash sends an **On** command, the light will turn on. If it sends an **Off** command, the light will go off. A small nightlight makes a good indicator light (fig. 7-25).

Tip In this garage door application, it's best to set the Powerflash and indicator light's appliance module to a house code different from the other modules in your house. Otherwise every time you use the All Off command to turn off the lights at night, you will also turn off the indicator light.

Close-Only Switch

A better solution, for security reasons, is to use X10 only to close the garage door and make it impossible to open it with X10 control. To do this, you will need to add a sensor that will determine if the door is open or closed. You can use a magnetic switch for this also. Mount the magnetic switch at the bottom of the door frame and attach the magnet to the door so that it lines up with the switch when the door is fully closed. Now wire the universal relay module and switch to the push-button terminals on the garage door opener as shown in fig. 7-26. Connect a two-conductor cable to the two push-button terminals on the garage door opener, leaving the original wires in place. Connect another piece of two-conductor cable to the **Com** and **NC** terminals on the magnetic switch. Run both cables to the universal relay module. Connect one of the wires from the magnetic switch to one terminal on the universal relay module. Connect one of the wires from the garage door opener to the other terminal on the universal relay module. Use a wire nut to connect the two remaining wires from the two cables. To complete the installation, set the house and unit code dials on the module and set the slide switches to **Momentary** and **Sounder and Relay**, then plug in the universal relay module.

When the door is open and you send an **On** command to the universal relay module, the module's contacts will close momentarily. Since the contacts are wired in parallel with the push button, the door will close just as if you had manually pushed the button. The sounder will beep, giving a warning that the door is closing. When the door is fully closed, the magnet lines up with the magnetic switch, opening the switch contacts. Because the magnetic switch is wired in series with one of the wires to the universal relay module, when the door is closed the universal relay module is disabled. Without this magnetic switch, the next time you sent an **On** command to the universal relay module, the door would open. With the magnetic switch, when you send an **On** command, the door will close if it is open, but nothing will happen if the door is already closed. You could also set up a mini-timer or a computer interface to close the door every night at a programmed time.

Fig. 7.25: A small nightlight makes a good indicator light at the remote location where you want to monitor the status of a device.

Fig. 7.26: This diagram shows how to wire a universal relay module with a magnetic switch to provide a close-only function.

Speaker Mute

You'll often see suggestions that you can simply place a universal relay module in the speaker line to mute speakers. While this method will work with many systems, you run the risk of damaging the amplifier in some systems. Check the instructions that came with the amplifier to see if they caution against disconnecting speakers with the amplifier turned on. Also, if you have multiple speakers in different rooms, when you cut off one set of speakers there will be a noticeable change in the volume of the other speakers. To minimize these problems, we recommend that you include an impedance-matching volume control in the speaker circuit ahead of the universal relay modules (fig. 7-27). However, you should always observe any cautions from the amplifier's manufacturer. An impedance-matching volume control is a speaker-volume control that presents a more constant load to the amplifier while varying the volume to the speaker. With this in the circuit, you can safely switch off speakers while the amplifier is running. An impedance-matching volume control is also handy if you have speakers in several rooms because it gives you independent control of the volume in each room. They even come in wall-mount models that look like a rotary dimmer switch.

 For an alternate method of muting speakers, see chapter 9. There, we'll show you how to use an IR interface to convert X10 commands to IR signals that mimic the signals from an IR remote control.

To build the speaker mute, you will need two universal relay modules and a stereo impedance-matching volume control. Begin by installing the impedance-matching volume control according to the directions that come with it. Note: A wall-mounted impedance-matching volume control requires fishing wires through the wall. If you don't want to go to this extra trouble, buy a surface-mounted control and install it in an inconspicuous location. After wiring the volume control, make sure it works properly, then install the universal relay modules. Attach two-conductor speaker cable to the terminals on one of the universal relay modules and run the cable to the impedance-matching volume control. Now go back to the impedance-matching volume control and disconnect the wire from the terminal marked **Output Right +** (this is the plus wire to the right speaker) (fig. 7-28).

Connect one of the wires from the universal relay module to this terminal. Use a wire nut to connect the other wire from the module to the speaker wire that you disconnected. Now repeat the procedure for the left speaker using the other universal relay module (fig. 7-29).

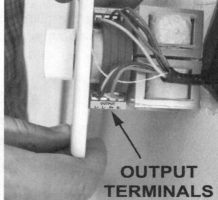

OUTPUT
TERMINALS

Fig. 7.29: This diagram shows how to use universal relay modules as speaker-mute controls.

Fig. 7.27: An impedance-matching volume control allows you to control the speaker volume separately in different rooms.

Fig. 7.28: To connect the universal relay modules to the impedance-matching volume control, pull the volume control out of the wall box and make the connections to the terminals inside.

Set both modules to the same house and unit code. Set the slide switches to **Continuous** and **Relay Only.** Now use a mini-controller to test the modules; you should hear them click as they turn off and on. Leave the modules in the on state and turn on the amplifier. The speakers should operate normally and you should be able to control the volume with the impedance-matching volume control. When you are sure everything is operating correctly, test the remote mute by sending an **Off** command from a mini-controller. Both speakers should mute.

 The universal relay module will respond to an All Off command, so you may want to use a different house code if you don't want to mute the speakers when you turn off all the lights.

With this setup, you can control the speakers from any controller in the house. If you have speakers in multiple rooms, you can repeat the procedure above in each room and assign the modules in each room different unit codes so that you can control each room individually. You can have an X10 controller by the amplifier to select individual speakers and you can also have a separate X10 controller in each room. You can also use the box-lid switch described below to activate the speaker mute.

This setup works best when you keep the volume control in the mid to low range. We measured the impedance and found that switching off the speakers when the impedance-matching volume control is set anywhere from off to about three-fourths of full volume had very little effect on the impedance. When the volume control is set to full volume, there is a slight change in impedance when you switch off the speakers but not as much as there would be without the volume control in the circuit.

Box-Lid Switch

At the beginning of this chapter we described a scenario where you could mute the stereo speakers when you opened a box containing a phone. You can build this system using a Powerflash module and a microswitch (fig. 7-30). Buy a decorative box that will fit your phone and drill a hole for the cord, as we described in chapter 1. Solder the wires from a two-conductor cable to the microswitch **Com** and **NO** terminals.

Position the switch on the side of the box so that the roller will be depressed when the lid is closed (fig. 7-31). Attach the switch with small screws. Run the cable to the Powerflash module and connect the wire to the two terminals. Set the module to the house and unit code for the stereo-mute system we described above. Set the slide switches on the Powerflash module to **Input B** (switch contact) and **Mode 3** (single unit code). Plug in the module and test the system. When the lid is opened, the Powerflash module should send an **Off** command, and when the lid is closed, it should send an **On** command.

Fig. 7.30: Using a decorative box, a Powerflash module, and a microswitch, you can build a system to mute your sound system speakers when you answer the phone.

Fig. 7.31: Position the microswitch on the side of the box where the roller will be depressed when the lid is closed. Attach the switch with small screws.

You can use this system to control anything under X10 control. In our example, it sends an **Off** command when the lid is opened to mute the stereo speakers, but you can change it to send an **On** command. To send an **On** command when the lid is opened, attach the wires to the **Com** and **NC** terminals on the microswitch. You could use this setup to turn on a spotlight over a display box to show off the box's contents when the lid is opened. The microswitch also works well on cabinet doors.

You now know how to use low-voltage modules to control a variety of things. The next chapter will introduce you to the use of X10 in home security systems.

Chapter 8

Wireless Home Security

It's late in the evening and you've just returned home from a weeklong vacation. You enter the front hallway and immediately realize that you've been burglarized. Thieves were able to open one of your ground floor windows, cut out the screen, and slip inside (fig. 8-1).

Being the victim of a burglary is a terrible experience; it makes you feel violated and vulnerable. But what can you do? The neighbors can't be expected to watch your house twenty-four hours a day, and the police have more pressing problems to deal with than the safety of your home.

The only answer seems to be purchasing a security system. Many thieves will not even bother with your home if they see security warning labels posted on your windows. Security systems are powerful deterrents, but most are expensive and require extensive wiring. It probably seems that only richer families in expensive neighborhoods can afford such systems.

However, for not much more than $100, you can set up a basic X10 security system, complete with motion detectors and an automatic phone dialer (fig. 8-2). The installation is quick and simple, and the system works. The next time you leave home for an extended amount of time, you can rest easy in the knowledge that your home is protected from intruders.

Basic X10 Security

A basic X10 security system comes with a dial-up security console, a main handheld security remote control, a keychain remote control, a motion sensor, and two door/window sensors (fig. 8-3). It also usually includes a lamp module. Companies often have sales or promotions on these systems and sometimes include for a nominal charge extra motion detectors, door and window sensors, and remote controls.

Fig. 8-1: An X10 alarm system can deter a thief from breaking into your home.

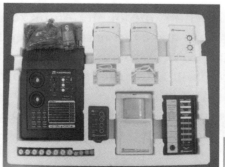

Fig. 8-2: A complete basic X10 security system kit.

Fig. 8-3: A basic X10 security system comes with a dial-up security console, a main hand-held security remote control, a keychain remote control, a motion sensor, and two door/window sensors.

Most security systems come with only two door/window sensors, so you will probably want to purchase more of these. Even if you find a special that includes extra motion sensors and door/window sensors, depending on the number of windows you have, you still might need more sensors. The sensors range in price from about $17 to $25, depending on the company. If you want to make do with the sensors that are included with the system, use the door/window sensors for your exterior doors, and use the extra sensors for just the windows on the ground floor. If you're still short on sensors, try using the motion detectors to cover areas near windows and doors that aren't equipped with sensors. With this type of setup, you will still have basic coverage, and you can add extra sensors later as you can afford them.

Security Console

The security console is the heart of the system (fig. 8-4). When the system is armed and the console senses a break in the system (i.e., when one of the door, window, or motion sensors is tripped), it automatically dials out to four preprogrammed numbers of your choosing to let someone know that the alarm in your home has been triggered. The console also has an 85-decibel siren that sounds for four minutes (unless you turn it off), and it flashes on and off all X10-controlled lights in the house that are set to the same house code as the console.

Fig. 8-4: The security console is the main component of the system.

The security console on a basic system will have a number keypad for entering phone numbers; a bank of sixteen zones with eight indicator lights; a house code dial; a unit code dial; record, arm, and bypass buttons; and a slide switch used to register remotes and sensors and to choose the basic run pattern.

The console keeps track of which zones are assigned to which sensors and will tell you if one of the first eight zones isn't responding (for example, if the batteries in the sensor aren't working properly) by flashing the corresponding zone light on the console. A steady zone light indicates that a window or door is open, a slowly blinking zone light indicates that a zone has a problem (such as weak batteries), and a rapidly blinking light indicates that a zone has been bypassed. The console also has a setting that sounds a chime in addition to turning on the zone lights when a door or window is open.

If you try to arm your system when one of the eight zone lights is on or blinking, the console will sound a trouble alarm. To make the alarm stop, you have two options. You can disarm the console and find out what the problem is with the zone and then correct it, or you can hit the bypass button. The bypass button will allow the system to bypass the zone that is reporting a problem. The system will then arm all other zones (note that the zone with the problem will not be armed). The bypass button is especially useful if you want to arm your system but want to leave a window open. A nice aspect of the system is that if you bypass an open window then later close the window, you don't have to rearm the system to make sure that this zone is activated. As long as the sensor is working properly, if you close a window that has been bypassed when setting the alarm, the system will automatically arm the closed window.

The system can also tell you if there is a problem with zones 9–16. If one of these zones is not working, the console will sound a trouble alarm when you try to arm the system. In this case, the trouble alarm will sound, but the zone indicators will not light. To find out which zone isn't working, press the bypass button. The indicator light that corresponds to the disabled zone will then blink rapidly, letting you know which of zones 9–16 isn't responding.

Handheld Security Remote

The handheld security remote that comes with a basic system has a series of **On/Off** rocker switches along with a **Panic** switch, an **Arm Home** switch, and an **Arm Away** switch (fig. 8-5). One of the **On/Off** switches (usually marked **Security Light**) controls a light set to the same house code and unit code as the security console. The other four **On/Off** switches control unit codes 1–4 of an X10 system. This means that you can use the security remote to control five different lights. There is also an additional rocker switch immediately below the four **On/Off** switches that allows you to dim the lights for unit codes 1–4.

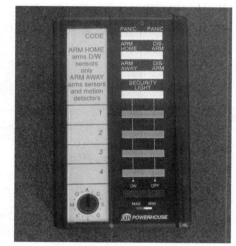

The **Panic** switch on the security remote allows you to trip the alarm even if it is not in the "armed" mode (fig. 8-6). If the system is not in the armed mode, the alarm will sound, but the system won't dial out. If you hit the **Panic** switch when the system is armed, the alarm will sound and the console will also dial out.

The handheld security remote also has a small slide switch marked **Max** and **Min** (fig. 8-7). The **Min** setting sets the alarm system to trigger instantly, whereas the **Max** setting sets the system to trigger after a delay, allowing you to exit or enter the house without setting off the alarm.

Fig. 8-5: The handheld security remote is the main remote. You can use this remote to arm the system either with a delay or without. It can also control X10 devices.

The **Arm Home** switch activates the door and window sensors, but not the motion sensors (fig. 8-8), so that your own movements around your house won't trip the alarm.

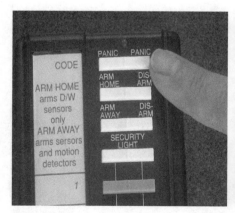

Fig. 8-6: The Panic switch on the security remote allows you to trip the alarm even if it is not in the "armed" mode.

Fig. 8-7: The Min setting sets the alarm system to trigger instantly, whereas the Max setting sets the system to trigger after a delay, allowing you to exit or enter the house without setting off the alarm.

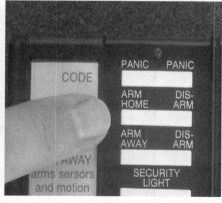

Fig. 8-8: The Arm Home switch activates the door and window sensors, but not the motion sensors.

The **Arm Away** switch activates door and window sensors along with motion detector sensors (fig. 8-9).

Keychain Remote

A basic keychain remote has four push buttons marked **Arm, Disarm, Lights On,** and **Lights Off** (fig. 8-10). The **Arm** button arms the security system immediately; there is no delay option with the keychain remote.

This type of remote is ideal for setting the alarm after you have closed your front door. Some keychain remotes also have a **Panic** mode; just press the **Arm** and **Disarm** buttons at the same time (fig. 8-11). The **Panic** mode is a really good feature for an elderly or disabled homeowner. The person should simply make sure to always carry the keychain remote. If the person has an accident and can't get to the phone, he or she can first arm the system with the **Arm** button, and then press **Panic** to set off the alarm and have it dial out. Remember that if the person presses the **Panic** button without first arming the system, the alarm on the console will go off, but it will not dial out.

The **Lights/On/Off** buttons control lights set to the same house and unit code as the console.

Installing a Basic X10 Security System

Installing an X10 security system is quick and simple, and in this chapter, we'll show you how to set up one of these systems. Depending on the type of system you purchase, some of the procedures might be slightly different, but the basics should be the same.

To set up your system, you will first want to pick an appropriate spot for the security console. The location you choose needs to be near a phone jack so that the system can call out in the event of a break-in. It also needs to be near a power outlet. The console, as is, is designed to sit on a table or counter, but wall-mount adapters are available.

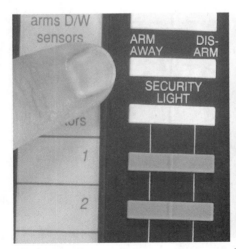 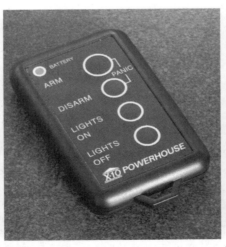 

Fig. 8-9: The Arm Away switch activates door and window sensors along with motion detector sensors.

Fig. 8-10: A basic keychain remote is ideal for arming the system after you have closed the front door.

Fig. 8-11: Some keychain remotes have a Panic mode that you activate by pressing two buttons at the same time.

Set up the security console by plugging it into the phone jack and power outlet (fig. 8-12). Install the backup battery, set the house code, and extend the antenna.

 When choosing a phone line for your transceiver, you might want to consider whether you would like a dedicated phone line for your system. Although a dedicated phone line isn't absolutely necessary, if you have one, you will never have to worry about the system not being able to dial out because the line is busy. If you don't want to go to the extra expense of a separate line, you can simply use an adapter (usually included) to add an extra jack if you already use the line for a telephone.

It's important to check out the coverage of the console; you don't want any dead spots in your home. In chapter 3, we discussed the positioning of base transceivers for wireless remote control, and the same principles apply here. If the signal has to go through several walls or through metal barriers (like a refrigerator), then you may have dead spots. To check for dead spots, hook up the console in the most convenient spot first because it's possible that you won't have any trouble from this location even if you have an upstairs and downstairs, or if you have a refrigerator and a few walls between your sensors and the console.

To check the coverage of the security console, make sure that the house code is set to the same house code as your other X10 modules and then carry a wireless remote to different spots around the house. Use the remote to turn on X10-controlled lights. If the lights work with the remote control from all parts of the house, then your coverage should be fine.

 The dial-up security console of an X10 security system can do double duty as a base transceiver for wireless remote control. This means that if you buy a security system, you probably don't need to also purchase a base transceiver, especially if your X10 system is not too complicated.

Now that the console unit is plugged in, you will need to have it recognize the security codes that have been preprogrammed into the handheld and keychain remotes. First, install batteries in the remotes. (Note: different brands may require different types of batteries; for example, one type of remote might require AAA batteries, whereas another type might require a 9V battery. Some systems will come with batteries already included.) Next, move the slide switch on the security console to **Install** (fig. 8-13).

Fig. 8-12: Plug the security console into a phone jack and power outlet.

Fig. 8-13: To register remotes and sensors with the security console, first move the slide switch on the console to **Install**.

Pick up the handheld security remote and press either **Arm Home** or **Arm Away** (fig. 8-14). The security console will beep to confirm that it has registered the remote's code.

If the base unit doesn't beep, you will need to have your handheld remote choose a new security code. The remote should have a hidden **Code** button that you can press with something pointed, like a pencil, to assign a new code (fig. 8-15).

Next, register your keychain remote. To register it, press the **Arm** button (fig. 8-16) and hold it down for about one second, then release it. The LED battery light on the remote should flash while you're holding the **Arm** button. Press **Arm** again; thesecurity console should beep once, acknowledging that you have added the remote to the system.

After the security codes have been registered, slide the base unit switch to **Run 1** or **Run 2** (fig. 8-17). In the **Run 1** position, if a door or window is opened when the system is in the unarmed mode, the corresponding zone indicator on the console will light up. In the **Run 2** position, the zone indicator lights up when a door or window is opened, and the console sounds a chime as well.

X10 security systems generally allow you to install anywhere from eight to sixteen remote controls, depending on the system you purchase, so each family member can have a remote.

Door/Window Sensors

The next step is to figure out which doors and windows you want to install the sensors on. Most basic systems come with just two door/window sensors, which of course are probably not enough. If you look for specials, you will often find deals where the company will include extra sensors (and other accessories) for a nominal charge. Most systems will accommodate a total of sixteen sensor combinations.

Fig. 8-14: To register the handheld security remote with the console, press either **Arm Home** or **Arm Away**.

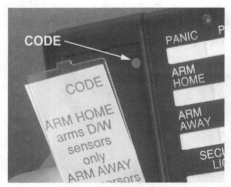

Fig. 8-15: The handheld security remote has a hidden Code button.

Fig. 8-16: Press the Arm button to register the keychain remote.

Fig. 8-17: If a door or window is opened, in the Run 1 position, the corresponding zone indicator on the console will light up. In the Run 2 position, the console sounds a chime as well as lighting up the corresponding zone.

The door/window sensors are magnetic switches attached by about a foot of two-conductor wire to a small transmitter pack that contains the batteries and the electronics that send an X10 signal to the security console when the window or door is opened (fig. 8-18).

The transmitter pack is mounted on the wall beside the door with screws; the magnetic switch has a built-in adhesive strip on one side of each of its two halves. Place the transmitter pack in the least visually obtrusive place; this is often right along the baseboard near the bottom of the door on the unhinged side (fig. 8-19). You can, of course, also mount the transmitter pack above the door frame if you want.

 Tip The mounting holes for some types of transmitter packs are inside the battery compartment, so you can't install the batteries in these packs and register them with the console before attaching them to the wall.

The wired half of the magnetic switch (it's attached to the transmitter pack) should be placed on the inside edge of the door frame. Here, you may run into a mounting problem with standard exterior doors with sloping casing molding. Because exterior doors on residential buildings swing inward, you have to make sure that the switch doesn't get in the way of the opening door (otherwise, your door won't open). However, there often isn't enough of an edge between the casing and the doorjamb to mount the magnetic switch, so you may have to chisel out a small notch in order to mount the switch flat enough to make a good connection with the other half of the switch (fig. 8-20).

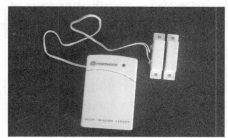

The other half of the magnetic switch should be mounted directly to the door. Make sure that the two halves line up with each other directly when the door is closed (fig. 8-21). Each side of the switch is marked with a small arrow, and the sides should be mounted so that these arrows face each other when the door is closed.

Fig. 8-18: The door/window sensors are magnetic switches attached by about a foot of two-conductor wire to a small transmitter pack.

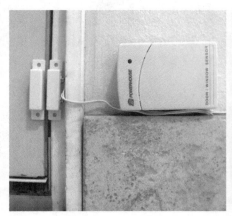

Fig. 8-19: The baseboard is often the least visually obtrusive place for the transmitter pack.

Fig. 8-20: You may have to chisel out a small notch to mount the switch flat on the door frame.

Fig. 8-21: The two halves of the magnetic switch should line up directly with each other when the door is closed.

Next, install batteries in the transmitter pack. Then, to register the sensor with the security console, press and hold the test button inside the transmitter pack for one second (fig. 8-22). The LED on the transmitter pack will flash, indicating that it has generated a security code. Next, go to the security console and slide the switch up to **Install**. Go back to the door sensor and once again press the test button. The console should beep and one of the zone LED indicators on the console should light up, indicating the zone to which the door sensor has been assigned.

The procedure for mounting window sensors is basically the same as that for mounting the door sensors. Mount the transmitter pack on the wall right next to the window where your window slides open. You should be able to hide the transmitter pack behind curtains or other window coverings (fig. 8-23).

If you push the sash up to open your window, mount the transmitter pack at the bottom of the window and stick the wired half of the magnetic strip at the edge of the window. Attach the other half of the switch to the edge of the window that slides up. Make sure that you line the magnets up so that the arrows point at each other and so that they are as close to each other as possible when the window is closed (fig. 8-24). The two
halves should be no more than 3/8 inch apart. If your window opens by sliding it to the side, you have more mounting options for the transmitter pack. You can place it near the top of the window at the side where it might be less visually obtrusive or at the bottom. Go through the same procedures described above for the door sensor to register the window sensor with the security console.

To test a door or window sensor, simply set the slide switch on the console to **Run 2**; then open the door or window. The corresponding zone light on the console should light up. The console will also sound a chime.

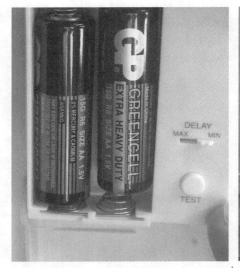

Fig. 8-22: Press and hold the test button inside the transmitter pack for one second to register it with the security console.

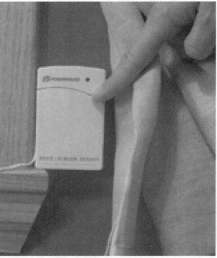

Fig. 8-23: You can hide the transmitter pack behind curtains or other window coverings.

Fig. 8-24: The two halves of the magnetic switch should be no more than 3/8 in. away from each other.

Special Wiring for Multiple Window and Door Combinations
The magnetic switches that come with the door/window sensors are quite versatile and will adapt to many applications, but in special situations you may want to use different or additional sensors. There are many different types of door and window sensors available for home security systems (fig. 8-25). The X10 transmitter packs are compatible with any sensor designed for a closed circuit (CC) installation. Such sensors may prove useful if you have a situation where the standard magnetic switch would be difficult to mount. Some types may require drilling holes in the jamb, but the electrical wiring will be the same.

You can add more than one sensor to a single transmitter pack. If you have two or more windows side by side or a door close to a window, you can make one door/window sensor do double duty simply by adding additional magnetic switches (you should be able to get an extra magnetic switch at a store that sells home security products) and running extra two-conductor wire between the switches. The transmitter pack can be mounted in an inconspicuous location like behind a curtain, and you can hide the wires to the additional locations by running them along moldings and baseboards.

When you add additional magnetic switches, the switches must be wired in series. To do this, disconnect one of the wires from the original switch and connect it to one of the wires to the additional switch. The other wire from the additional switch should be connected to the terminal on the original switch that you first disconnected (fig. 8-26).

To make wire connections in the alarm system, use crimp-on connectors. These are similar to wire nut connectors, but instead of screwing on, they slip over the wire ends and you use a special crimping tool to squeeze the connector tight on the wires (fig. 8-27). These connectors work better than wire nut connectors on the small wires used in alarm systems.

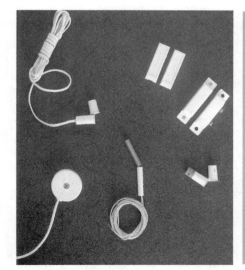

Fig. 8-25: There are a variety of door and window sensors that you can use with home security systems.

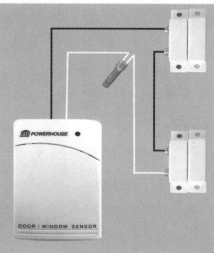

Fig. 8-26: When you add additional magnetic switches, the switches must be wired in series.

Fig. 8-27: Use a special crimping tool to squeeze the connector tight on the wires.

Glass-Breakage Detectors

In many cases a thief will simply break a window to gain entrance to a home. If this happens, a magnetic switch won't set off the alarm. There are special X10 glass-breakage detectors available, but they are expensive. A less expensive alternative is to connect standard CC glass-breakage detectors to an X10 transmitter pack. These detectors cost about $10 and simply stick onto the corner of the glass (fig. 8-28). They have a sensitive switch that detects the vibration caused by breaking glass. Because they are tuned to the vibration frequency of breaking glass, other vibrations like passing trucks won't cause false alarms.

If you are just replacing the original magnetic switch that comes with the door and window sensor, simply remove the two wires from the switch and connect them with crimp-on connectors to the two wires coming from the glass-breakage detector (fig. 8-29). If you have several windows close together, you can wire the detectors in series just as we described for magnetic switches above. In fact, you can mix glass-breakage detectors and magnetic switches in a single circuit. So if you had a door with two windows nearby, you could use a single transmitter pack with one magnetic switch and two glass-breakage detectors to protect all three openings.

To wire this example, mount the transmitter pack near the door and mount the original magnetic switch on the casing. Remove one of the wires from the switch and use a crimp-on connector to connect it to one conductor (in this example we'll call it the red wire) of a two-conductor cable. Attach the other conductor of the cable (we'll call it the black wire) to the screw terminal on the magnetic switch. Run the cable over to the first window and connect the black wire to one of the wires from the glass-breakage detector. Connect the other wire from the glass-breakage detector to the black wire in another piece of cable that runs to the second window. Connect the two red wires from the two cables together with a crimp-on connector. At the second window connect the two wires from the glass-breakage detector to the two wires in the cable (fig. 8-30).

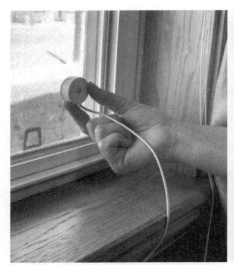

Fig. 8-28: A closed-circuit glass-breakage detector is a less expensive alternative to standard X10 glass-breakage detectors.

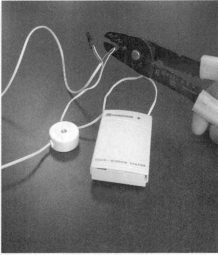

Fig. 8-29: Connect the two wires from the switch to the two wires from the glass-breakage detector with crimp-on connectors.

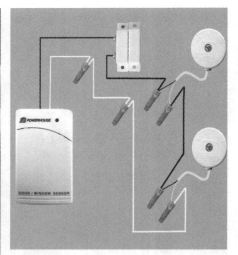

Fig. 8-30: You can use a single transmitter pack with one magnetic switch and two glass-breakage detectors to protect two windows and a door.

Motion Detectors

A single motion detector can cover a large area (fig. 8-31). Rather than install sensors on every door and window, you can aim a motion detector at an area like an entrance hall and protect several openings. Area sensors, such as motion detectors, are more prone to false alarms than perimeter sensors like those on doors and windows.

A good place to mount motion detectors is near outside doors or near windows where an unauthorized person is likely to try to gain entrance. You should place motion detectors fairly high up on walls, about six feet above the floor. They are equipped with a special lens that looks downward, so you don't need to tip them toward the floor. They generally have a range of about thirty to forty feet. Since most motion detectors work by detecting the heat of a moving body, it's a good idea to avoid installing motion detectors above heating ducts or near air conditioners; you also don't want to install them in a spot where the sun will shine directly on them.

Before you mount the motion detector, you should install its batteries and register the detector with the security console. To register the motion detector, press the **Code** button on the back of the detector in order to generate a security code (fig. 8-32). Next, on the security console, slide the switch up to **Install.** Press the **Test** button on the detector. The console will beep and assign the next available zone to the motion detector.

Some motion detectors come with a swiveling wall-mounting bracket that screws into the bottom of the detector (fig. 8-33). When you mount the detector on the wall, the face of the detector should be parallel to the wall; however, to get the best coverage, you may want to adjust it a little. The bracket swivels, so it's possible to tip the face of the detector up or down slightly if you need to. The swiveling bracket can also make installation easier if you want to mount the detector on the underside of an interior sofit.

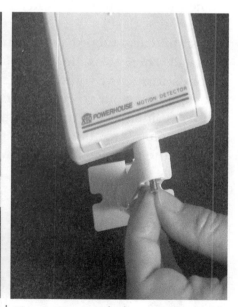

Fig. 8-31: Mount motion detectors about 6 ft. above the floor.

Fig. 8-32: Press the Code button on the back of the detector to generate a security code.

Fig. 8-33: Attach the swiveling wall-mounting bracket into the bottom of the detector with the screw.

You can adjust the sensitivity of the motion detector with a slide switch on the back of the detector. In the maximum setting, which is marked with the number 1, one motion triggers it instantly; in the minimum setting (marked by the number 2), it ignores the first motion and trips the alarm on the second motion (fig. 8-34).

To test the motion detector, make sure the slide switch on the back of the detector is set to the instant trigger option; then push in the **Test** button (also on the back) for one second. The LED on the detector should flash. Wait twenty seconds to give the sensor time to arm itself; then walk in front of it. The LED on the top of the sensor should flash whenever it senses movement. You may want to adjust the position of the detector to obtain the greatest coverage. When you are done testing the sensor, push the **Test** button again and it should be ready for normal operation in about two minutes.

Programming the Console to Make Calls
Use the number keypad on the console to program it to call four telephone numbers. To program the numbers, first slide the switch on the console to **Install**, and then press the **Prog** button on the keypad (fig. 8-35). Enter your first phone number, press the **Mem** button, and then press 1. This enters the number in the first memory location. To enter your next number, press **Prog**, enter the phone number, press the **Mem** button, and then press 2. Repeat for the next two numbers, using 3 and 4 for the memory locations.

It's a good idea to program a number in all four memory locations because if an intruder trips the alarm, the console will cycle through all four and call each number that's programmed. If you only have one number that you want to have called, enter the same number in all four locations. If you don't program a number for all four locations, the console will still cycle through each memory location, which could waste time in the event of a break-in.

If you want to change a number that you've programmed, slide the switch to **Install**, press the **Prog** button, enter the new number, press the **Mem** button, and then press the appropriate number for the memory location.

You should also record a voice message. To do this, make sure the slide switch on the console is set to Install. Then press the **Record** button (fig. 8-36). Once the **Busy** light comes on you'll have fifteen seconds to record your message, then the **Busy** light will go out. Say your message slowly and clearly, aiming your voice into the microphone on the console. Here is a sample message: "This is the Smiths' residence and the alarm has been triggered." Most systems come with a small earphone that you can plug into the console and listen to your message after you have finished recording it. To listen to the message, slide the switch from **Install** to **Run 1** or **Run 2**.

Fig. 8-34: The maximum setting is marked with the number 1, and the minimum setting is marked by the number 2.

Fig. 8-35: Press the Prog button on the keypad before entering a phone number.

Fig. 8-36: Press the Record button to record your message.

Your message should play automatically. At this point, if you have finished installing all of your sensors, you can simply leave the switch in **Run 1** or **Run 2**. Remember that in the **Run 1** position, the corresponding zone indicator on the console will light up when any door or window is opened when the system is unarmed. In the **Run 2** position, the console sounds a chime as well as lighting the indicator light.

Note: It's possible for the person being called to listen in to your home by pressing 0 on his or her telephone dial. When the person called presses 0, the system switches off the siren for seventy-five seconds so that the person can monitor what's happening in your home and determine whether it's necessary to call the police. After the seventy-five seconds, the system switches the siren back on for another four minutes, and then rearms itself. Be advised that if a person does listen in, the alarm system won't call any of the other numbers on your call list.

You should not program the console to call the police directly because in the event of a false alarm, you could have to pay a fine if the police respond.

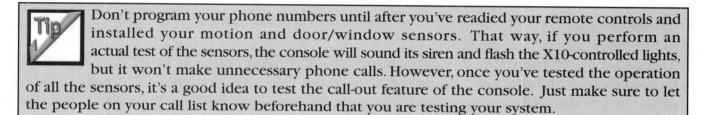

Don't program your phone numbers until after you've readied your remote controls and installed your motion and door/window sensors. That way, if you perform an actual test of the sensors, the console will sound its siren and flash the X10-controlled lights, but it won't make unnecessary phone calls. However, once you've tested the operation of all the sensors, it's a good idea to test the call-out feature of the console. Just make sure to let the people on your call list know beforehand that you are testing your system.

Outdoor Motion Sensor with Floodlights

You might like to have an advance-warning system that will scare off intruders before they try to break into your home. One option is an outdoor motion sensor equipped with floodlights that you can use in conjunction with your X10 security system or as a stand-alone deterrent (fig. 8-37).

Fig. 8-37: You can use an X10 outdoor motion sensor equipped with floodlights in your X10 security system.

This device can be programmed to turn on interior lights as well as outdoor floodlights, a feature that is useful as an extra precaution or as a stand-alone security measure. Ordinary outdoor motion detectors equipped with lights but no other security features sometimes don't deter thieves because when the lights go on, a thief can simply toss a rock at the outdoor lights and break them. But with an X10 motion sensor, you can program the detector to also turn on interior house lights or a loud radio, or even trigger the recorded sound of a barking dog.

You don't want to have an outdoor motion sensor tied into your alarm system because every stray cat and dog in the neighborhood will trip it, and you'll be plagued with false alarms. Likewise, you probably wouldn't want to have an interior light, radio, or dog alarm activated to go off while you are home—you probably wouldn't get much sleep. However, if you're not home, it makes sense to tie the X10 motion sensor to floodlights, interior lights, or noises to scare away would-be intruders.

The motion sensor with floodlights requires that you mount it in a standard round electrical box. (If the box is controlled by a switch, make sure you leave the switch in the **On** position.) Follow the wiring and installation procedures included in the owner's manual. The motion detector has a special panel inside that allows you to choose the X10 settings that you prefer (fig. 8-38). To test the motion detector and adjust it to the ranges that work best for you, first turn the **Dusk** control knob to **Light**, turn the **Range** control knob to **Max**, and set the **Time delay** dial to 0.1 minutes. Wait for one minute to allow the system time to reset itself, then walk around in the area covered by the detector. The floodlights should turn on.

Fig. 8-38: Use the special panel inside the motion detector to choose the X10 settings that you prefer.

After checking that the floodlights work, turn the **Dusk** knob to the setting already marked on the dial. Reset the **Range** knob to your preferred setting. **Max** will probably result in more false alarms than **Min**. Set the **Time delay** to the number of minutes you would like the floodlights to stay on after the sensor detects no additional motion.

This unit comes with several control options. For example, you can choose to have the floodlights stay on from dusk until dawn, you can choose to have the lights triggered when the sensor detects motion, or you can turn them on and off with X10 commands.

You can use the motion sensor to turn on up to four other appliance or light modules along with the floodlights. You can also set it so that four modules turn on at dusk and off at dawn.

More Sophisticated Systems

You can also buy systems that are professionally monitored by a security company. These systems are usually more expensive, ranging from about $200 to $300 and up, but the monitoring service itself is relatively inexpensive. One company offers a monitoring service for less than $10 per month. In some cases, you can add professional monitoring to a basic system like the one we've described above. The monitoring company would provide you with a special phone number for your console to dial if the alarm is triggered.

If you want to spend the extra money, X10 systems that are specifically designed to be monitored by a security company offer more features than you get with a basic system. Some of these systems are fairly advanced and are more like having a central home command center. You can use them to leave messages and instructions for other household members, to monitor when your children arrive home from school, and to control X10 lights and appliances.

With a professionally monitored system, the security company will be able to tell exactly which zone has been triggered. It's also possible to add fire or smoke alarms and personal panic buttons to systems like this. When an alarm goes off, the security monitoring company will be able to tell which door or window has been opened or if the alarm was triggered by the fire or smoke alarm or by someone pushing a panic button.

More-sophisticated systems also let you assign zones within your house. With this feature, instead of each window in a room having its own zone, you can assign one zone to all of the windows in a room. The systems also typically accommodate more than the standard sixteen zones on a basic system.

No matter which type of system you choose, with an X10 security system installed in your home, you should be able to go on vacation without having to worry about coming home to a burglarized house. In the next chapter, we'll discuss how to use X10 to control all those devices in your home that use infrared remote controls.

Chapter 9

Infared Interface

It seems that every new piece of electronic equipment you buy comes with its own infrared (IR) remote control. Although each by itself is convenient, eventually people tend to get overwhelmed with having too many separate remote controls (fig. 9-1).

Although universal remotes can help solve the problem, you still can't automate functions or use the remote from another room. Adding an X10 infrared interface will allow you to automate IR functions, control several different devices from a single remote, and use remotes in any location in the house (fig. 9-2).

There are two types of X10 IR devices that deal with IR signals. The most useful is the IR interface, which allows you to control IR devices with X10 commands. The other type is the IR mini-controller, which allows you to use an IR remote to send signals to X10-controlled devices. The next few pages discuss the IR interface; at the end of the chapter, we'll discuss the IR mini-controller.

IR remotes operate by sending a coded signal on a beam of invisible infrared light. Even though IR light is outside the range visible to our eyes, it behaves like regular light. That means you must have a direct line of sight between the remote and the receiving sensor on the piece of equipment. If the light is blocked by a wall or cabinet door, the remote will not work. One of the big advantages of an X10 IR interface is its ability to overcome this limitation. An IR interface acts like a go-between between the device receiving the IR signals and the device sending the X10 commands. The interface learns the IR signals that control a specific device. The power line adapter that comes with the interface receives the X10 commands and the interface converts these commands to IR signals. Since X10 signals travel over the power line, they will travel anywhere in the house to get to the interface.

What can you do with an IR interface? Back in chapter 1, we described how to use X10 to turn off the family room TV from your bedroom. With many modern TVs, however, simply turning off the

Fig. 9-1: Remote controls are convenient, but you can become overwhelmed if you have too many of them.

Fig. 9-2: An X10 IR interface will allow you to automate IR functions, control several different devices from a single remote, and use remotes in any location in the house.

TV with an X10 command to an appliance module will cause your TV to lose its memory settings. Instead, you can use an IR interface to perform the same task without losing the settings. Remember our gas log example in chapter 7? If your gas log already has an IR remote, it won't be necessary to wire a universal relay module to the thermostat. Instead, you can use an IR interface to set up the gas log so that you can control it with X10 commands. You can also use an IR interface to add remote control to your stereo system. In chapter 7, we discussed how to mute stereo speakers by adding universal relay modules. However, if your system has an IR remote control, you can use an IR interface to add X10 remote control.

Why, you might ask yourself, do I want to use X10 to control my equipment instead of just using the IR remote controls that I already have? Besides being able to turn things off and on from another room, when you use X10 to control devices that normally use IR remote controls, you gain the ability to program several different functions to happen all at once.

As home entertainment systems have become more complex, just turning the system on and starting a movie has become a multistep procedure. Instead of using separate remotes to turn on each device in the system and set them to the proper configuration, wouldn't it be nice to press a single button on an X10 controller and have all of the appropriate devices turn on and be ready to go? You can do this using the macro function of an IR interface. For example, you can press a button labeled "play DVD" that will turn on the TV and set it to AV input, turn on the surround sound system and set it to DVD input, and turn on the DVD player and start the DVD. In chapter 11, we'll show you how this macro can be nested within a larger macro that can also adjust the lighting in a room for optimum viewing and perform other functions like opening or closing curtains.

Setting Up the IR Interface

Installing the IR interface is simple: just connect the IR interface and the power line adapter with the supplied cable, plug in the power line adapter to an outlet, and it is ready to go (fig. 9-3); however, deciding where to position the IR interface requires some thought.

The interface transmits IR signals in two ways: through built-in IR blasters and through IR stick-on emitters that plug into the interface. The IR blasters are on the front of the interface and are powerful IR emitters that send the IR signals (fig. 9-4).

Fig. 9-3: To install the IR interface, simply connect it to a power line adapter with the supplied cable, and then plug in the power line adapter to an outlet.

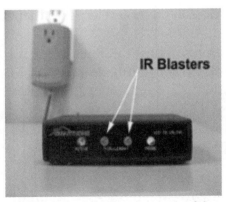

Fig. 9-4: IR blasters are powerful IR emitters that send IR signals.

These blasters require a direct line of sight to be effective, so to use the blasters, you should pick a location for the IR interface that will be visible to the equipment you want to control. The built-in blasters are powerful enough that you could place the IR interface on a shelf directly across the room from the equipment it controls, but you should be aware that a person standing in front of the IR interface could block the signal that the interface sends to the equipment.

For the most reliable operation, use the stick-on emitters. These are IR emitters on the end of a wire several feet long that plug into the IR interface. They use a self-adhesive tape to stick to the front of the controlled device directly over the device's built-in sensor (fig. 9-5). You can plug up to three of these stick-on emitters into one interface. The built-in IR blasters still work when the stick-on emitters are plugged in, so you can use both stick-on emitters and IR blasters to control different devices (just remember that the IR blasters require a line of sight to the device you want to control). This can be useful when some devices are inside a cabinet and others are in a different location in the same room.

You can place the IR interface outside the cabinet facing the equipment you want to control with the IR blasters, and then run the stick-on emitter wires inside the cabinet and attach the emitters to the equipment inside (fig. 9-6).

 Like visible light, IR light can be reflected by some surfaces. You may be able to find a location for the IR interface that covers a larger area than expected because the signals are reflected by walls. However, the reflected signal will be weakened and may not be as reliable as one that is in a direct line of sight.

For stick-on emitters to work reliably, you must find the location of the IR sensor on the controlled equipment and place the emitter directly over the sensor. Sometimes the location is obvious; the sensor will look like an LED on the front panel (fig. 9-7).

Fig. 9-5: Attach the stick-on emitters to the front of the controlled device directly over the device's built-in sensor.

Fig. 9-6: You can place the IR interface outside the cabinet facing the equipment you want to control with the IR blasters, and then run the stick-on emitter wires inside the cabinet.

Fig. 9-7: The sensor will look like an LED.

If it is not in plain sight, the sensor is often hidden by a dark red plastic panel (fig. 9-8).

Sometimes it's hidden behind the plastic faceplate of the equipment. You may be able to find the sensor by closely examining the face of the equipment with a flashlight (fig. 9-9).

If you can't find the sensor by examining the faceplate, you can try blocking the sensor to find its location. Use something opaque, like a piece of cardboard, to block the IR signal from the remote from reaching the sensor (fig. 9-10). Have someone aim the remote at the equipment and press one of the buttons while you hold the cardboard in front of the face of the equipment. Choose a function that is rapidly repeatable like volume or channel. Move the cardboard around until the remote stops working. By moving the cardboard slightly and observing when the remote works again, you can pinpoint the location of the sensor.

 The stick-on emitters don't completely block the sensor on the device, so even though you have placed the emitter over the sensor, in most cases the original remote will still work.

Programming
The IR interface is similar to the learning remote described in chapter 3. You use the original remote control to teach the IR commands to the IR interface. Once the interface has learned the command, you use a mini-controller or a maxi-controller to assign an X10 code to trigger the IR command.

 When you're programming the IR interface, only press the set button briefly. If you hold the set button for more than five seconds, it will erase all commands that are already in the memory.

Fig. 9-8: The sensor is often hidden by a dark red plastic panel.

Fig. 9-9: Use a flashlight to see the sensor behind the plastic panel.

Fig. 9-10: Use a piece of cardboard to block the IR signal from reaching the sensor.

Follow the exact learning procedures in the instructions that come with the IR interface. As an example, we will give the general procedure for teaching the IR interface to turn on a TV. Start by pressing the "Set" button on the back of the interface for about one second (fig. 9-11).

The red "Active" LED should start blinking. Holding the TV remote about an inch away from the front of the IR interface, press the power button on the remote (fig. 9-12).

If the IR interface has learned the command successfully, the red LED will turn off and the green "Probe" LED will begin blinking. We want to assign this function to X10 house code A, unit code 6. To do this, we press the **ON** side of the rocker switch for unit code 6 on a mini-controller set to house code A (fig. 9-13).

If the interface has successfully received the X10 signal, the green LED will stop blinking and stay on for a few seconds, then turn off. Now you can press the A6 button on any X10 controller in the house and send a "Power" command to the TV.

You can use the **On** and **Off** X10 commands to control different devices. For example most remotes have a power button that serves to turn the unit on and off, so you don't need separate on and off commands assigned to the X10 buttons. In the TV example mentioned above the **On** side of the X10 button will turn the TV on if it is off and off if it is on. This leaves the **Off** side of the button on the controller unassigned. You could program the **Off** side to control the power function of the DVD player. This gives you the ability to control twice as many devices.

Fig. 9-11: To begin the general learning procedure for an IR interface, press the "Set" button on the back of the interface for about one second.

Fig. 9-12: Next, press the power button on the remote.

Fig. 9-13: Press the **On** side of the rocker switch for unit code 6 on a mini-controller set to house code A.

Using the Bright/Dim Buttons

Functions that need a continuous up or down command (like volume or channel) can be assigned to the **Bright/Dim** buttons on an X10 controller. In this case, it is best to use a controller like the maxi-controller to do the programming because it sends the unit code separately from the **On** and **Off** commands (fig. 9-14). Once the IR interface is programmed, you can use any type of X10 controller to operate the device.

To program the IR interface to control the TV volume, you use the same procedures that you used to program the TV to turn on. Again, start by pressing the "Set" button on the back of the interface. The red "Active" LED will blink. Hold the TV remote about an inch away from the interfaceand press the "Volume Up" button on the remote (fig. 9-15).

The red LED should turn off and the green "Probe" LED will blink. Next assign the X10 code by first pressing the unit code 6 button and then pressing the **Bright** button (fig. 9-16). To program Volume Down, repeat the procedure and assign it to unit code 6 **Dim.**

Once the IR interface is programmed, the **Dim/Bright** button will control the TV volume as long as the last X10 command sent was an A6. This is the same way the normal **Dim/Bright** command operates—after you turn on a light, the **Bright/Dim** button will control the light until another unit code is sent; then the buttons will control the light associated with that unit code. In the case of the TV, this can be a slight problem if you are using a mini-controller; for example, after you turn on the TV, you can adjust the volume with the **Bright/Dim** buttons, but if you later turn on a light with an X10 command, the **Bright /Dim** buttons will dim the light instead of controlling the TV volume. To return to TV volume, you need to send another A6 signal, but if you press 6 **On** again, the TV will turn off. One way around this problem is to use a maxi-controller. Then you would simply press the 6 button and then **Dim** or **Bright** to control the TV volume. If you would rather use a mini-controller, leave the **Off** side of the button unassigned, and then you can press 6 **Off** without affecting the TV. Sending the 6 **Off** signal will reset the IR interface to control the TV volume in response to **Bright/Dim** commands.

 |  |

Fig. 9-14: It is best to use a maxi-controller to do the programming because it sends the unit code separately from the On and Off commands. | **Fig.** 9-15: Hold the TV remote about an inch away from the interface and press the "Volume Up" button on the remote. | **Fig.** 9-16: Assign the X10 code by first pressing the unit code 6 button and then pressing the **Bright** button.

Programming Troubleshooting

Most of the time the learning process will go smoothly, but occasionally there will be a problem getting the IR interface to learn a command. Here are a few tips to solve common learning problems. The most common source of problems is weak batteries in the remote control that you are using to teach the commands. If you run into any programming glitches, the first thing to try is to replace the remote's batteries. Next, make sure that the remote is directly in line with the two IR LEDs on the front of the IR interface. Experiment with different distances from the front varying from one to three inches. Light sources can interfere with the learning process. Darken the room or shield the remote and IR interface with a dark towel. Even the glow from a TV screen or computer monitor can cause problems. If there is a probe connected to the IR interface, unplug it during the learning process (we'll discuss probes later). Usually you continue pressing the remote button until the IR interface signals that it has learned the command by switching off the red LED, but sometimes it works better to press the remote button and then quickly release it.

Once the green LED starts flashing, the next X10 command that is sent will be assigned. Occasionally, someone else may press a button on an X10 controller elsewhere in the house before you press the one you intended. As a result, the IR command will be assigned to the wrong X10 command. If this happens, just start the learning process over and tell everyone to refrain from using any X10 controls for a few minutes.

Macros

A macro is a series of commands initiated by a single trigger command. This is a powerful function of the IR interface that allows you to perform a multistep procedure by simply pressing one X10 button. The only limitation is the size of the IR interface's memory. The memory can hold about thirty-one commands, so there should be ample memory for two or three separate macros.

To program a macro, you simply follow the procedure given above for each remote function. Each time you reach the step where you press the X10 controller button, press the button that will trigger the macro. You can add steps to a macro at any time. For example, if we wanted to add a command to turn on the DVD player to the TV power command that we programmed above, we would teach the IR interface the DVD Power command and then press the **On** side of the rocker switch for unit code 6 on a mini-controller set to house code A. Now when you press the A6 **On** button, the TV and the DVD player will both respond.

Fig. 9-17: In our example home, we use an IR macro to turn on the sound system and set it to play our favorite station on the satellite radio. Some equipment like this satellite radio won't accept additional IR commands until it finishes a start-up sequence. In this case, when the XM logo disappears, it is ready to accept a channel command.

In our example home, we use an IR macro to turn on the sound system and set it to play our favorite station on the satellite radio (fig. 9-17). This way, we can simply press a button on any mini-controller in the house to start the music on our whole-house sound system.

> **Tip** The IR interface will send the IR signals in the order they are learned. If a particular sequence is necessary to operate the equipment successfully, be sure to program the commands in the correct order. Sometimes it takes a few seconds for a device to start up before it will respond to another command. In this case you can sequence the commands to give the device time to start up. For example, the satellite radio in our example home won't respond to the command to change stations until it has gone through its start-up sequence. If we sent the channel command immediately after the power command, nothing would happen. To solve this problem, we programmed the satellite radio power command first, then the power commands to the other sound system components. The last command in the macro sequence sets the satellite radio to the desired station. This gives the radio enough time to start up before receiving the stationcommand. If you need more time, you can insert dummy commands to nonexistent equipment into the macro. A dummy command is simply any command from a remote that is used for other equipment and that won't have any effect on the equipment you want to control. We saved the remote from an old CD player that we don't use any more to create dummy commands. The dummy commands just pad out the time between the actual commands.

You can use a mini-timer or a computer interface to trigger an IR macro at a preset time. If you are a TV news junkie, for example, you could program a macro that turns on the TV to your favorite news channel, and then set the mini-timer to trigger the macro when you want to wake up in the morning.

Using Probes

One problem with most IR remotes is that they usually do not have separate on and off buttons. Instead, the power button turns the unit on and off. This is fine if you are manually controlling the device, and you can either see or hear if the unit is off or on. However, if you want to control a device in another room and you can't tell if it is on or off, how do you know whether you are turning it on or not? The IR interface solves this problem with optional probes that can determine the actual state of the controlled device (fig. 9-18).

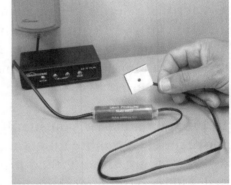

Fig. 9-18: You can use optional probes to determine automatically the state of a controlled device.

The probe is useful when you automate a macro. Take our example of the TV news junkie who wants the TV to turn on automatically in the morning. Suppose she awakens early one morning before the alarm on the mini-timer goes off. She gets up and manually turns on the TV. However, when the alarm goes off on the mini-timer, it will trigger a macro that will send an on/off command to the TV. If the macro doesn't know whether the TV is on or off, it will simply send a command that turns the TV on if it is off, off if it is on. In this situation, without the probe, the macro will turn off the TV. However, with a probe wired to the IR interface, the probe will send a signal indicating that the TV is already on, which will in turn tell the macro not to send the IR power command.

The probe plugs into a jack on the back of the IR interface marked "Probe" (fig. 9-19). Several types of probes are available: TV detector probes, light detector probes, video detector probes, low-voltage probes, and contact closure probes. The TV detector probe can indicate whether a TV is on by sensing the high frequency RF (radio frequency) that leaks from an operating TV. The light detector probe can sense when an indicator light is on. It can be attached directly over the power indicator light of a device. The video detector probe plugs into the video-out jack of a device and senses the presence of a video signal. (Note: This probe won't work correctly if the device outputs a blank blue screen signal when it is in stand-by mode.) The low-voltage probe detects between 3V and 28V AC or DC. Some AV equipment may have low-voltage output terminals that this probe can connect to. The contact closure probe can be used if the controlled device has relay terminals.

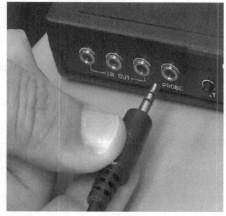

Fig. 9-19: Plug the probe into the jack on the back of the IR interface marked "Probe."

To program the IR interface to check the probe status, follow the general procedures for programming the interface to recognize IR remotes. When you get to the point where you assign the X10 code, use a maxi-controller to send the unit code first and then either an **All On** or **All Off** command. At this point, you might think that using **All On** or **All Off** in the IR command will turn off everything in your house every time you turn on the TV; however, when programming an IR interface, the **All On** command just tells the interface to check the probe when an **On** command is received. If the probe detects that the device is already on, the IR interface will not send the IR command. If the probe detects that the device is off, the IR command will be sent. The **All Off** command has the opposite effect. It programs the IR interface to check the probe when an **Off** command is received and only sends the signal if the probe determines that the device is on.

You will turn on or off everything on that house code while you are programming the IR interface, but this shouldn't be a big problem since it will only happen once. Once you have programmed the probe function, you don't use an **All On** or **All Off** command to activate it. You simply use regular **On** and **Off** commands.

The probe function also sends an X10 signal when the probe status changes. You can use this feature to provide remote monitoring of a device's status. For example, suppose you have an AV system in the basement and your kids tend to leave it on all day when no one is using it. You could set up an indicator light similar to the one we described for the garage door in chapter 7. Plug a night-light into an appliance module and put it somewhere visible upstairs. Above the kitchen counter might be a good location. Now if someone turns on the AV system and the probe detects the power light coming on, it will send an X10 **On** signal for the unit code assigned to the AV system. With the appliance module upstairs set to the same unit code, the night-light will turn on whenever the AV system in the basement is running. If you see the light on and know that no one is using the system, you can use an X10 remote to turn it off from upstairs. The night-light will turn off, confirming that the AV system is indeed off. This feature is also useful when programming computer macros (see chapter 10). In this case, you could use a conditional statement to trigger a macro based on the state of a device controlled by the IR interface.

Do-It-Yourself IR Interface

If you only want to control one IR function by X10, you can make a rudimentary IR interface using a standard remote control and a universal relay module. For example, in chapter 7, we talked about using X10 to mute a sound system when you answer the phone. With an IR interface, it isn't necessary to install impedance-matching volume controls or universal relay modules for each speaker because with the interface, you are in effect using the stereo's IR remote control. If you only want to use an IR interface to mute your stereo speakers or perform some other one-function application, you could make this simple do-it-yourself interface.

To build the interface, you will need an extra remote for the device; you can use an inexpensive universal remote for this. Open up the remote's case and examine the keypad area on the circuit board. Find the contacts that correspond to the button you want; in our case we will use the mute button. Solder two-conductor cable to the contacts (fig. 9-20). You may need to scrape off a coating on the circuit board to get down to bare copper. After you have attached the wires, cover them with a piece of electrical tape. If you don't cover the wires, one of the button contacts could short-circuit them. Cut a small exit notch for the wire in the side of the remote case. Route the wire through the notch and reassemble the remote.

Now connect the other end of the wire to the two terminals on the universal relay module (fig. 9-21). Keep this wire as short as possible—three feet is about the maximum you should use. A longer wire could pick up interference that will make the remote erratic.

To finish the installation, place the remote near the device you want to control (in our case the sound system amplifier) with the IR emitter facing the sensor, and set the house and unit code dials on the universal relay module to the desired settings. Set them to the same settings as the Powerflash module used for the telephone box project in chapter 7. Set the slide switches to **Momentary** and **Relay Only**, and then plug in the universal relay module. Now when you send the assigned X10 code, the universal relay module's contacts will close momentarily. This will have the same effect as pressing the mute button on the remote. If you use this with the phone box project we described in chapter 7, you will need to connect the wires to the microswitch in the box differently. Solder the wires from a two-conductor cable to the microswitch **Com** and **NC** terminals. This will cause the Powerflash module to send an **On** signal when the box lid is opened. The operation will be slightly different also. When you lift the lid, the music will mute, but when you close the lid, the music will still be off. To get the music to start again, lift the lid slightly after you have closed it and then let it down again. This will send another **On** signal activating the mute button, and the system will go off mute.

Fig. 9-20: Solder two-conductor cable to the mute contacts in the extra remote.

Fig. 9-21: Connect the other end of the wire to the two terminals on the universal relay module.

X10 IR Mini-controller

So far we have concentrated on converting X10 signals to IR signals, but what if you want to use an IR remote to control an X10 device? You can use an X10 IR mini-controller to convert IR signals to X10 signals (fig. 9-22). You can achieve the same goal by using the universal remote described in chapter 3 to send RF signals to a base transceiver. The IR mini-controller is just another way to do this.

The X10 IR mini-controller performs the opposite function of the IR interface. It receives IR signals from a remote control and converts them to X10 signals. This device has a limited application. Unless you have a special need for this, you probably will be better served by a base transceiver and RF remote system like that described in chapter 3. In fact, you must use one of the X10 universal remotes described in

Fig. 9-22: An X10 IR mini-controller converts IR signals to X10 signals.

chapter 3 to send the IR signals to the IR mini-controller, so the only component that you are replacing is the base transceiver, and you don't get the multiroom capability that an RF remote offers. You may think of other applications for this unit; however, you would be most likely to use this device if there is so much RF interference in your area that an RF remote won't work.

To set up the X10 IR mini-controller, simply set the house code dial and plug in the cord. Place it somewhere that will give it a good line of sight to the IR remote. On top of the TV is a good spot. Next program an X10 universal remote to send the appropriate IR codes. Look up the three-digit programming code for the mini-controller in the instruction manual that comes with the universal remote. In our case, the code for the mini-controller is 013. Start programming the remote by pressing the **setup** button on the remote until the LED lights steadily, then release the **setup** button. Next press and release the **X10** button on the remote. Finally enter the three-digit code for the IR mini-controller. The LED should turn off after you enter the last digit. Now the remote is programmed to control X10 devices via the IR mini-controller.

To use the remote for X10 control, first press the X10 **Mode** button, then enter the unit code of the device you want to control on the number keypad. You don't need to enter an initial zero for single digit numbers. After you've entered the unit code, press the function key you want. The keys serve dual purposes on the remote, but they are all clearly labeled. Here is a list of the dual-function keys:

A/V	X10
Channel+	On
Channel–	Off
Volume+	Bright
Volume–	Dim
Power	All On
Mute	All Off

You now have a good understanding of IR interfaces and what you can use them for. The next chapter discusses controlling X10 devices and settings using your computer.

Chapter 10

Computer Control

Even though you now have various lights and devices through-out your home under X10 control, they still require a bit of human intervention. For example, you still have to push buttons on remotes, mini-controllers, or wall switches to make things do your bidding. Even if you have a mini-timer, its scheduling and controlling capabilities are fairly limited. Wouldn't it be nice if there were some sort of autopilot that could take over the controls for you? Fortunately, such a thing exists—a computer power line interface module with the appropriate soft-ware is just the ticket to help you reach the next level of home automation (fig. 10-1).

Fig. 10-1: A computer power line interface module will help you reach the next level of home automation.

A computer power line interface module is a plug-in module about the size of an appliance module. You can think of it as a mini-timer that you can program from your computer. The computer power line interface module contains all of the electronics to generate X10 commands and an interface that connects it to your computer. The software that comes with the interface allows you to enter information about how and when you want X10 commands sent. The computer transfers this information to the computer power line interface module, where it is translated into actual X10 commands and sent over the power lines to the modules in your home.

Some computer interface modules have internal memory to store the programming. With this type you can download a schedule of timed events into the module and then disconnect the cable to the computer. The module will operate as a stand-alone timer without any help from the computer. You will only need to connect it to your computer again if you want to change the scheduling. In our example home, we have set up different schedules for spring, summer, fall, and winter. At the beginning of each season we connect the computer interface module to the computer and download the new schedule. Then we disconnect the module from the computer and let it run independently until the next season change.

With computer control, you can send any X10 command to any of the 256 possible house and unit code combinations, at any time, and schedule such commands to run automatically. This chapter will cover the basics of computer control and home automation software and will also introduce you to the concept of programming macros. In chapter 11, we will discuss macros and scenes in greater detail, and in chapter 12, we will talk about voice activation, another way to expand your X10 system using your home computer.

Choosing a Computer Power Line Interface Module

There are two basic considerations when you buy a computer interface module: how the computer interface will connect to your computer and where the scheduling information will be stored. Computer interface modules connect to computers via either USB ports or serial ports. The modules are available with or without internal memory, although most have an internal memory.

Most newer computers have a USB connection, so it is preferable to buy a USB computer interface (fig. 10-2) unless you will be using it with an older computer that has only a serial port. Early X10 computer modules with a USB connection had one major drawback: they couldn't be used on a "stand-alone" basis (without being connected to the computer) because they had no internal memory. However, this drawback has been solved with the introduction of USB X10 controllers that can store as many as a thousand commands in a 32 kilobyte (KB) nonvolatile memory chip. The device also uses a backup battery to keep its internal clock running.

If you don't mind having home automation software always running in the background on your computer and you aren't particularly concerned about the power going off, you can use the cheaper USB controller without internal memory. However, if you want an extra measure of stability and reliability, you may want to spend a bit extra and invest in a controller that has internal memory. These computer controller modules have backup battery power to "remember" every X10-related command or procedure scheduled. Thus, they will continue to work even after the computer that was used to program them has been shut off. This feature is particularly useful if you are going to be away from home on vacation and want to make sure that a power failure doesn't disable your entire system. Although your computer won't be able to turn itself back on after a power outage, the X10 computer controller's battery backup will ensure that the basic events in your X10 schedule will still be carried out. Keep in mind, however, that some higher-level functions (such as voice control) do require that the computer be on all the time.

Older computers that don't have USB ports require a serial port computer interface (fig. 10-3).

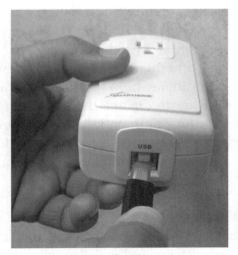

Fig. 10-2: It is preferable to buy a USB computer interface if you have a newer computer.

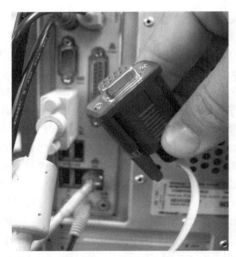

Fig. 10-3: Older computers that don't have USB ports require a serial port computer interface.

The serial port is used to connect a variety of devices, typically a mouse or a modem, to the computer. Most older PCs have at least one or two serial ports. Older Macintosh computers have a different type of serial port, but there are adapters available that allow you to connect the serial port interface to these types of computers (fig. 10-4).

Fig. 10-4: Adapters are available that will allow you to connect a serial port interface to an older Macintosh computer.

Serial port computer interfaces are the least expensive; however, they only have a tenth of the memory available in the USB interface. The increased internal memory available in USB interface modules makes them well worth the increased cost.

A serial port interface has a battery backup and internal memory that can store about a hundred commands, so you can disconnect it from the computer and let it run as a stand-alone controller.

 If you aren't going to leave your computer turned on all the time, be sure to disconnect the cable from the serial port interface module before you turn off the computer. Some serial interfaces have a quirk that causes them to behave erratically if they are connected to a powered-down computer.

Software

Regardless of which type of X10 computer controller you buy, it will likely come with basic home automation software. You can also download programs from the Internet for free or for a nominal charge. The programs that come with the computer modules have enough features to give you a fairly wide range of controlling capabilities. Although such programs may differ in appearance, most are fairly similar in functionality and ease of use.

When you want to go beyond the basic features, you can buy advanced home automation software that has a sleeker-looking interface and features more bells and whistles. For example, advanced software programs allow more complicated macros that involve conditional procedures and statements like "if-then" and "or else." Advanced software can also be used for voice control, voice announcements by the computer, and sending e-mail notifications.

Free home automation software programs available for PCs include ActiveHome and Smarthome Manager Essential. There are dozens of advanced home automation programs available for purchase, including Home Control Assistant, HomeSeer, Smarthome Manager Plus, Firecracker, Premise Home Control, and HAI. Macintosh users can try free programs like Xtension or pay for more advanced software such as Indigo, Thinking Home, or Mouse House.

Most of the basic software that is available will do a lot. In fact, it will probably do just about everything you need it to do. We recommend that you try out one or two free programs before you pay for a more advanced one. Only buy a more advanced program if you need to run more complex macros involving multiple conditionals, or if you want to be able to monitor continuously the state of a two-way module.

There are common elements in all home automation software. Even the most basic software will likely include the following features.

Module Selection

Basic home automation software will have a menu that lists various types of X10 modules, including lamp modules, appliance modules, motion detectors, and heavy-duty modules. Choosing the correct module type is important because it sets the parameters that a particular module can recognize. For example, an appliance module won't recognize a **Dim** command. When you choose the appliance module, the program will not list **Dim** as an option for that module.

After selecting the appropriate module from the menu, you can then use the program to enter the module's settings, including its assigned house and unit codes and the desired dim level (if applicable).

You can usually select from various icons for a given module. These icons represent different types of light fixtures and appliances that you might control with X10 modules. They don't affect the operation of the program; they are simply graphic reminders to show you what type of device is connected to the module. For example, you could choose a picture of an outdoor light to represent the front porch light or a chandelier icon to represent the dining room lights.

Timed Events

The core of any home automation software is the timed-event function. You use this to schedule the times you want modules to turn on or off. The software will also configure the computer interface to calculate the sunrise and sunset times for a particular area. You enter the geographic coordinates (latitude and longitude) of the place where you live (or simply choose the nearest city from a menu), and the program will use this data to figure out the correct sunrise and sunset times.

The software will also have a dialogue box for you to enter your time zone. Most programs have a dialogue box you can check to adjust automatically for daylight savings time.

With this time information loaded into your program, you can create timed events to turn a device on or off or set the dim level. The timed events can be either onetime or recurring. You can also set the specific days on which the timed event will occur, so you can have complete control over when each event takes place. For example, if you have an event that turns on your bedroom lights to wake you up for work, you can choose to disable the event on Saturday and Sunday.

Timed events also have a security option. When you select this option, the event happens at a random time around the programmed time. This is a useful security feature, since it makes it so the lights do not always go on or off at exactly the same time each night. You can program some lights with this security feature to make your home look occupied when you're away.

> **Tip** If you are using a serial port computer interface, you may need to limit the number of sunrise-sunset events that you include. The sunrise-sunset timer function occupies a larger portion of a serial port computer interface's limited built-in memory than specific timed events (some serial port controllers are able to store only about a hundred commands). However, you really don't need to worry about this unless you start to run out of memory. In our example home, we have three sunrise-sunset-dependent events, fifteen other timed events, and three macros, which combine to take up only 70 percent of the serial port interface's memory.

Most home automation programs have a "tolerance" feature that determines the precision of the event timing. For example, if you set the dusk tolerance setting to twenty minutes, the light will go on some-time within twenty minutes of sunset. The higher the precision, the more memory the event will use. The USB interfaces with greater memory will allow you to use higher precision and still have enough memory to store all of the events.

Macros

Most computer control programs have some form of macro capability. A macro is a series of related instructions that are carried out in response to a trigger event. In X10-related contexts, the trigger event can be an X10 command sent from a controller anywhere in the house, a light going on or off, the sun going down or coming up, a motion sensor, a command sent via touch-tone phone, or even a person's voice. Chapter 11 discusses macros in greater detail, and chapter 12 discusses voice- and phone-activated commands. To better understand how macros work, let's consider a simple example. Arriving home from work, a homeowner drives into her driveway and presses a single button on her wireless keychain remote control. As soon as this signal is received by the computer interface, it activates a "welcome home" macro, enacting the following sequence of steps: the driveway lights, front porch light, front room light, and stereo all turn on, and five minutes later (once the person has come inside the house), the driveway lights and front porch light automatically turn off. This macro is an example of how a chain of events separated by a five-minute delay can be initiated by a single command. Even though this macro may seem quite complex, it is well within the capabilities of basic home automation software.

Logging

If you leave the computer on and the computer control software program running (in other words, the communication link or bridge to the interface module remains open), you can keep a continuous log of all X10 activity. For example, you could use the software to keep track of lighting and usage patterns. With this information, you would be able to see exactly what's running at specific times of the day, which would allow you to analyze your energy usage. If you live in an area that has a variable rate for energy usage, this feature would give you the necessary knowledge to make changes to lessen your energy consumption at peak-rate times.

Basic Software Setup

To give you a better idea of what's involved in setting up basic home automation software, we'll run through the step-by-step procedures for a typical program. Although the interfaces and menus depicted in the illustrations are generic, they are similar to those of actual software.

Begin by plugging in the power line computer interface. Next connect the interface to the computer with the cable.

Tip—Do not plug the interface into a surge protector. The surge protector treats X10 signals like line interference and filters them out. Instead, you should plug the interface into the wall outlet first. The interface has a pass-through outlet that you use to plug in the computer; however, you can also plug the surge protector into this pass-through outlet. The computer and other components can then simply be plugged into the surge protector.

Once the software is installed and running, you can begin setting it up to automate your home. First you need to tell the computer what type of interface you are using. If the software came with the interface, you may be able to skip this step; the software may be preprogrammed with the correct information. If you are using a program designed for more than one type of interface, select the appropriate one from the drop-down menu. Next, enter your geographic location. This tells the computer how to calculate sunrise and sunset times. You can either enter your longitude and latitude or choose from a drop-down menu of cities. You can find the longitude and latitude of your city by looking at a topographic map at the local library or doing an Internet search for your city's name and the keywords longitude and latitude (fig. 10-5).

Now enter all of the modules that you want to control with the computer. You can organize the modules in different ways; for example, you can arrange them by type of module or by room if you like. Click on the tab for the room you want. The program will come with standard room names, but you can rename the tabs to suit your home or arrangement preferences (fig. 10-6).

Select the module type from the drop-down menu (fig. 10-7). It is important to select the correct type because each module responds to commands differently. For example, as noted earlier, an appliance module won't respond to **Bright/Dim** commands.

Once you select the module type, a window will appear where you can select more detailed data about the module. After choosing the specific type of module, you can give it a name—we will call this one "Table Lamp" (fig. 10-8).

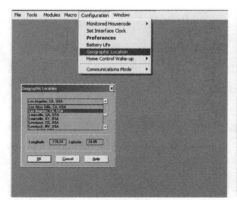

Fig. 10-5: You can either enter your longitude and latitude or choose from a drop-down menu of cities.

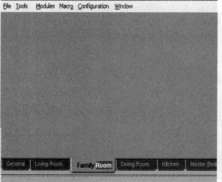

Fig. 10-6: The program comes with standard room names, but you can rename the tabs if you want.

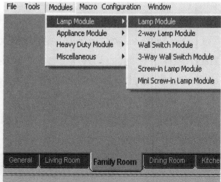

Fig. 10-7: Select the module type from the drop-down menu.

Next enter the house code and unit code for this module. In our example we use house code A and unit code 6 for this lamp. You can also choose an identifying icon for this module. Click on the icon window to scroll through the available icons (there are numerous options). We chose a basic table lamp.

Repeat this procedure for the rest of the X10 modules in the house. Now you are ready to set up timed events for the modules. Click in the "On Time" window of the module, and a time set window will appear. We want the table lamp to come on at 7:30 on weeknights, so we will enter that time and select all of the week days and unselect Saturday and Sunday (fig. 10-9).

If we wanted to have the light come on at sunset instead of at a specified time, we could select the Dawn/Dusk option (fig. 10-10).

You can set an offset time if you want the light to come on sometime before or after sunset. For example, it usually doesn't get totally dark until sometime after sunset. For an outside light, you might want to include an offset after sunset to account for this twilight time. For interior rooms, you might want to use an offset before sunset if the room tends to get dark a little while before it is completely dark outside.

You also have the option of setting the brightness level of the lamp. For example, you may want the lamp to come on at 50 percent brightness. You can set this by clicking on the brightness button and moving the slider to the desired brightness (fig. 10-11).

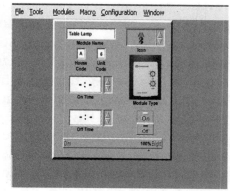

Fig. 10-8: After choosing the specific type of module, you can give it any name you like.

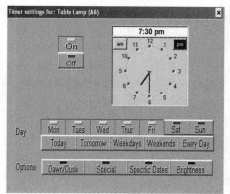

Fig. 10-9: Unselect Saturday and Sunday if you want the table lamp to come on only on weeknights.

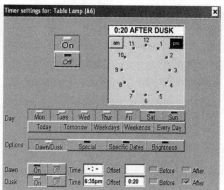

Fig. 10-10: You can also select the **Dawn/Dusk** option.

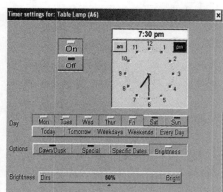

Fig. 10-11: Click on the Brightness button and move the slider to choose your desired **brightness** level.

Next you can set the off times. You can choose different rules for off times and on times. For example if you choose to have the light turn on at sunset, you can choose to have it turn off at a specified time. We want the table lamp to turn off at 11:30 every night. Even though we only have it turn on on weekdays, we will set the off time for every day of the week. That way if someone turns the table lamp on manually, it will still turn off automatically at the designated time (fig. 10-12).

Now suppose we are going away on vacation and we want the house to look lived in. Having the light come on after dusk will look natural, but if the light goes off every night at the same time, it will look automated. To solve this we can use the Security setting. Click on the "Special" button and some check boxes will appear. Check the security box to add some randomness to the off time. Now the light will turn off at a different time between 11:00 and 12:00 each night (fig. 10-13).

Following these same basic procedures, you can now program timed events for any of the other modules in your home.

A basic program can also perform simple macros. For example, when we watch TV, we like the family-room ceiling lights set to 70 percent brightness and the table lamp set to 50 percent brightness. We can make a macro that will set both lights with one push of a button. Select "New Macro" from the Macro drop-down menu. The macro-generator window will appear with small graphics called placeholders that represent the macro and the modules that you have installed in your home. The macro placeholder has a box to enter the house code and unit code that will trigger the macro. We will use house code A, unit code 8 for this macro, so we will type A8 into the box. You can also give the macro a name. We will call this one "TV Lights" (fig. 10-14).

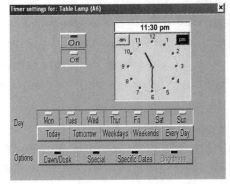

Fig. 10-12: Choose an off time for your lamp so that it will turn off automatically if someone leaves it on.

Next, select one of the module placeholders from the list of installed macros and drag it over to the macro. This installs the module in the macro. In fig. 10-15, we've added the table lamp to the macro.

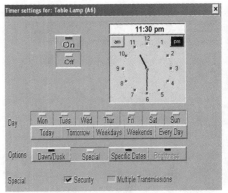

Fig. 10-13: Check the Security box to turn off a light automatically at a different time between 11:00 and 12:00 each night.

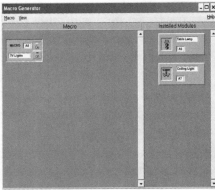

Fig. 10-14: Give your macro a name of your own choosing.

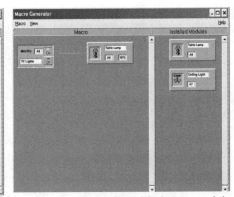

Fig. 10-15: Drag the table lamp module from your list of installed modules into your macro and adjust the brightness. Note: even though you may have already set the brightness level for a timer function (fig. 10-11) you will need to set it separately each time you set up a macro. Each macro can have a different brightness level.

There is a brightness selector in the module placeholder; since we want this macro to dim the table lamp to 50 percent, we will adjust the brightness level on the table lamp placeholder to 50 percent. Next, drag the ceiling lights placeholder into the macro and adjust the brightness to 70 percent (fig. 10-16). We now have completed a simple macro that will dim the family room lights to our preset levels when we press the A8 **On** button on an X10 controller.

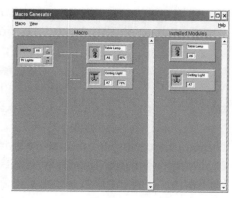

Fig. 10-16: Continue to drag modules into the macro to add additional steps.

Advanced Software

After you've used the basic free software that comes with the computer interface for a while, you may find that you want functions that aren't included in the basic package. Here are a few features that are available in more advanced home automation software:

- An overall summary screen

- A status and control screen that shows the current status of lights, appliances, sprinklers, and other X10 devices

- An events log screen that lists all X10 activities or events and the exact time that they occurred

- A temperature status screen showing all thermostats and temperature sensors

- A message setup screen allowing you to record, set up, or otherwise control system messages (either vocal or written)

- A list of conditions or rules for macros or scenes, which can be set or changed by the user

- An options screen that can be used to change certain preferences and other configurable items

Most advanced home automation software programs give you a wide range of monitoring and testing options. For example, some programs will display all of the available unit and house codes in one 16 x 16 grid, with icons in each occupied square indicating the status of each module. Most software programs can also display detailed statistics and event logs to help you track all X10 activity within your home. If you have advanced software, you can generate a series of responses based on X10 events. For example, the software can be used to generate an automatic e-mail message.

X10 events can also create responses in the form of voice messages spoken by the computer. Also, if you have voice-recognition software, you can send X10 commands in response to your spoken commands. See chapter 12 for more details.

Some advanced home automation software has an Internet access feature. For a monthly fee, sites like smarthome.com will monitor your system for you and provide online support. You can access a password-protected Web site to see the status of your system or choose to receive automatic e-mail notifications. That way you can monitor and control your home from any computer with Internet access. PDAs and cell phones can also be used. See chapter 12 for a more detailed description of how Internet-based X10 control works.

Computer control allows users to delegate tasks to their computers. Such tasks can range from the simple to the sophisticated. The idea is to set everything up according to your desired schedule and let the computer do the "button pushing." Your computer can be used for virtually any X10 task, but to achieve this level of automation you may need to give the computer more decision-making power. You can do this with conditional macros. A conditional macro incorporates "if-then" conditions that trigger the macro in response to actual conditions in the home.

Here is an example of a more complicated macro that involves a conditional situation. This macro is designed for a family with two younger children, each with her own bedroom. The two bedrooms exit into the same hallway, and there is an adjoining bathroom next to one of the bedrooms. After the girls have been tucked into bed and their bedroom lights turned off, they like to have the hallway light on (dimmed to 30 percent) as sort of a night-light so that they can still get up and go to the bathroom, if necessary. After midnight, however, the girls are asleep and no longer need the hallway light. In this example, a macro can be used to turn on the hallway light at a designated time (say, 9:30 p.m.) and dim it to 30 percent, but only if the following conditions are met: both children's bedroom lights must be turned off, and it must be after 9:30 p.m. and before midnight. If either of the children's bedroom lights is still on, there is no need for the hallway light to be engaged, since one or both children are presumably still awake and using the bedroom light(s). You can use computer controller software, a pair of two-way X10 switch modules for the two bedroom lights, and a simple screw-in lamp module for the hallway light. Using the software, you can set up the macro to trigger when one of the bedroom lights is turned off. It then checks the time to see if it is past 9:30 p.m., and it checks the status of the other bedroom light. If the other bedroom light is still on, the macro does nothing. If they are both off, the program sends an **On** command to the hallway light, followed by a **Dim** command reducing the bulb to 30 percent brightness. At midnight, the hallway light is switched **Off**.

The next chapter talks about macros and scenes in greater detail, and Chapter 12 discusses voice, telephone, and Internet control.

Chapter 11

Macros and Scenes

Using a computer or scene-enabled modules, you can program complex events involving several different devices. You will be able to set several devices to turn on, turn off, or dim in response to a single button. For example, you could have three scenes for your family room. One would turn on all lights at full brightness. The second, for TV viewing, would dim some lights and close the curtains. It could also lower a screen for a projection TV or energize a lift to raise a TV out of a cabinet. The third, for reading or relaxing, could dim most lights, turn on a reading light next to your easy chair, and turn on soft music (fig. 11-1).

Fig. 11-1: At the touch of a button, you can activate different lighting scenes programmed for your family room.

The terms "macro" and "scene" are often used interchangeably, but for the purposes of this book we will make the following distinction. A macro is a series of X10 commands that are executed in sequence in response to a trigger; in other words, they occur one after the other. A scene is a combination of preset conditions that individual modules execute simultaneously in response to a trigger; in other words, they happen all at the same time. Both a macro and a scene can have the same result, but they achieve that result through different methods. Macros are stored in a central controller like a computer interface and can control any type of X10 module. Scenes require the use of scene-enabled modules, and each module is individually programmed to respond to a scene trigger. After a scene is programmed, the trigger for that scene can then be incorporated within a computer macro.

Macros

The exact programming details for a macro vary depending on the type of computer program or controller you are using, but many general principles apply to all types of macros. We will cover the general principles here, but you should refer to the documentation for your program for exact details.

Planning a Macro

The first and most obvious consideration when planning a macro is whether the desired event can be achieved with X10. Throughout this book, we have shown you various ways to control devices using X10. All of these methods come together in this chapter. If you have wondered why you would want to add X10 control to a device that already has an infrared (IR) remote, one answer is so you can include that device in a macro. Once all of the desired devices are under X10 control, the next step in planning is to determine exactly what you want the macro to do. Remember that a macro is executed in sequence, so you will need to plan the sequence carefully, especially if there is something that must be turned on before another command can be executed.

As an example we'll create a macro for watching movies. When we decide it's time to watch a movie, we can simply press a button and the family room will go into "home theater" mode. The lights will dim, the drapes will close, and the TV and DVD player will both turn on. The background music will turn off, and we'll be ready to sit down and watch the movie. We'll even set up the popcorn popper to start popping automatically (fig. 11-2).

To achieve everything in the scenario, we'll first determine how to control the devices with X10. We'll need X10 wall switches for the ceiling lights (which consist of both track lights and recessed lights) and a lamp module for the table lamp. To close the drapes, we will need an appliance module controlling a motorized drape control. The TV, DVD, and sound system can be controlled with an IR interface. We'll use an appliance module to control the popcorn popper.

Now let's think about the sequence of events. We want to use this when we have a home theater party; after the guests arrive, we'll push a button on a mini-controller to start the sequence. The event that starts a macro is called the "trigger." We'll talk more about triggers later in this section. For now we'll simply use an X10 command as the trigger. We've chosen house code A unit code 4 as the trigger. You can use any unit code you want, but we wanted ours to be in the first group of codes on a mini-controller (fig. 11-3).

So, what is the first thing that should happen? Since we'll want the popcorn ready when the show starts, let's begin with the popcorn popper. This will actually take a little advance planning because we'll need to have the popcorn loaded in the popper before the party starts. Once everything is set up, we'll plug the popper (a hot-air type) into an appliance module. In this example we'll use unit code 9 for the popcorn popper. (Note: in this example all modules are set to house code A.) Next, we want the curtains to close. We'll use a motorized drape control plugged into an appliance module. We'll assign unit code 10 to the curtains.

Before we start dimming the lights, we want to turn on the TV and DVD player. This will give them time to run through their start-up sequence while the room lights dim. We've programmed a macro into the IR interface to send a TV ON and DVD ON IR command when it receives an X10 unit code 14 ON signal (fig. 11-4).

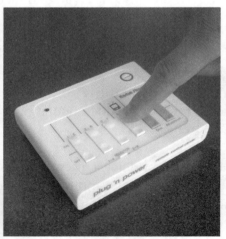

Fig. 11-2: You can program a popcorn popper to start popping automatically as part of a home theater macro.

Fig. 11-3: We want to use a code in the first group on a minicontroller to trigger our macro.

Fig. 11-4: We'll use an IR interface to translate X10 signals from the macro into IR signals that the TV and DVD player will respond to.

We'll nest this IR macro within the X10 macro. This means that we only need to include one X10 command in the macro to turn on both the TV and the DVD player. Now, we can dim the lights. Two X10 switch modules control the ceiling lights. One is set to unit code 11, which controls the track lights, and the other to unit code 12, which controls the recessed lights. The table lamp is controlled by a lamp module set to unit code 13. After experimenting with different levels, we've decided that the best light for TV viewing in our room is 50 percent brightness for the ceiling lights and 70 percent brightness for the table lamp.

It's about time to start the show, but first we need to turn off the background music. The IR interface is programmed to send a **Power** command to the amplifier when it receives an X10 unit code 7 OFF. We will have already loaded a DVD disc into the player before the party, so all that's left is to have the IR interface send the play command. We've set this up to happen when the IR interface receives an X10 unit code 15 ON.

Here's what the finished plan for the macro looks like (fig. 11-5):
A4 Trigger
A9 ON (starts the popcorn popper)
A9 DELAY OFF 5 min. (Turn off the popcorn popper five minutes later)
A10 ON (closes curtains)
A14 ON (turns on TV and DVD player)
A11 DIM to 50% (dims track lights)
A12 DIM to 50% (dims recessed lights)
A13 DIM to 75% (dims table lights)
A7 OFF (turns off music)
A15 ON (starts the DVD playing)

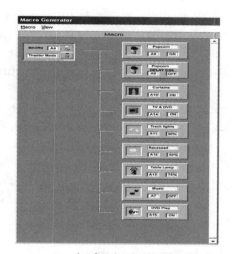

Fig. 11-5 The finished macro will look like this.

Now that we have the macro planned, we can enter it into the computer interface software. To enter the macro, we'll select "New Macro" from the Macro drop-down menu and choose a placeholder to represent it. We'll enter A4 as the trigger for the macro, which we'll name "Theater Mode." Next, we'll drag the modules from the list of installed modules over into our new macro.

Triggers
In the example above, we used an X10 command from a mini-controller as the trigger for a macro, but there are other ways to trigger a macro:

Time
You can use a time trigger to start a macro at a specific time on a recurring interval. For example, you could create a "wake up" macro that runs at 6:00 a.m. Monday through Friday. Such a macro could turn on the bedroom light, turn on the TV news, and start the coffee maker.

Sunrise/Sunset
The computer interface can calculate the time it will get dark or light each day. You can use this to trigger a macro that is more dependent on whether it is light or dark than on a specific clock time.

Change in Status of a Device

The computer interface monitors all X10 signals, so it can tell when a device changes status. For example, when someone turns on a specific light, you can have that event trigger a macro. You will need two-way modules if you want this to work from a wall switch or to monitor local control status..

Conditionals

Some of the most powerful macro triggers are conditional statements. These check the status of other things before triggering the macro. Conditionals are like if-then statements in computer programs. If the test conditions are met, the macro will be triggered. You can include several conditionals in a single trigger. This allows you to design a trigger that is very specific. For example, you could design a macro that will close the living room curtains when the living room lights are turned on but only if it is dark outside. Here is a list of some of the conditionals you will find in more sophisticated software:

Is it a specific time?
Is it before a specific time?
Is it after a specific time?
Is it daytime (light outside)?
Is it nighttime (dark outside)?
Is it sunrise?
Is it sunset?
Is a specific device on?
Is a specific device off?
Has a specific device been on for a specified number of minutes?
Has a specific device been off for a specified number of minutes?
Has a specific device changed its status (on, off, dim, bright)?

Code Translation

In chapter 7, we showed you how to use a universal relay module and a Powerflash module to perform a code translation. Using macros, you can do the same thing without all the hardware. This enables you to have as many code translations in your system as you wish. As we explained in chapter 7, a code translation is using one house code / unit code combination to trigger a different house code / unit code. For example, in our example home we have a light over the kitchen sink and an overhead kitchen light. Sometimes we want to be able to turn on just the sink light, but whenever we turn on the overhead light, we also want the sink light to come on. We can use code translation to achieve this. In this example, the overhead light is house code A unit code 2, and the over-the-sink light is house code A unit code 3. To set up the code translation, we would program the following simple macros (fig. 11-6):

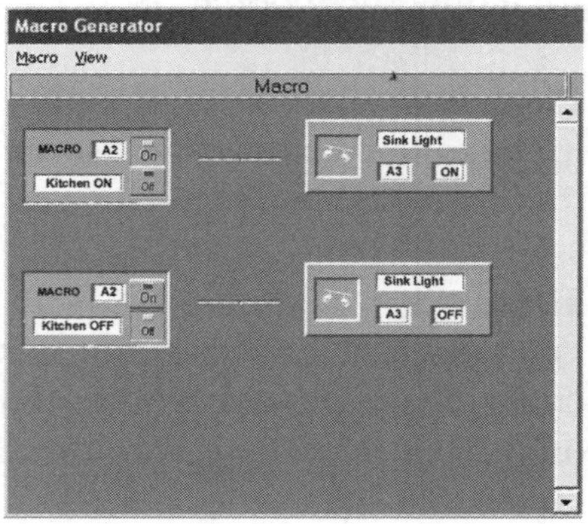

Fig. 11-6: This code translation will enable you to turn on both the kitchen and sink lights with the A2 unit code button.

Trigger: A2 ON
        A3 ON
Trigger: A2 OFF
        A3 OFF

Now, sending an X10 signal to control the overhead light will also control the over-the-sink light. However, sending a signal to the over-the-sink light will have no effect on the overhead light.

One of the most useful things you can do with code translation is to reassign buttons on controllers. Code translation isn't limited to unit codes within the same house code; you can use code translation to control devices with different house codes. Many of the controllers we have described in this book require that unit code numbers for the buttons be sequential. This means that a four-button controller could control unit codes 1, 2, 3, and 4 but not, for example, unit codes 1, 7, 9, and 11 together. Even with careful system planning, you often end up wishing you could swap buttons around on some controllers. To get around this problem with code translation, you set the controller to a different house code. For example, we want to place a mini-controller in the family room that will control every light in the room. Unfortunately in this system the lights are assigned to unit codes 1, 7, 9, and 11, and the mini-controller only controls codes 1 to 8 and can only control four of these codes at a time. The normal house code is A, so we will set this mini-controller to house code B and program the computer with the following macros:

Trigger:	B1 ON
	A1 ON
Trigger:	B1 OFF
	A1 OFF
Trigger:	B2 ON
	A7 ON
Trigger:	B2 OFF
	A7 OFF
Trigger:	B3 ON
	A9 ON
Trigger:	B3 OFF
	A9 OFF
Trigger:	B4 ON
	A11 ON
Trigger:	B4 OFF
	A11 OFF

With these code translations programmed into your software, you can use the mini-controller to control unit codes 1, 7, 9, and 11. To turn on unit code 9, you simply push the **On** side of the unit code 3 button on the mini-controller. The software interface recognizes that you pushed the B3 trigger and that this trigger should be translated as house code A unit code 9, so it does the translation and then transmits A9 ON.

Scenes

If you use scene-capable devices, you can set up complex lighting scenes that are triggered by a single X10 command. One of the advantages of scenes is that all of the events happen simultaneously. In the home theater macro we described earlier, there are three commands to dim lights in the room. Because a macro performs each action in sequence, you will notice that the track lights dim first, then the recessed ceiling lights dim, and finally the table lamp dims. If we programmed the same action using a scene, all of the lights would dim at the same time. Scenes work well with lighting; however, it is harder to integrate IR commands into a scene. All of the devices associated with a scene must have a scene-capable module, either hardwired in or plugged into an outlet.

You can use scenes and macros together, using one to trigger the other. This way you can have the best of both systems. As an example, we'll create a scene that dims the lights for our home theater macro. Then, instead of listing all three lights in the macro, we can simply list the trigger command for the scene and all three sets of lights will dim simultaneously.

First we will need to install scene-capable modules in the room. Most X10 product catalogs will let you know if a module is scene-capable, but if you are unsure, it's best to call the company.

For the table lamp, we'll simply plug a scene-capable lamp module into an outlet (fig. 11-7).

We'll replace one of the wall switches with a scene-capable rocker switch (fig. 11-8). This switch controls the track lighting. We have something special in mind for the second wall switch, which controls the recessed lighting.

The switch shown in figure 11-9 is a keypad that can control eight different unit codes. It includes a scene-capable light control so it can be a direct replacement for the original light switch that controlled the recessed lighting. The codes can be assigned individually to each button on the keypad, so they don't need to be sequential. We'll assign buttons for each of the lights in the room, and we'll still have buttons left to assign to the trigger codes for the home theater lighting scene and other lighting scenes for the room.

Fig. 11-7: To control the table lamp, simply plug in a scene-capable lamp module.

Refer to chapter 6 for directions for installing the rocker switch. The keypad is installed in about the same way. This keypad requires a neutral connection, so be sure there is one available in the box you plan to use. Begin by turning off the circuit breaker and removing the old switch. Identify each wire and label it as explained in chapter 6. Connect the black pigtail from the keypad to the hot wire from the old switch (fig. 11-10).

Fig. 11-8: Replace one of the wall switches with a scene-capable rocker switch.

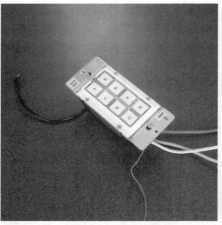

Fig. 11-9: This keypad wall controller can control eight different unit codes.

Fig. 11-10: Connect the black pigtail from the keypad to the hot wire from the old switch.

Connect the red pigtail to the load wire from the old switch (the wire that connects to the light) (fig. 11-11).

Add the white pigtail to the bundle of white neutral wires in the box and replace the wire nut (fig. 11-12).

If there is a ground connection in the box, connect the bare copper pigtail to the ground wire (fig. 11-13).

Finally, cap off the yellow wire with a wire nut (fig. 11-14). You would use the yellow wire if you wanted to use this keypad as a replacement for a three-way switch.

Now you are ready to program the modules. Each module, including the keypad, must first be programmed with a primary address. This is the address that a module will respond to under normal conditions when it is not responding to a scene command. In our example, the table lamp module is A13, the rocker switch is A11, and the keypad is A12.

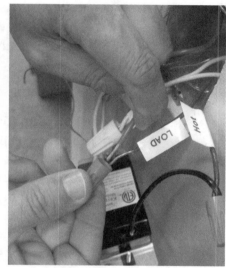

Fig. 11-11: Connect the red pigtail to the load wire from the old switch.

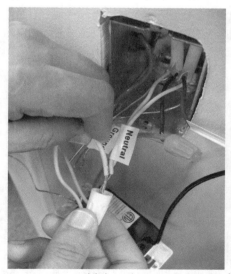

Fig. 11-12: Add the white pigtail to the bundle of white neutral wires in the box.

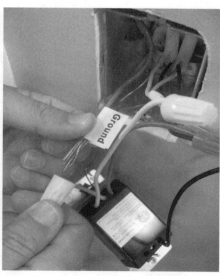

Fig. 11-13: Connect the bare copper pigtail to the ground wire.

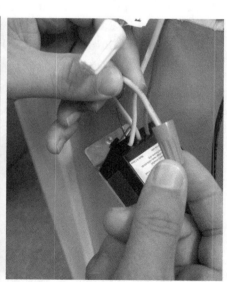

Fig. 11-14: Cap off the yellow wire with a wire nut.

Follow the directions that come with the module for setting the primary address. The process basically involves pressing a "set" button and then transmitting the desired house and unit code from an X10 controller (fig. 11-15).

Once the primary addresses have been programmed on all the modules, you can begin setting up the scenes. Each module can belong to a maximum of sixty-four different scenes, which gives you plenty of versatility. The modules can be set to different dim levels; when the scene is activated, each module will go to its individually preset dim level.

 Tip If you want a light module to turn off in response to a scene trigger, turn the module on and dim it to zero.

To program the scenes, you can use a maxi-controller, a special wall controller or a computer program that includes a wizard for setting up scenes. To set up the scenes manually, use a controller that sends the house and unit code separately from the **ON** and **OFF** codes. The maxi-controller will do this, but the mini-controller will not.

Using a maxi-controller to program the scene is rather cumbersome; for example, sending the code that starts the scene programming process involves using a screwdriver to turn the house code wheel to O and then pressing unit 16. Using the screwdriver, you then have to reset the house code to N and press 16, reset the house code again to M and press 16, and finally reset the house code to P and press 16 (fig. 11-16). However, if you use a keypad wall controller that has scene-programming capabilities, you can automate the procedure.

The keypad controller we installed includes a feature that speeds up scene setup. To use this feature, you set one of the buttons on the keypad to the scene trigger code. To set up the scene, push the scene trigger button for about three seconds and the button will begin to blink. This indicates that you can start setting up the scene (fig. 11-17). Using an X10 maxi-controller, turn on and adjust the dim level of each light in the scene (in this case, you'll use the primary addresses of the light modules that you programmed in earlier: A13, A11, and A12). You have about four minutes to complete this operation. When all of the lights are set to the desired level, press the same trigger button on the keypad again. This will lock in the scene.

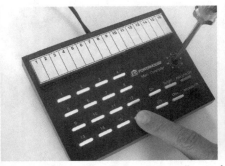

Fig. 11-15: To set the primary address for the keypad controller, press the "Set" button, and then transmit the desired house and unit code from an X10 controller.

Fig. 11-16: Using a maxi-controller to program the scene is rather cumbersome.

Fig. 11-17: Press and hold the scene button for three seconds. When the button begins to blink, you can start setting up the scene.

Scenes don't need to be on the same house code as the primary address of the modules. In fact, it's probably best to put them on a different house code, so you don't use up all of the unit codes on your primary house code.

You can program each button of the keypad controller to a different house code if necessary. This means that you can choose a different house code for scene triggers while still being able to assign buttons to the other lights and modules in the room. In our example we've chosen house code B unit code 1 as the address for the home theater lighting scene. The lights and other modules in the room are on house code A.

Before you begin programming the keypad, you need to understand how the buttons operate. The buttons can be set in either of two modes, nontoggle or toggle. In the nontoggle mode each button always sends the same command and the button will not light up. In this case, you would need two buttons for each unit code, one to send an **On** command and one to send an **Off** command. This is just like most controllers that we have already discussed in this book. In toggle mode, one button can be used for both **On** and **Off**. For example, the first time you press the button, it will send an **On** command and the light inside the button will light up and stay on. The next time you press the button, it will send an **Off** command and the light in the button will go off.

Refer to the keypad's instructions for complete directions for programming. Basically, you press any two buttons and hold them for five seconds to enter the programming mode. Next press the button to be programmed. The button should be blinking to indicate it is in toggle mode. If it isn't blinking, press it again. Now use a maxi-controller to transmit the desired house and unit code for the scene.

 You'll have to change the house code dial on the maxi-controller twice because you're programming the scene to a different house code from the individual light modules. Before you begin programming the scene, set the house code dial on the maxi-controller to the desired house code that will trigger the scene. However, keep in mind that once you've programmed the house code for the scene trigger, you'll have to switch the maxi-controller's house code back to the house code for the individual lights.

For our scene, having already set the house code dial to B, we will press the 1 button on the maxi-controller. Now send a second signal that will determine the mode the button on the keypad is set for. We want this button to be in "scene mode." To set the button on the keypad to scene mode, press the unit code 8 button on the maxi-controller.

Now we can set up the scene. Press the button assigned to the scene for three seconds and release. The button will start blinking. Using the maxi-controller (be sure to set it back to house code A) press the unit 13 button, then press the **Dim** button and set the table lamp to the desired dim level. Next press the unit code 11 button on the maxi-controller and dim the track lights to the desired level. Now press the unit code 12 button on the maxi-controller and dim the recessed ceiling lights to the desired level. With all of the lights set to the desired level, press the scene button on the keypad again. The lights will blink momentarily indicating that they have enrolled in the scene. The scene button light on the keypad will stop blinking and go off.

Now we can include the scene in our computer macro. Instead of listing the three lights separately, we will simply include the scene trigger command of house code B unit code 1. On your X10 computer software create a new placeholder for the scene and choose a name for it; for example, you might want to use "movie lighting." Here is what the revised macro would look like (fig. 11-18):

A4 Trigger

A9 ON (starts the popcorn popper)

A9 DELAY OFF 5 min. (turns off the popcorn popper five minutes later)

A10 ON (closes curtains)

A14 ON (turns on TV and DVD player)

B1 ON (dims ceiling lights and table lamp)

A7 OFF (turns off music)

A14 ON (starts the DVD playing)

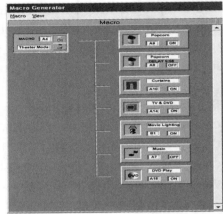

Fig. 11-18: A Revised macro that includes the placeholder for the new scene will look like this.

Now that you can program macros and scenes, you're ready to go one step further with X10 control. The next chapter will discuss controlling your home by phone and through the Internet. We'll also show you how to talk to your home and even have it talk back!

Chapter 12

Controlling Your Home by Phone, Internet, or Voice

Now that you've installed an X10 system that lets you control many things in your home with the touch of a button, the next step is to be able to control these things in other ways—for example, by telephone, through the Internet, or by voice.

Suppose you work for an airline and you've just discovered that you'll be flying home tomorrow for an unexpected long weekend. You'd like to soak in your hot tub when you arrive. Unfortunately, you haven't been home in three weeks, and you don't keep the water in the hot tub heated when you're away. You know you're going to want to use the hot tub this weekend, but you also know that it takes twenty-four hours to get the water hot.

Luckily, you have an X10 telephone controller in your apartment, and your hot tub is controlled with an X10 module. This means that you can call your apartment from a touch-tone phone, push a few buttons on the telephone keypad, and start the heater for your hot tub. When you get home twenty-four hours later, the water in your tub will be at the perfect temperature for a long, hot soak (fig. 12-1).

Or, instead of using the phone, you could set up a computer system that will allow you to control X10 devices over the Internet. You could then simply log on to the Internet, go to your secure Web server, and turn on your hot tub this way.

Fig. 12-1: With an X10 telephone controller and a hot tub controlled with an X10 module, you can call home from a touch-tone phone, push a few buttons on the telephone keypad, and start the heater for your hot tub.

Doing something like this might seem to be a complicated task, but in fact it's fairly easy. Probably the simplest and most foolproof way is to install an X10 touch-tone controller. To control X10 devices by phone, all you have to do is purchase an X10 touch-tone controller, set the house code, and plug it into a power outlet and a phone jack. You now have the ability to call from a remote location and control up to ten lights or appliances simply by pushing the touch-tone buttons on any telephone keypad. The Internet option isn't much harder. The installation is simple: just plug in a computer interface module of the sort we described in chapter 10. The programming will be more time consuming than for the touch-tone controller, but you will have more options. The touch-tone controller is limited to 10 unit codes, all on one house code. The computer options will control any of the 256 available codes.

You can use telephone or Internet controllers with any X10-operated device, but they are probably most useful for controlling hot tubs, heating and cooling systems, and water heaters in homes that are vacant for long periods of time. If you are away from home a lot or have a vacation home, you can save on energy costs by setting back the thermostat and turning off the water heater and hot tub while you're away. The only problem is that these systems take a long time to get up to a comfortable temperature after you turn them back on. With a telephone or Internet X10 controller, you can turn them on the day before you arrive and find everything ready when you get home.

Touch-Tone Controller
The touch-tone controller responds to the tones generated when you press a button on a touch-tone keypad (fig. 12-2).

These tones are technically called DTMF (dual-tone, multifrequency) tones. Any phone that generates true DTMF tones will operate the X10 controller (fig. 12-3). In the United States, DTMF phones are almost universal, but you will still find some phones that use the older pulse-dialing system. You can't tell the difference just by looking because modern pulse phones use buttons just like DTMF phones (older pulse phones used a dial); however, you can tell by listening. If you hear tones in the earpiece of the phone when you press a button, it is a DTMF phone; if you hear a series of clicks, it is a pulse phone.

Installation is simple. Simply plug the unit's phone cord into a telephone jack and plug the power cord into an outlet (fig. 12-4). Using a screw-driver, choose the house code (make sure the house code on the phone controller is set to the same house code as the lights or appliances you want to control).

Next, choose a three-digit security code using the three dials on the top right of the unit's control pad (fig. 12-5). The third number of the security code will cause one of your X10-controlled lights to flash on and off when the phone rings. For example, if your desk lamp is X10 controlled and you control it with unit code 7, the lamp will flash on and off if the third number of your security code is a 7.

Fig. 12-2: This touch-tone controller responds to the tones generated when you press a button on a touch-tone keypad and sends X10 signals to control modules in your home.

Fig. 12-3: Any phone that generates true DTMF tones will operate the X10 controller.

Fig. 12-4: To install the touch-tone controller, plug the phone cord into a telephone jack and plug the power cord into an outlet.

Fig. 12-5: Set a three-digit security code using the three dials on the top right of the unit's control pad.

Because a module that has the same unit code as the third digit of your security code flashes on and off, you may want to leave that unit code unused unless you want the flashing light to get your attention when the phone rings. If you need to use all of the available unit codes, you can disable the flashing feature by setting the third dial to **Off**. However, this means that you will only have a two-digit security code.

After programming your security code, set the answer delay mode to either fifteen seconds or thirty-five seconds (fig. 12-6). If you have an answering machine, it's best to set the delay mode to the maximum thirty-five seconds, so that your answering machine can answer the phone first. You can use the controller without an answering machine, but it may be confusing to people who call your home when you are away. They will hear the controller beep and won't know what it means. You can partially solve this by setting the controller to the maximum delay. This equals about six rings, so most people will give up before the controller answers.

 If you don't have an answering machine but instead use a voice mail service, a telephone controller is probably not the answer for you. If your voice mail service answers your phone before it rings in your home, the controller will never be able to answer. Conversely, if your voice mail service allows calls through to your home before answering, the controller will always answer, so your calls will never be forwarded to the voice mail service. In this situation, you should either use a different phone line for the telephone controller or use Internet control.

You're now ready to call your home from work or some other remote location and turn your X10 modules on or off. Did you forget to turn off your bedroom light before you left for work? Simply call home and follow these steps.

Let your answering machine answer the phone and let your message play. Then, instead of leaving a message, enter your security code. You should hear three beeps. If you don't have an answering machine, the telephone controller will answer and you will hear three beeps indicating that it is ready for you to enter the security code.

After entering your security code, you should hear three more beeps. Enter the unit code of the light that you want to turn off. Your bedroom light is unit code 3, so enter 3 on the touch-tone pad of the telephone and then push the # button. You will hear two beeps to confirm that the light has been turned off. If you want to turn a module on, enter the unit code on the touch-tone pad and then press the * key. You will hear three beeps to confirm. If you press an invalid button on your touch-tone pad, the controller will let you know by sounding just one long beep.

The telephone controller can also be used in your home like a mini-controller to control up to eight unit codes, although you can't use it to dim lights (fig. 12-7).

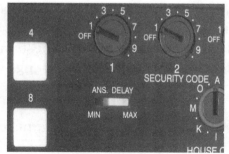

Fig. 12-6: Set the answer delay mode to either fifteen seconds or thirty-five seconds with the slide switch.

Fig. 12-7: Under the lift-up lid, the telephone controller has buttons so you can also use it like a mini-controller to control up to eight unit codes.

You may have noticed that the first paragraph of this chapter indicates that you can control ten lights or appliances via telephone. This is true. With a touch-tone pad on a telephone, you can use the number 9 to control a light or appliance set to unit code 9, and you can use the number 0 to control a light or appliance set to unit code 10. However, the telephone controller pad itself has only buttons 1 through 8, so at home you can use it to control only eight unit codes.

Internet Control

Although the touch-tone controller is easy to use and reliable, it is limited to 10 unit codes on the same house code. If you need to control more that ten things, you may want to use Internet control. With this technology, you'll be able to control any of the 256 available codes in your home from anywhere you have Internet access (fig. 12-8).

Fig. 12-8: With an Internet control program, you'll be able to control any of the 256 available codes in your home from anywhere you have Internet access.

There currently are two main ways of accessing your home through the Internet; one involves using special software that has a built-in Web server and the other is a system where you subscribe to a monthly service which provides a remote Web server. No matter what system you use, you must have an Internet connection that is always on, like a DSL or cable modem. Both systems will work with an X10 interface connected to a computer. With the monthly service option, you can also use a stand-alone interface that doesn't require a computer. With this system you won'tneed an additional computer interface. You can program the module with timed events from any computer with an Internet connection. This means that you can change the schedule of timed events in your house even when you are away from home.

The downside of Internet control is that in its present state, the Internet is not as reliable as the telephone system. If the system you subscribe to should have server-related problems, you will lose the ability to control your home.

Controlling Heating and Cooling Systems

As we mentioned earlier, controlling heating and cooling systems (HVAC) with X10 can result in significant savings because you can reduce energy consumption when you are not at home. As an added bonus, you can control the temperature without having to get out of bed or get up from your chair. You can also use a computer interface to set up a timed schedule for routine temperature control and then only use the Internet or phone controller to override the timed settings when you will be at home unexpectedly.

Anything that can plug into an X10 module can be controlled with a telephone or Internet controller. For example, you might like to turn on your window air conditioner before heading back to your apartment from work. With a phone controller, simply call home, enter your security code, listen for the beeps, and then enter the unit code that corresponds to the appliance module that you've plugged your air conditioner into.

Most furnaces or air-conditioning systems are controlled by a thermostat, and you can control even these types of appliances when you aren't home. You'll need to invest in a special thermostat control for the furnace or air conditioner. If you're on a limited budget, you can add what's called a thermostat-setback module, which costs about $20 (fig. 12-9).

This device, which mounts directly under your thermostat and plugs into a power supply that is plugged into an appliance module, contains a tiny heater that tricks your existing thermostat into thinking that your home is warmer than it really is. It has a three-position switch that lets you choose a setback of roughly 5, 10, or 15 degrees (fig. 12-10).

To use the setback module in the winter, you would first set the thermostat to a comfortable temperature (say, 72 degrees) and then turn on the setback module when you leave home. (You could set up a timed event on your computer that would automatically turn on the setback module about the time you leave for work.) The setback module will heat up and trick the thermostat into registering a temperature warmer than the actual room temperature. With the module set to the middle setting, the actual room temperature would be about 62 degrees while the thermostat thinks it is 72 degrees. So the furnace would not kick on even though the room temperature was 10 degrees lower than the thermostat setting. Then, in the afternoon, before heading home, you could simply call your home and turn off the setback module. The thermostat would then be able to register the real temperature and cause the furnace to turn on.

The device would work in the opposite way during the summer for the air-conditioning. First, you would set the thermostat to a high temperature (say, 85 degrees). The air-conditioning wouldn't turn on because the house would be much cooler. In the afternoon, you could call home and turn on the setback module, which would start warming the thermostat. Once the thermostat registered a temperature of 85 degrees, the air-conditioning would start cooling the house.

You can also purchase X10-controllable thermostats that take the place of your standard thermostat, but they are more expensive, generally costing about $250. These devices can be used to set individual temperatures, with one unit code representing a specific temperature; for example, unit code 8 might equal 72 degrees.

Fig. 12-9: A thermostat setback module mounts directly under your thermostat. It contains a tiny heater that tricks your existing thermostat into thinking that your home is warmer than it really is.

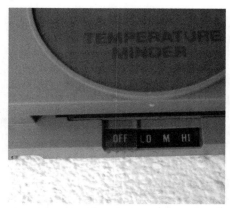

Fig. 12-10: The thermostat setback module has a three-position switch that lets you choose a set back of roughly 5, 10, or 15 degrees.

Controlling Hot Tubs and Water Heaters

Water heaters are notorious energy wasters. Whether it is the large tank-type that supplies hot water to your whole house or the small heater that warms the water for your hot tub, it will continue to use energy to keep a supply of water warm whether or not you actually need to use it. Turning off electric water heaters with X10 modules can save you a significant amount on your electric bill while still giving you the convenience of coming home to hot water (fig. 12-11).

Electric water heaters and hot tubs generally run on 240VAC and 30 amps or more. If you have a very small hot tub that plugs into a 240VAC 20 amp outlet, you can use a plug-in heavy-duty appliance module, but most of the time a hot tub is hard wired to a GFCI (ground fault circuit interrupter) circuit breaker box. To control this type of hot tub or a water heater, you will need to use a hardwired 240VAC 30 amp module. Be sure to check the amp rating on the water heater or hot tub. If it is more than 30 amps, you can't use this module.

Unless you have experience working on 240VAC circuits, you may want to hire an electrician to install this hardwired module. The module mounts near the circuit breaker box or the GFCI control for the hot tub and must be connected to the box with conduit (fig. 12-12).

Once you have the module installed, you can simply call home and enter the appropriate unit code on your telephone's touch-tone pad or log on to your Internet control and click on the appropriate icon. The water in your hot tub will be warming up by the time you reach home.

Voice Announcements and Voice Control

A home that speaks and responds to voice commands has been a staple of science-fiction movies for years. With X10 voice control, reality has almost caught up with fiction, but the voice recognition technology is still not perfect.

There are a variety of home automation devices on the market that allow you to use voice control in your home. Some systems allow you to phone home and give voice commands; and in others, all commands are given and announcements made within the confines of the home itself.

Although they are usually thought about in conjunction with each other, the technology used to make voice announcements is very different from the technology used for voice recognition. We will cover the two subjects separately.

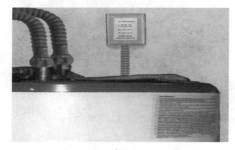

Fig. 12-11: Water heaters are notorious energy wasters. Turning off electric water heaters with an X10 module like the one shown here can save you a significant amount on your electric bill while still giving you the convenience of coming home to hot water.

Fig. 12-12: Usually a hot tub is hard-wired to a GFCI circuit breaker box. To control this type of hot tub or a water heater, you will need to use a hardwired 240VAC 30A module. The module mounts near the GFCI control for the hot tub and must be connected to the box with conduit.

Computer-Generated Voice Announcements

The first way of using voice in connection with X10 involves the computer or controller speaking in response to X10 commands. For example, when you come home, you could have a button on a remote that activates a coming home macro to turn on lights and other devices the way you like them when you are at home. As part of this macro you could have the computer say, "Welcome home, I hope you had a pleasant day." The technology involved in computer speech is mature and reliable, so it's not difficult or expensive to use voice announcements with your X10 system. Many X10 computer software interfaces have some sort of audio capability. You can set up the program so that certain sentences are spoken by the computer whenever an X10 event occurs (fig. 12-13). At

their most basic level, such voice commands can be used to provide simple factual acknowledgments of on and off switching. For example, when the porch light (A3) is switched on via an X10 command, the X10 signal is also detected by the computer or voice-control device, which then causes the following sentence to be played aloud: "The porch light is on."

Turning off the same light causes a different response, such as, "The porch light has been turned off." In some cases, the number of speakable commands may be limited, as may the number of different types of voices built into the system software. Some programs and devices, however, allow you to make custom recordings of messages. There are also stand-alone message controllers available, which can operate without a computer. Such controllers are capable of delivering messages up to four seconds long (longer messages can be created by playing two or more shorter ones back-to-back).

Fig. 12-13: You can set up some X10 computer control programs so that certain sentences are "spoken" by the computer whenever an X10 event occurs. As part of a "welcome home" macro you could have the computer say, "Welcome home, I hope you had a pleasant day."

For more sophisticated announcements, it may be necessary to set up macros with computer-control software. For example, let's suppose H1 is your chosen command for your "movie time" scene. Sending H1-On via any X10 controller causes a series of steps to take place, such as turning on the TV and DVD player (using the infrared [IR] interface, if necessary) starting the popcorn popper, closing the electric drapes, and dimming the overhead lights in the family room. You could add one more command to the macro that would have the computer announce, "Please take your seats. The show is about to begin."

 Use house code J for all voice-announcement macros. J has become the default setting for most voice-related devices and applications; many are preprogrammed to house code J. Make sure that no other devices in the house are set to house code J and set up your macros so that all voice commands are assigned to the J house code.

You can use timed events to activate voice announcements, so you can use them to provide audible reminders. The computer can say things like "It's Tuesday morning, time to put the garbage cans on the street," or "Kids, it's bedtime."

As long as the computer is close enough to be heard, setting up voice announcements will only involve setting up a computer program. If you want the announcements to be heard in other parts of your home, you will need to add additional remote speakers to your computer. This may involve running speaker wires around your home, but a simpler method is to use wireless speakers. These have a base station that plugs into the speaker jack on your computer and speakers that simply plug into an ordinary outlet in another room. The speakers are linked to the base by radio. Just be careful to choose wireless speakers that won't interfere with X10 signals. If the speakers use radio frequency (RF) transmission over the air, they probably won't interfere. If they send the signal over the house wiring, they might interfere with your X10 system.

Controlling X10 with Voice Recognition

In the second type of X10 voice control, the user speaks the desired commands to the computer and the computer carries out the X10 commands. Ideally, voice control is supposed to allow you to simply speak a command and have the home automatically perform that action (fig. 12-14). For example, you could say a sentence like, "Computer, I'm home," and the lights would come on, music would start, and a computerized voice would say, "Welcome home, I hope you had a pleasant day."

Fig. 12-14: Voice control allows you to speak a command and have the home automation software send an X10 command.

That's how it's supposed to happen anyway. In actuality, it can be difficult to get the computer's attention in the first place, particularly if there are other people at home or if there is a TV or radio turned on. Voice recognition has come a long way, but it is still not a mature technology. Using voice control can be fun, and if you already have a computer and X10 home control program with voice recognition capabilities, it won't cost you anything to experiment with it. However, don't expect the voice recognition system to work flawlessly. Also, you need to be near the computer's microphone for the computer to hear you. If you want to use voice control in rooms other than the one where the computer is located, you will be faced with the complex and costly project of adding microphones throughout the house.

Most voice-activated systems are enabled when an attention word is spoken first (usually the word "computer" or the computer's name, like "Hal"). Speaking the code word "wakes" the computer up and places it in a state of alert—ready to receive, interpret, and execute the desired command.

 If you want to use another attention word, you can change the name of the computer (you should be able to change your computer's name in your computer's control panel). For example, if you named the computer Hey, you could say, "Hey, turn on the bedroom light."

Several factors can affect whether voice commands are successfully executed, including the quality and abilities of the voice-recognition software, the level of ambient noise in the room, the sensitivity of the microphone, and how well the speaker enunciates the command. If the computer for some reason does not respond, a frustrating situation could result, with the person loudly repeating the command, "Computer, turn off the light!" over and over again while continually walking closer to the microphone. For all that effort, the person might as well have gone and switched off the light by hand (or simply pressed a button on a remote control).

In addition, wiring your house with the microphones and speakers necessary for full-fledged voice control is still relatively expensive. In some systems, the hardware alone (including wiring, microphones, mixers, and speakers) can easily cost well over $2,000 even if you do all the labor yourself. Also, in most cases, you have to have a dedicated computer running with the necessary voice-recognition software to make it work.

However, a single-room setup can be inexpensive. If you already have a computer program with voice-recognition capabilities, there would be no additional cost to set it up for voice control. This type of setup could be useful for people who are in a wheelchair or are otherwise confined to a single room in the house. Voice control could enable such users to turn on or off the sprinklers, TV, and virtually any other type of device just by voice alone.

For most users, the X10 voice-control devices on the market are not yet at the level of sophistication needed to make voice control a completely convenient home automation tool. Even so, there are a number of potentially useful applications for in-home voice control, especially for those who are physically disabled. However, voice control is an emerging technology, and we expect that soon there will be stand-alone plug in modules with built-in microphones that will deliver X10 commands on cue.

Do-It-Yourself Voice Control Module

If you'd like to experiment with voice control without investing in computer software and hardware, we've developed a simple and fairly reliable system that will respond to one voice command. There are stand-alone voice-activated products that look like X10 modules but don't actually send X10 signals. They are simply light switches that you activate by speaking a phrase rather than by pushing a button. You plug a lamp into them and say a phrase like "Lights on" to make the lamp turn on. You can use one of these voice-control modules in connection with a Powerflash module to make a simple X10 voice controller (fig. 12-15).

You will need a plug-in low-voltage power supply to activate the Powerflash module. Its output should be rated between 6 and 12Vand can be either AC or DC. You can buy these power supplies at Radio Shack, but if you're like most of us, you already have a drawer full of them from dead tape players and radios. We used a salvaged transformer that has an 8VAC output (fig. 12-16).

Cut off the plug and strip the ends of the wires. Connect the bare ends of the wires to the terminals on the Powerflash module (fig. 12-17).

Fig. 12-15: This stand-alone voice-activated module recognizes simple phrases and will control a device directly plugged into the module, but it doesn't send X10 signals. You can use one of these voice control modules in connection with a Powerflash module to make a simple X10 voice-control device.

Fig. 12-16: Use a plug-in low-voltage power supply to activate the Powerflash module. Its output should be rated between 6 and 12V and can be either AC or DC.

Fig. 12-17: Connect the bare ends of the power supply's wires to the terminals on the Powerflash module.

If, like us, you use a transformer with AC output, you don't need to worry about polarity. If you use a power supply that has DC output, you must connect the wires correctly to the terminals marked + and –. You can find the polarity of the wires by connecting them to a voltmeter. If no voltmeter is available, the wires from the DC supply can be connected to the terminals without regard to polarity. If the wires are connected backward, the installation won't work, but nothing will be damaged, and when the wires are later reversed and reconnected, everything will be fine.

When you buy the voice-activated module, make sure you get one that is rated for appliances. There are two types: one is for lamps only and includes a dimming feature, the other is for lamps or small appliances and does not include a dimming feature. Because you will be plugging a transformer into the module, you don't want one that has the dimming feature.

Plug the transformer into the outlet on the voice-activated module, and set the house code and unit code dials on the Powerflash module. Set the slide switches on the module to **Input A** (voltage detect) and **Mode 3** (single unit code) (fig. 12-18).

Now you're ready to install the system. The voice-activated module has a built-in microphone, so pick an outlet near where you will usually be when you want to give a voice command. We use this system in our example house to start the "welcome home" macro, so we placed the module near the front door. If you want to hide the modules in a cabinet or behind a curtain, you can get an optional extension microphone that plugs into the module (fig. 12-19). Place the microphone somewhere where it will pick up your voice clearly. Plug in both the voice-activated module and the Powerflash module and you are ready to test the system. Say "Light on" to send an X10 **On** command and "Light off" to send an X10 **Off** command. This system has worked well in our application because there is not a lot of background noise when you first come home to an empty house and the module only needs to recognize a few words.

The voice-activated module is preprogrammed to respond to "Lights" or "Lights on" and "Lights off." If you want, you can program it to respond to other words. If you say "Program" during the first five seconds after you plug in the module, it will go into a learning mode. In this mode you can teach it to recognize any word or phrase. You repeat the word several times until the LED flashes amber indicating that the command has been learned. In our experience with the module, it seems to be selective enough for most uses. Occasionally it might mistake a similar word for the trigger word. For example, it might turn on if you said "fights" instead of "lights."

Chapters 1 through 12 discuss many of the ways you can use X10 in your home, but what if a module suddenly decides not to respond to a command? The next chapter, which discusses troubleshooting, has the answer.

Fig. 12-18: Plug the power supply into the outlet on the voice-activated module. Set the slide switches on the Powerflash module to Input A (voltage detect) and Mode 3 (single unit code).

Fig. 12-19: An optional extension microphone that plugs into the module allows you to hide the module in a cabinet or behind a curtain and place the microphone in a more favorable location.

Chapter 13

Troubleshooting

Troubleshooting

Your X10 system has been working perfectly for months—then, one night when you press the **All Off** button as you go to bed, one persistent light in the living room stays on. What went wrong? How do you fix it? Although X10 is easy to use and relatively trouble-free, on occasion you may have trouble with a particular module not responding to commands. Fortunately, most X10 problems can be easily diagnosed and solved with a few plug-in modules. In this chapter, we will discuss some of the common problems and tell you how to fix them.

Problems

To understand the causes of X10 problems, let's use the analogy of an AM radio. Have you ever been listening to the radio and then turned on a vacuum cleaner? That loud buzzing you hear on the radio is **interference** caused by the vacuum's motor (fig. 13-1). Also, when you are listening to a local radio station, the signal is loud and clear, but when you try to pick up a station from a distant city, the signal is weak and fades in and out. This is called **signal attenuation**. In addition, sometimes you may be listening to a local station, and then another station on the same frequency from a different city breaks in. This is **signal conflict.** These three problems (interference, signal attenuation, and signal conflict) are the most common causes of X10 problems.

Interference

Because X10 signals travel over the power lines in your home, anything that plugs into the power lines can be a potential source of interference (sometimes called **noise**). Fortunately, the engineers at Pico foresaw this problem and designed the X10 protocol to use the area of the AC wave called the zero crossing. This portion of the wave generally has the least amount of interference. Most normal household appliances won't cause interference in the zero crossing area. However, some electronic devices do generate interference that can affect X10, most notably, computers, wireless intercoms, and baby monitors.

Fig. 13-1: Just as a vacuum cleaner's motor can cause interference on an AM radio, some electronic devices can cause interference with X10 reception.

Attenuation

In the AM radio analogy above, signal attenuation occurs when the signal must travel over a long distance. The same thing occurs with an X10 signal, but the distance involved is not necessarily the physical distance. Since the X10 signal travels over the power line, the signal is attenuated by the electrical distance between the controller and the module. You may have a controller in the same room with a module, but because of the way most homes are supplied with electricity, the electrical distance between them might involve the distance from your house to the power pole down the street and back.

The standard outlets and lights in your home are supplied with 120VAC, but large appliances like electric dryers and ranges need 240VAC. If you look at the wires that come from the power pole to your house, you will notice that there are three wires. One is neutral and the other two are hot legs. If you were to connect a voltage meter to the neutral and one of the hot legs, it would read 120VAC, but if you connected the meter to the two hot legs, the meter would read 240VAC (fig. 13-2). After the three wires pass through the service entrance to your home, they connect to three buses, one neutral and two hot, inside the circuit breaker cabinet (fig. 13-3). About half of the circuit breakers are connected to one of the two hot buses and the rest are connected to the other hot bus. Cables that supply power to 120VAC outlets and lights have one wire connected to the neutral bus and one hot wire connected to a circuit breaker that connects to one of the hot legs. The cable from a 240VAC outlet (like the dryer outlet) includes two hot wires that connect to a special type of circuit breaker. This breaker is like two standard breakers combined into one. It connects each of the hot wires to a separate hot leg. When a house is initially wired, the electrician tries to balance the 120VAC loads between the two hot legs. This means that about half of the outlets in your home will be connected to one hot leg and the other half will be connected to the other hot leg. For an X10 signal to travel from one leg to the other, the signal must travel out to the power transformer and back. This usually isn't a problem, but if the transformer is far away, the signal path may be so long that the X10 signal will become too weak to be effective (fig. 13-4).

Another type of signal attenuation occurs when devices connected to the power line absorb part of the signal. Every X10 transmitter absorbs a small portion of the signal from other transmitters. This usually isn't a problem unless you have an abnormally large number of transmitters or the signal is already weak. Every two-way module has a transmitter in it, so using many two-way modules can weaken the signal. Electronic devices like TVs and computers may also have internal circuits that absorb X10 signals.

Surge protectors are one of the biggest culprits (fig. 13-5). The less expensive types only use metal oxide varistors (MOVs) or silicon transient voltage suppressors (TVSs) to protect the equipment that is plugged into them, and they won't attenuate the X10 signals. Others, however, bypass the mains to ground with capacitors or parallel the MOVs or TVSs with capacitors, which can seriously degrade the X10 signals.

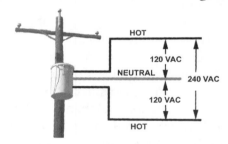

Fig. 13-2: Most homes have three wires coming from the power transformer. The three wires provide two 120VAC legs to power most lights and appliances and 240VAC to power large appliances like dryers and ranges.

Fig. 13-3: A circuit breaker cabinet. The 240VAC circuit breakers connect to the two hot buses. The 120VAC circuit breakers connect to one of the hot buses.

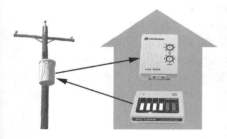

Fig. 13-4: If the X10 signal must travel out to the power transformer and back again it may become too weak to be effective.

Fig. 13-5: Surge protectors have circuits that filter out line noise; unfortunately they may also block or absorb X10 signals.

Signal Conflict

As X10 systems become more popular, the chances that you will have a neighbor with X10 become greater. If X10-controlled devices in your home turn on or off at unexpected times, you may have a signal conflict problem (fig. 13-6).

Diagnosis

Most of the time, you can diagnose a problem with a little logical deduction. If you have a very large system, you may want to get a signal strength meter to simplify troubleshooting. If your system has been working correctly and you suddenly notice a problem with a particular module, the first step is to unplug the module where the problem is suspected and replace it with one that you know is working correctly. If the problem persists, you should then think about what you have changed recently. Did you plug in a new TV or computer? Have you added any new X10 controllers or two-way modules? Did you install a wireless intercom or a baby monitor? If you have recently added a new device, try unplugging it and see if that corrects the problem.

If you notice a problem while you are installing an X10 system for the first time, your diagnosis procedure will be a little more complicated. A signal strength meter will be helpful here, but you can do it without one. Begin by analyzing the problem. Is it confined to a specific location? Are all of the problem outlets controlled by a single circuit breaker? A good way to determine if you have a long-signal-path problem is to turn on a 240VAC appliance like an electric clothes dryer. If the problem gets better, then a long signal path is the problem (turning on the dryer provides a signal path between the two legs). Once you have narrowed down the possibilities, start looking for devices that could create interference or absorb signal. One by one unplug computers and surge protectors, TVs, intercoms, and extra X10 controllers. Each time you unplug a device, try sending a command from an X10 controller to the X10 module that isn't responding. When it starts working, you have found the problem device. Refer to the "Solutions" section of this chapter to determine how to solve the problem.

If you can't find the source of the problem by logical deduction, then you may need to use a signal strength meter (fig. 13-7). The signal strength meter we use has a green LED that lights when a valid X10 signal is received and an LED bar graph meter that shows the signal strength.

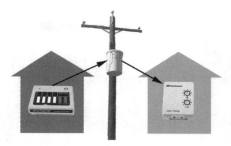

Fig. 13-6: When you share a transformer with a neighboring house that uses X10, the signal can travel into the other house. You may have a signal conflict problem if your neighbor uses the same house code that you use.

Fig. 13-7: A signal strength meter.

To use the meter, begin by plugging its cord into one of the outlets that has a problem. If the bar graph meter shows some activity but the green LED doesn't flash on briefly, there is interference on the line (fig. 13-8). Start unplugging things nearby and watch the meter. When the interference stops, you've found its source. If you can't find the source, the interference may be coming from outside your house. Try moving to different outlets throughout the house and plugging the meter into them. If the signal strength of the interference stays about the same, the interference may be coming from outside. If the signal strength varies, try to pinpoint the strongest area, then look for devices that could cause interference. X10 devices can tolerate some interference if the signal strength is higher than the interference. If you can't eliminate the interference, then you can try boosting the signal. See the "Solutions" section for details.

Next check for signal strength. Press a button on an X10 controller and watch the signal strength meter. The green LED should light briefly, and the red meter will indicate the signal strength (fig. 13-9). As long as the meter is in the mid-range or above, the strength is OK. If you get a weak signal, try moving the meter to different locations and note any change in the signal strength.

When you perform a signal strength test, you can either have someone assist you by pressing the controller button each time you move to a different location or you can set up a Powerflash module to send a signal every few seconds. Connect the two terminals on the Powerflash module with a short piece of wire and set the slide switches on the module to **Input B** (switch contact) and **Mode 2** (flash). When you plug in the Powerflash module, it will send a signal every few seconds (fig. 13-10).

If you find a noticeable difference in signal strength between outlets, you may have a long signal path through the power transformer. If the signal strength is lowest in a particular room, there may be some device in the room that is absorbing the signal.

If you think you might have a signal conflict problem with signals from a neighbor's house, try using the logging feature of an X10 computer program for a day (fig. 13-11). This will give you a list of all of the X10 activity. Look over the log to see if there are commands listed at times you know you didn't use an X10 controller. If you notice commands listed that shouldn't be there, then you have a conflict. Some programs also have a feature that searches for other computer interfaces on the line. The simplest solution is to choose a different house code. The log will tell you what house codes are already in use. If you want to completely isolate your house from your neighbor's signals, we'll tell you how in the "Solutions" section below.

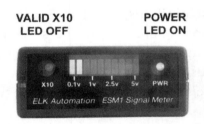

Fig. 13-8: There is interference on the line if the bar graph meter shows activity but the green LED doesn't flash.

Fig. 13-9: The green LED will flash on briefly when the meter receives a valid X10 signal. The red meter will indicate signal strength.

Fig. 13-10: To help trace a problem using a meter, you can use a Powerflash module to send a signal every few seconds. Use a short piece of wire to connect the two terminals on the module.

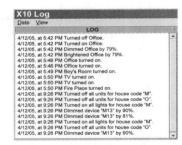

Fig. 13-11: Use the logging feature on your X10 computer program to track down a signal conflict problem from your neighbor. In this log, we noticed activity at times when we were not at home and activity on two house codes that we don't use. This is a clear indication that one or more of our neighbors is also using X10.

Solutions

Once you have found the source of the problem, the solutions are usually simple. Plug-in modules will solve most of the problems. Only the most difficult problems will require the services of a qualified electrician.

Plug-in Noise Filter

Probably the most useful problem solver is the plug-in noise filter (fig. 13-12). Whenever you have a problem with a device creating interference or absorbing signal, try this first. It's usually best to eliminate the problem at its source. This filter will do that. The filter acts as a wall that won't let interference or X10 signals through. Any interference that the device is generating can't get past the filter, and X10 signals in the line can't get past the filter to be absorbed by the device (fig. 13-13). The filters are available in several ratings. Most devices will only need the 5 amp type. For larger devices, you can get a 15 amp plug-in module. If you need a higher rating, there is a 20 amp module available, but it must be hardwired. Plug the noise filter directly into the wall outlet, and then plug the offending device into the filter. The filter won't let any X10 signals through, so you can't plug in any X10 devices to a plug strip that is isolated by a filter. For example, you can isolate all of your computer equipment by plugging the surge protector into a filter, but if you want to use an X10 computer interface, you can't plug it into either the surge protector or the filter. Instead, plug the interface directly into a wall outlet.

Plug-in Coupler

If you've determined that there is a long signal path between the two 120VAC legs in your house, the simplest way to solve the problem is with a plug-in coupler (fig. 13-14). This is a module that plugs into a 240VAC outlet and provides a short path for the X10 signal between the two legs.

The module has a pass-through outlet on the front so you can plug the original device back into the outlet. Typically, you plug the coupler into the outlet for an electric clothes dryer. There are two types available: one is for a three-wire outlet and the other is for a four-wire outlet (fig. 13-15).

Fig. 13-12: The plug-in noise filter is a useful problem solver.

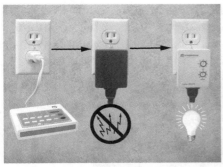

Fig. 13-13: In this diagram, interference from a TV plugged into the middle outlet was blocking the signal from the controller to the lamp module. With the noise filter installed, the interference is blocked.

Fig. 13-14: A plug-in coupler.

Fig. 13-15: The two types of plug-in couplers.

Look at your outlet before you order the coupler and get the one that matches. To install the coupler, turn off the circuit breaker for the outlet and unplug the dryer. Plug the module into the outlet; then plug the dryer cord into the module. Now turn the circuit breaker back on. The plug-in coupler contains electronic components that provide a low-resistance path for X10 signals between the legs while blocking 60-hertz current. With the coupler in place, X10 signals on one leg only need to travel to the dryer outlet before they are transferred to the other leg. This is a much shorter path than it would be if the signals had to travel all the way to the power transformer.

Tip You don't need to have anything plugged into the coupler for it to work. If you have an unused 240VAC outlet, you can simply plug the coupler into it.

Automatic Gain Control

Many high-end modules include an AGC, or automatic gain control, circuit, which is a way to overcome interference problems (fig. 13-16). To understand AGC, let's go back to our AM radio analogy. Most AM radios also include an AGC circuit. When you tune to a strong station, the AGC reduces the gain (amplification) of the signal to a point where the background noise is inaudible, but the desired program is still at a comfortable listening volume. This will only work when the desired signal is stronger than the interference. When you tune to a weak station, the desired signal and the background noise are about the same intensity, so the AGC can't distinguish between them and you hear the background noise. AGC in X10 components works a little differently, but the concept is the same. It allows strong signals through while suppressing weaker signals and background interference. It may be difficult to tell if a module has AGC because the product description may not specifically mention it. Some manufacturers use a trade name to describe their type of AGC; for example Leviton calls its AGC "Intellisense." You might need to look at the specification sheet for the product to find out if it includes AGC. Some catalogs have a chart that compares the features of all the modules. This is a good way to find which ones include AGC.

Using modules with AGC can be an effective way to overcome generalized interference problems, but it is still a good idea to try to minimize the interference by using noise filters. If the interference level is about the same as the X10 signal level, the AGC won't be able to distinguish between the signal and the interference.

Booster Repeater

If you have a weak-signal problem that you can't solve by isolating signal-absorbing devices with plug-in noise filters or coupling the legs, you can try a booster repeater. This is a device that receives a weak signal and retransmits it at a higher level. Some booster repeaters are separate modules; others combine a booster repeater with other functions. For example, the keypad we used in chapter 11 is available with an optional built-in booster repeater. You can also get a booster repeater built into a plug-in coupler (fig. 13-17).

Fig. 13-16: Most high-end switch modules like the one pictured have AGC.

Fig. 13-17: Booster repeaters receive weak signals and retransmit them at higher levels. Booster circuits can be included in wall controllers or plug-in couplers or they can be separate modules. You can plug it in near the problem area.

Whole-House Blocking Coupler

When you have a signal conflict problem or interference that is originating outside of your house, you can have a whole-house blocking coupler installed (fig. 13-18). The blocking coupler also couples the hot legs, so you won't need a plug-in coupler if you have a whole-house blocking coupler. The blocking coupler must be installed by a qualified electrician. It must be placed between the meter and the circuit breaker panel, and it requires the installation of an additional circuit breaker.

Case Studies

Now that you know the concepts of troubleshooting, let's go through several case studies that are based on actual problems we've run into in different X10 systems.

Case 1

We'll start with the problem we described at the start of the chapter. One light in the living room is not responding to commands from the controller in the bedroom. This problem is a little puzzling because the light worked normally until a few days ago, and it does respond to commands sent from a controller in the living room. To start the diagnostic procedure, ask yourself if you've added any new electronic equipment recently. In this case the answer is yes, you bought a new TV and plugged it into an outlet in the living room near the lamp that won't respond. It seems obvious that the new TV is creating the problem. The first thing to do is unplug it and see if the lamp responds normally to X10 commands. In this case, the lamp works correctly when the TV is unplugged. The solution to the problem is to buy a plug-in noise filter and use it to isolate the TV from the power line (fig. 13-19). The controller in the living room still operated the lamp because it was close enough to the lamp module that some of the signal still got through even though the TV absorbed much of the signal. The controller in the bedroom was farther away, so the TV could totally absorb the weaker signal.

Case 2

In this case, you're installing a new X10 system. You test each module with a nearby controller and they all work correctly. Then you notice that some of the modules don't respond to commands from controllers in other parts of the house. This could be another case of an electronic device absorbing much of the signal or it could be something different. How can you tell? Because it is affecting several modules in different parts of the house, it seems that the problem could be caused by a long signal path between the hot legs of the power line. To test this theory, turn on a 240VAC appliance like an electric dryer or range. In this case the problem improves with the 240VAC appliance turned on. The solution is to buy a plug-in coupler and plug it into the dryer outlet (fig. 13-20).

Fig. 13-18: A whole-house blocking coupler.

Fig. 13-19: A plug-in noise filter isolates the TV from the power line.

Fig. 13-20: A plug-in coupler bridges the two 120VAC legs.

Case 3

Here, you've got a working X10 system and you are in the process of adding a computer interface. You plug the interface into the surge protector with all of the other computer equipment and set up the program. When you test the computer interface, you notice that none of the modules respond to it. You can't figure out what's wrong, but then you remember that surge protectors can block X10 signals. So you remove the computer interface from the surge protector and plug it directly into the wall outlet. Many times, that's all it takes to solve the problem, but this time the computer interface still doesn't work. It's possible that the surge protector is absorbing most of the signal from the computer interface because of its proximity. Some surge protectors will do this and others won't. If your computer interface has internal memory, try disconnecting the interface from the computer and moving it to an outlet in another room. If scheduled events that you have programmed into the computer interface start working after you move the module, the surge protector is probably the problem.

If you can't easily move the computer interface, try temporarily removing the surge protector. Use a plug strip without surge protection to plug in all the computer components. If the modules respond to the computer interface now, the surge protector was the problem.

In this case, you determine that the surge protector is absorbing the X10 signal. The solution is to isolate the surge protector with a plug-in noise filter. If you only have one outlet close to the computer, it might be difficult to fit both the computer interface and a plug-in noise filter into the same outlet. The computer interface has a pass-through outlet on the front and you could plug the filter into it, but the combined weight and size of the two units can make it easy to bump the units and cause them to come out of the outlet. A better solution is to buy a plug strip that doesn't have any surge protection and plug it into the wall outlet. Then plug the computer interface and the plug-in noise filter into the plug strip. Next, plug the original surge protector into the plug-in noise filter (fig. 13-21). Now the computer interface can send signals into the power line and the surge protector is isolated from the power line.

Fig. 13-21: To isolate a computer from an X10 interface, plug the computer's surge protector into the plug-in noise filter. Plug the filter and the computer interface into a plug strip that is not a surge protector.

Case 4

You're sitting in your living room reading the paper when the lights suddenly turn off. You reach over to the controller by your chair and turn them back on. They come on, but then turn off again. It's like you're fighting with someone for control of your lights. You look out the window and notice that every time you turn on the living room lights, your neighbors' bedroom light comes on. You have a signal conflict problem. When you talk to the neighbors, it turns out that they have been so impressed with your X10 system that they just installed their own. The trouble is that both of you are using house code A. After talking it over, the two of you decide that you will continue to use house code A, and for future expansion you reserve house codes A through H, and your neighbor agrees to change his house code and use codes I through P.

This solves the problem, but you would really like to completely isolate your home from your neighbor's signals, so you hire an electrician to install a whole-house blocking coupler (fig. 13-22). Now you can use any of the sixteen house codes without interference, and you get the added benefit of signal coupling between the two legs of the power line, ensuring increased the signal strength that you may need because you are planning to install several two-way modules soon.

Case 5

You have a large X10 system that has been working correctly for years. Now you are upgrading to two-way modules. After you've installed several new two-way modules, you notice that the response to several controllers has become erratic. Most of the time they control everything just fine, but occasionally they just won't work. You plug in a signal strength meter and notice that there is interference on the power line. You move the meter to other outlets, but you can't pinpoint the source of the interference. At the same time you notice that the signal is weaker in the areas around the two-way modules (fig. 13-23). You decide that the interference problem has been around all along, but before you installed the two-way modules, there was enough signal strength to overcome the interference. Now the two-way modules are absorbing some of the signal. Most of the time there is still enough signal to get through the interference, but occasionally the interference is strong enough to block the signal, causing theerratic operation. In this case a booster repeater will solve the problem.

You could buy a separate booster repeater module, but you are already planning on adding a wall-mounted keypad. Luckily, this type of keypad is available with an optional booster repeater built in (fig. 13-24). Once you install the new keypad, the problem is solved.

Case 6

You've installed a very small X10 system with just a few of the most inexpensive modules. You're happy with the system, but you've noticed that occasionally the operation is erratic. Now you are planning to expand the system and install wall-switch modules, but you wonder if you should invest in high-end modules with AGC or if you can get by with the less expensive modules. Fortunately, you have a friend who owns an X10 signal strength meter. You ask him to analyze your system, and he determines that there is a slight amount of interference constantly on the power line (fig. 13-25).

Fig. 13-22: Have an electrician install a whole-house blocking coupler to isolate your home from the neighbors' X10 signals.

Fig. 13-23: The meter shows that the X10 signal strength is weaker near the two-way modules.

Fig. 13-24: Some wall-mounted keypads have built-in signal booster repeaters.

Fig. 13-25: With an X10 signal strength meter, you can determine whether there is interference on the power line.

After testing several outlets, he decides that it isn't coming from anything he can pinpoint in your home and it may be coming from outside your house. This is a problem that can be solved with AGC, so you decide to invest in the more expensive modules to ensure reliable operation of your expanded system (fig. 13-26).

Now that you know how to detect and solve the most common X10 problems, you can be considered a seasoned X10 expert, just like our example family. In the afterword, Rob and Diane describe their new automated X10 home theater system. For in-depth workings and specifications of the X10 protocol, please see appendix A. For a list of Web sites that sell X10 products, refer to appendix B.

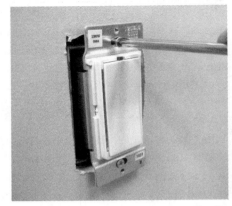

Fig. 13-26: Modules with AGC can solve some interference problems.

Afterword: Example Home Theater System

Back in our example home, Rob and Diane have brought their years of X10 expertise into an impressive home theater project (fig. AF-1) that incorporates much of the technology and devices discussed in this book.

Fig. AF-1 The home theater system in our example home uses many of the X10 devices discussed in this book.

"When we refinished our basement last year, we decided to upgrade our family room to include a home entertainment system," explains Rob, noting that the system includes a wide-screen HDTV-ready television, home theater amplifier with surround-sound, and an array of surround-sound speakers mounted in the corners of the room. Nestled in the custom-made wooden cabinets are a DVD player, a VCR, and a CD player, plus shelves for the family's extensive library of VHS and DVD titles. Using X10 products, they were able to enhance their home theater viewing experience to closely match that of an actual theater.

"After dinner, we often like to sit down and watch a movie together," explains Rob, adding, "With this new system, we wanted to be able to activate the 'home theater' mode in several different ways, so that it wouldn't matter which remote someone was holding, or even if they didn't have one at all. Anyone could still get a movie started with one simple action." Continues Rob, "The only thing we have to do ahead of time is make sure the right disc is in the DVD player and that the popcorn is ready to go in the hot air popper."

The family's home theater system uses the following X10 products, which cost under $400:
- Two-way USB computer interface
- IR interface
- Two appliance modules (for popcorn popper and motorized drape controller)
- Plug-in lamp module
- Scene keypad
- Two scene-capable wall switches (for ceiling lights)
- Powerflash X10 module (with non-X-10 voice-recognition module)

After the wall-switch modules for the ceiling lights were installed and the various modules were plugged in, macros were set up so that the following steps occur:

- The automatic drapes close.
- The hot-air popcorn popper starts popping a batch of popcorn (it turns on for five minutes—enough time to pop an entire batch of kernels—then turns off), as described in chapter 11.
- If the home's music system is on, the music turns off. The computer then announces, "Please take your seats. The movie will start in two minutes."
- The DVD player turns on and after allowing a minute or so to give the disc time to get to its main menu, the "play movie" command is automatically activated. Note: although the macro's default is the DVD player, the VHS player can be activated via a separate macro. Both macros use the IR interface.
- As the film begins, the ceiling lights begin a thirty-second dim, just like they do in a real movie theater. At the same time, the table lamp on the end table next to the couch dims to off.
- Family members on the couch salt the popcorn and pass around the bowl as the show starts.

All of these procedures and steps are activated in sequence by a single command (in this case, **H-1 On**), which can be entered via the universal remote control or any other mini- or maxi-controller in the house. Or the user can press the "Movie" button on the scene keypad (fig. AF-2) located on the wall in the family room or the "Home Theater" button on the X10 handheld remote (fig. AF-3). If no remote is handy, the user can simply say the code word "showtime," and the Powerflash module (with the non-X10 voice-recognition controller wired to it, as described in chapter 12) will send the appropriate **H-1 On** signal to activate the movie macro.

Rob notes that they originally were going to use their existing serial port computer interface, but they soon discovered that it didn't have enough memory to store all of the desired commands and conditions. To add the additional home theater macros, the family recently upgraded to a two-way USB interface, which has more memory and includes built-in conditional capabilities. It even doubles as a two-way base transceiver (fig. AF-4).

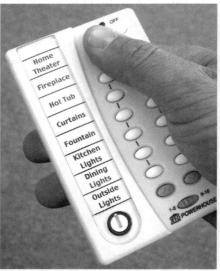

Fig. AF-2: One way to activate the home theater mode is to press the "Movie" button on the scene keypad.

Fig. AF-3: Another way to activate the home theater mode is to press the button labeled "Home Theater" on the X10 handheld remote.

Fig. AF-4: This two-way USB computer interface has more memory and includes built-in conditional capabilities. It also doubles as a two-way base transceiver.

The family sees its automated home theater system as a practical way to utilize the many applications of X10 to their fullest logical extent. "It's not just so that we can show off our home theater system to our friends," Diane explains. "We did it for the added convenience; plus it really does set the mood and enhance our whole movie-watching experience."

"It's awesome," says teenage son Gary, who invites his friends over almost every weekend to watch the latest DVD releases. "It's actually better than watching them in the movie theater," he says, adding that he also likes watching football and baseball games on the wide-screen TV.

Younger sister Jenny agrees, although she sometimes has trouble scheduling the use of the room around Gary and his friends. "I definitely get to go to a lot more parties now, since I'm usually asked to be the host," she comments.

With myriad X10 devices (old and new alike) working together, the house has achieved a level of sophistication and automation that the family hardly dreamed would be possible.

Even so, Rob doesn't see his home theater as the pinnacle of X10 achievement. "Right now, I'm working out how to make it so the movie will automatically pause when the phone rings or the doorbell is pressed," he says, adding, "I'm always trying to think up new applications, and I enjoy trying out the new modules that come out on the market. Even though a newer module might replace an older one in a particular application, I am always able to find a use for the old module in some other part of the house. The possibilities are almost endless."

Start Code

X10 in Depth

X10 Operation

X10 signals travel over the power line in the form of binary data. The data frame consists of a start code followed by 1 byte (8 data bits) and a 1-bit function bit. To respond to a command from a controller, an X10 module must receive two data frames. The first, called the unit code frame, transmits the house code and unit code, and the second, called the command frame, transmits the house code and the command code such as **On, Off, Bright,** or **Dim.**

The binary data is sent in 1 millisecond (ms) pulses of 120 kilohertz (kHz). Each pulse is timed to occur around (within 200 microseconds of) the point where the voltage on the sine wave of the 60Hz line is approaching zero. This is called the zero crossing (fig. A-1). To synchronize all of the transmitters and receivers, every module has a zero crossing detector. The receiver listens for a command twice each sine wave cycle around the zero crossing. A binary 0 is represented by the absence of a pulse on the rising edge of the cycle, followed by the presence of a pulse on the falling edge of the cycle.

A binary 1 is represented by the presence of a pulse on the rising edge of the cycle, followed by the absence of a pulse on the falling edge of the cycle (fig. A-2). Note: For the sake of consistency we will always refer to the beginning of a transmission as being on the rising edge of the cycle; however, some X10 products may actually start transmission on the falling edge of the cycle. In any case the pattern will be the same.

The start code that begins every data frame begins with at least six clear zero crossings, then a start code of pulse, pulse, pulse, absence of pulse (fig. A-3).

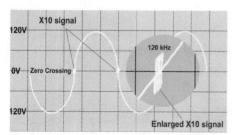

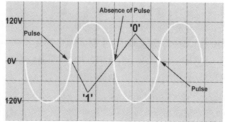

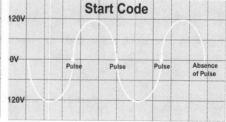

Fig. A-1: The X10 signal pulse is timed to occur around the zero crossing of the sine wave.

Fig. A-2: A binary 0 is represented by the absence of a pulse at a rising zero crossing followed by the presence of a pulse at the next falling zero crossing. A binary 1 is represented by the presence of a pulse at a rising zero crossing followed by the absence of a pulse at the next falling zero crossing.

Fig. A-3: The start code that begins every data frame is pulse, pulse, pulse, absence of pulse.

After the start code has been transmitted, the data frame is sent. The first four bits of data, called a nibble, represent the house code letter (fig. A-4). The second nibble represents the unit code. The last bit is a function bit.

A 0 designates the preceding nibble as a unit code; a 1' designates the preceding nibble as a command code (fig. A-5). To increase reliability, each frame of data is transmitted twice. This helps to overcome interference on the power line.

The data frames must be separated by at least six clear zero crossings (three full AC cycles) (fig. A-6). **Bright** and **Dim** commands are exceptions to this rule; they are transmitted continuously with no pause between data frames. After a module has received a unit code frame, it waits to receive a command frame. The command data frame also begins with the start code.

The first nibble after the start code represents the house code letter and the next nibble represents the command code such as **On, Off, Bright,** or **Dim.** The function bit (the last bit) will be 1 to designate the preceding nibble as a command code (fig. A-7).

As an example, a complete sequence to turn on house code B unit code 16 would be:

Send address code:

START CODE, HOUSE CODE (1110) UNIT CODE (1100) FUNCTION BIT (0)

Repeat address code:

START CODE, HOUSE CODE (1110) UNIT CODE (1100) FUNCTION BIT (0)

Pause for three full AC cycles

Send command code:

START CODE, HOUSE CODE (1110) COMMAND CODE (0010) FUNCTION BIT (1)Repeat command code:

START CODE, HOUSE CODE (1110) COMMAND CODE (0010)

FUNCTION BIT (1)

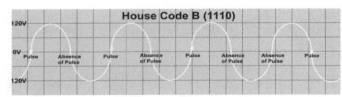

Fig. A-4: The first 4 bits of data represent the house code letter.

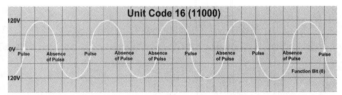

Fig. A-5: The second 4 bits of data represent the unit code. The last bit is a function bit.

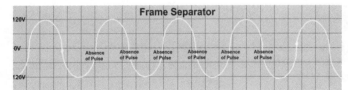

Fig. A-6: The data frames must be separated by at least six clear zero crossings.

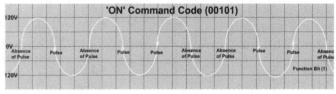

Fig. A-7: A command code will be followed by a 1 function bit.

Receiving Modes

A module has three receiving modes. In the first mode, it will not respond to a command code until it has been activated by receiving its assigned unit code. Once it receives a valid unit code, it switches to the second mode and is ready to receive a command code. In this second mode, it will ignore additional unit codes and will respond to the first command code it receives. After it receives a command code, it switches to the third mode. In this mode it will respond to any command code it receives, but if it receives a unit code other than its own, it will reset to the first mode.

A lamp module will continue to respond to the **Dim** command long after the initial **On** command was sent because it stays in the third mode until you press a button that sends a different unit code. This also means that it is possible to send several unit codes before you send a command and all of the modules with corresponding unit codes will respond to the command. For example, a maxi-controller sends the unit code data frame when you press the numbered buttons and the command data frame when you press one of the command buttons (like **On** or **Dim**). If you press buttons 1, 8, and 16 before you press the **On** button, all modules assigned to unit codes 1, 8, and 16 will turn on at the same time (fig. A-8). The modules will now switch to the second mode and continue to respond to commands simultaneously. If you press **Dim**, they will all dim at once, and if you press **Off**, they will all turn off. However, if you press another unit code button after you have sent an **On** command to the three units, the modules will reset to mode one. For example, if you pressed the button for unit code 5 after you pressed **On** for the other three, the modules set to the three original unit codes will reset to mode one. Now if you press **Dim**, only the module set to unit code 5 will respond.

Three-Phase X10

For an X10 module to work with three-phase power, a controller must send three pulses spaced to hit the zero crossing of all three phases (fig. A-9).

X10 Command Codes

The original X10 protocol has been expanded to include extended codes that add more commands. The extended codes aren't used in most common X10 devices, but they allow manufacturers increased flexibility in designing X10-compatible devices that require other commands besides the standard **On, Off, Bright, Dim, All On,** and **All Off.** Table A-1 shows all of the codes, including the extended codes.

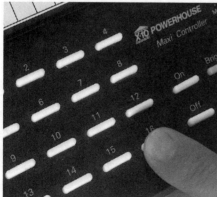

Fig. A-8: A maxi-controller sends the unit code data frame when you press the numbered buttons and the command data frame when you press one of the command buttons.

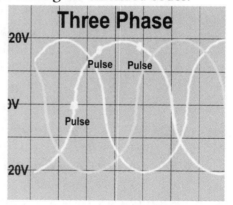

Fig. A-9: For an X10 module to work with three-phase power, a controller must send three pulses spaced to hit the zero crossing of all three phases.

Table A-1. X10 Command Codes

House Codes

A	0110
B	1110
C	0010
D	1010
E	0001
F	1001
G	0101
H	1101
I	0111
J	1111
K	0011
L	1011
M	0000
N	1000
O	0100
P	1100

Unit Codes (including function bit)

1	01100
2	11100
3	00100
4	10100
5	00010
6	10010
7	01010
8	11010
9	01110
10	11110
11	00110
12	10110
13	00000
14	10000
15	01000
16	11000

Command Codes (including function bit)

On	00101
Off	00111
Dim	01001
Bright	01011
All Lights On	00011
All Units Off	00001
All Lights Off	01101
Hail Request1	10001
Hail Acknowledge	10011
Status Request	11111
Status Is On	11011
Status Is Off	11101
Extended Code 2	01111
Extended Data (analog) 3	11001
Preset Dim 4	101X1

Notes

Manufacturers may implement the extended codes in different ways. All X10-compatible products are compatible with the standard codes, but they may respond to the extended codes in different ways. When you are using extended-code products, you may need to stay with one brand.

1. Hail Request is a request to any X10 transmitters within range to send a "Hail Acknowledge." This is a diagnostic tool used to determine if there are other transmitters that could cause a conflict.

2. Extended Code (also called Extended Code 1) is a way to expand beyond the 256 standard codes. Additional information is sent in 8 bit bytes following the initial "Extended Code" (there are no gaps between the bytes). This code has also been designated for data and control.

3. Extended Data (also called Extended Code 2) can be used to send data that has been converted from analog to digital, such as analog meter readings. Analog information is sent in 8 bit bytes following the initial "Extended Data Code" (there are no gaps between the bytes).

4. Preset Dim is a command that sets a module to a predetermined dim level. The X in the code can be either 1 or 0 indicating the most significant bit of the dim level. The part of the code usually used for the house code represents the least significant bits of the dim level. Most manufacturers have not implemented this code. The code 1010 (called Extended Code 3) has also been designated for security messages, but it hasn't been implemented yet.

X10 Minimum Specification

Carrier Oscillation Frequency	120kHz +/- 5%
Zero Crossing Detection	100 microsecond (µs) +/- 100µs
Width of Transmitted Carrier	1 millisecond (ms) +/- 50µs
Transmitter Output Power	60 milliwatt (mW) average (5V peak to peak)

X10 RF Remote Frequency

North America	310 megahertz (MHz)
Britain and some parts of Europe	418 MHz
Most of Europe	433.92 MHz

Suppliers

Advanced Control Technologies, Inc.
http://www.act-solutions.com

Applied Digital, Inc.
http://www.appdig.com

Home Automated Living (HAL)
http://www.automatedliving.com

HomeLink Vehicle Interface
http://www.homelink.com

Home Security Store
http://www.homesecuritystore.com

HomeSeer Technologies, LLC
http://www.homeseer.com

Improving Tomorrow
http://www.improvingtomorrow.com

Leviton
http://www.leviton.com

Lowe's Home Improvement
http://www.lowes.com

Marrick Limited
http://www.marrickltd.com/

Motorola Premise™ Home Control Software
http://www.premisesystems.com

Radio Shack
http://www.radioshack.com

Smarthome
http://www.smarthome.com

X10.com
http://www.x10.com/home

Index

A

ActiveHome 133
Air Conditioner 8, 13, 28, 37, 40, 41, 113, 154, 155
Alarm 18, 39, 40, 97, 103, 104, 105, 106, 113, 114, 115, 116, 126
All off command 14, 25, 26, 28, 31, 35, 38, 42, 47, 48, 49, 91, 145
All on command 25, 26, 28, 30, 38, 47, 48, 49, 69, 90, 91, 92, 145
Appliance 6, 7, 17, 18, 19, 21, 23, 24, 25, 26, 27, 28, 30, 31, 35, 36, 37, 38, 41, 42, 43, 45, 48, 64, 67, 79, 99, 116, 127, 131, 134, 136, 139, 142, 149, 151, 154, 155, 156, 160, 161, 162, 163, 167, 171
Attenuation 12, 161, 162
Attic 44
Audio 8, 11, 37, 38, 48, 157
Automatic gain control 12, 79, 166

B

Back-wired 58, 59
Backyard 15, 36, 51, 53, 80, 93
Base transceiver 8, 43, 44, 45, 46, 47, 48, 49, 107, 129, 172
Batteries 17, 41, 46, 47, 49, 50, 52, 81, 104, 107, 109, 110, 113, 125, 132, 133
Bedroom 17, 28, 31, 39, 40, 41, 44, 77, 119, 134, 140, 143, 153, 158, 167, 168
Blaster 120, 121
Booster 80, 166, 169

Booster repeater 166, 169
Box 7, 9, 10, 13, 15, 24, 26, 32, 33, 36, 38, 51, 55, 56, 57, 61, 64, 65, 67, 68, 69, 70, 71, 72, 73, 75, 76, 81, 82, 83, 84, 85, 86, 87, 89, 92, 93, 100, 101, 102, 116, 128, 134, 138, 146, 147, 156
Bright 11, 23, 25, 26, 30, 38, 46, 47, 49, 69, 70, 77, 78, 124, 129, 136, 137, 138, 139, 140, 141, 143, 144, 149, 175, 176, 177, 178

C

Christmas 16, 35, 36
Circuit breaker 6, 55, 56, 63, 64, 66, 68, 81, 83, 87, 146, 156, 162, 163, 166, 167
Close only switch 10, 99
Code translation 10, 11, 96, 144, 145
Companion switch 9, 75, 76, 78, 83, 84, 85
Computer 6, 11, 12, 13, 14, 15, 16, 17, 18, 19, 21, 38, 44, 78, 79, 80, 92, 93, 96, 99, 125, 126, 127, 129, 131, 132, 133, 134, 135, 136, 137, 139, 140, 141, 143, 144, 145, 148, 150, 151, 154, 155, 157, 158, 159, 161, 162, 163, 164, 165, 168, 171, 172
Computer interface 17, 18, 38, 92, 96, 99, 126, 131, 132, 133, 134, 135, 139, 141, 143, 154, 168, 171, 172
Conditionals 11, 133, 144,
Coupler 12, 165, 166, 167, 169

D

Diagnosis 163

Dimming 9, 28, 31, 50, 65, 70, 77, 78, 79

Door 10, 13, 17, 18, 21, 28, 43, 44, 51, 67, 77, 91, 95, 97, 98, 99, 102, 103, 104, 105, 106, 108, 109, 110, 111, 112, 113, 115, 116, 119, 127, 160

Door sensor 110

Doorbell 10, 92, 94, 95, 98, 173

Driveway 13, 44, 46, 135

DSL 154

DVD 13, 14, 18, 20, 48, 120, 123, 125, 142, 143, 150, 157, 171, 172, 173

E

Electronic addressing 9, 46, 50, 52, 79

Emitter 120, 121, 122, 123, 128

F

Faceplate 122

Family Room 13, 14, 15, 18, 20, 28, 29, 30, 43, 48, 138, 139, 141

Fan 8, 28, 35, 37, 44, 62, 67, 79

Feed through 9, 64, 67

Firecracker 133

Fireplace 10, 35, 48, 94

Fixture box 70, 72

Fixture relay module 9, 70, 72

Flag 36

Floodlight 10, 115, 116

Fountain 8, 15, 35, 36, 51, 53

Four-way switch 9, 67, 75, 76, 85

Front porch 29, 32, 39, 41, 134, 135

G

Garage 10, 17, 21, 24, 43, 51, 97, 98, 99

Garage door 10, 21, 43, 97, 98, 99

Gas fireplace 10, 94

GFCI 36, 156

Glass 10, 112

Glass breakage detector 10, 112

H

Halloween 16, 36

Handheld 8, 10, 43, 47, 103, 105, 107, 108, 172

Hardwired controls 9, 55, 57, 59, 61, 63, 65, 67, 69, 71, 73, 75

Heater 8, 12, 17, 28, 35, 37, 151, 152, 155, 156

High-end switch module 62, 67

Holiday 8, 16, 35, 36, 40

Home security 18, 19, 25, 102, 103, 105, 107, 109, 111, 113, 115, 117, 181

HomeSeer 133, 181

Hot tub 12, 78, 151, 152, 156

Hot wire 9, 56, 65, 68, 71, 72, 73, 74, 81, 82, 83, 146

House-code 28

I

Incandescent 26, 70

Infrared 11, 17, 21, 31, 37, 48, 121, 123, 125, 127, 129

Infrared Interface 121, 123, 125, 127, 129,

Interface 11, 12, 17, 18, 38, 46, 92, 94, 96, 99, 100, 119, 120, 121, 122, 123, 124, 125, 126, 127, 128, 129, 131, 132, 133, 134, 135, 136, 139, 141, 142, 143, 145, 154, 157, 168, 171, 172, 181

Interference 12, 44, 45, 79, 129, 135, 161, 163, 164, 165, 166, 167, 169, 170, 176

Internet 12, 14, 21, 24, 25, 133, 136, 139, 140, 150, 151, 152, 153, 154, 155, 156, 157, 159

IR Blaster 120, 121

K

Keychain 8, 10, 13, 14, 46, 52, 103, 106, 107, 108

Keychain remote 8, 10, 13, 46, 52, 103, 106, 107, 108

Keypad 48, 49, 69, 70, 104, 114, 128, 129, 146, 147, 148, 149, 151, 152, 166, 169, 171, 172

Keypad controller 148, 149

Kitchen 18, 28, 51, 52, 70, 127, 144

L

Lamp 7, 17, 19, 23, 24, 25, 26, 27, 29, 30, 31, 32, 35, 37, 43, 51, 61, 62, 66, 80, 96, 103, 134, 136, 137, 138, 139, 140, 142, 143, 145, 146, 147, 149, 150, 159, 160, 165, 167, 171, 172, 177

Learning Remote 48, 49

LED 46, 47, 48, 49, 50, 79, 108, 110, 114, 121, 123, 124, 125, 129, 160, 163, 164

Light switch 8, 15, 16, 28, 49, 51, 55, 68, 146, 159

Living room 15, 24, 28, 29, 30, 32, 38, 43, 46, 144, 161, 167, 168

Local control 7, 27, 29, 30, 80

Low-Voltage 8, 10, 23, 26, 28, 36, 37, 51, 62, 79, 87, 89, 90, 91, 94, 95, 96, 97, 99, 101, 102, 127, 159

M

Magnetic switch 96, 97, 98, 99, 109, 110, 111, 112

Master switch 74, 75, 78, 86, 87

Maxi-controller 8, 35, 38, 79, 124, 148, 149, 177

Microphone 158, 159, 160

Microswitch 89, 96, 97, 98, 101, 102, 128

Mini-controller 7, 11, 23, 24, 25, 26, 28, 29, 30, 31, 32, 38, 39, 41, 42, 67, 69, 123, 125, 129, 142, 145, 148, 153

Mini-timer 8, 35, 36, 38, 39, 40, 41, 42, 53, 99, 126, 131

Momentary 90, 95, 128

Motion 8, 10, 18, 20, 51, 52, 53, 103, 104, 105, 106, 113, 114, 115, 116, 134, 135

Motion detector 8, 10, 51, 52, 103, 104, 106, 113, 114, 115, 116, 134

Movie 18, 21, 78, 120, 142, 150, 156, 157, 171, 172, 173

Multiple Relay Controller 10, 92

Music 13, 14, 15, 16, 18, 21, 37, 43, 89, 125, 128, 141, 142, 143, 150, 158, 172

Mute 10, 15, 29, 49, 89, 100, 101, 102, 120, 128, 129

N

National Electrical Code 55, 68

NEC 55, 68, 72

Neutral wire 9, 56, 65, 67, 68, 69, 71, 72, 85, 86, 147

Night-light 127, 140

Nightstand 28, 31, 39

Noise 9, 12, 79, 115, 158, 160, 162, 165, 166, 167, 168

Noise filter 12, 165, 168

Noise reduction 9, 79

O

Outdoor 8, 10, 17, 26, 32, 35, 36, 37, 51, 52, 80, 115, 134
Outdoor lighting 8, 35, 36, 37, 51
Outlet module 8, 9, 55, 64, 65, 67, 73
Overhead light 144, 145, 157

P

Panic 105, 106, 116
Patio 15, 44, 51, 53, 78, 80
Photocell 8, 17, 35, 41, 42, 52
Photocell controller 8, 17, 35, 41
Pigtails 61, 64, 65, 75, 76
Placeholder 138, 139, 143, 150
Plug-in modules 19, 53, 55, 77, 80, 161, 165
Porch 13, 14, 20, 29, 32, 39, 41, 42, 46, 94, 134, 135, 157
Power line interface module 11, 131
Power tap 30
Powerflash 10, 94, 95, 96, 98, 99, 101, 128, 159, 172
Probes 11, 125, 126, 127
Pull-chain 17, 51

R

Rain delay 10, 92
Reflected light 49
Remote control 8, 11, 13, 16, 19, 20, 24, 25, 27, 30, 31, 35, 37, 38, 42, 43, 48, 55, 61, 62, 66, 75, 89, 92, 94, 97, 98, 100, 103, 107, 108, 115, 117, 119, 120, 122, 125, 128, 129, 135, 158, 172
Remote doorbell 10, 94
Remote thermostat 10, 95
Repeater 12, 45, 47, 166, 169
Rewire 69
RF 12, 43, 44, 45, 47, 48, 127, 129, 179

RF Repeater 45, 47
Rocker 25, 29, 30, 31, 32, 38, 40, 41, 50, 51, 62, 77, 105, 123, 125, 146, 147
Rocker switch 25, 29, 30, 31, 32, 38, 40, 41, 50, 51, 62, 77, 105, 123, 125, 146, 147

S

Satellite radio 125
Scene lighting 9, 78
Scenes 11, 67, 70, 78, 131, 139, 140, 141, 143, 145, 146, 147, 148, 149, 150
Scent trigger ????
Security code 107, 113, 152, 153, 154
Security console 10, 45, 103, 104, 105, 106, 107, 108, 109, 110, 113
Security remote 10, 103, 105
Security system 10, 18, 21, 45, 102, 103, 104, 106, 107, 108, 111
Serial port 132, 133, 134, 172
Signal conflict ????
Smarthome 24, 133, 139, 181
Software 11, 17, 18, 21, 38, 133, 134, 139, 140, 145, 150, 154, 157
Speaker mute 10, 100, 101
Special-purpose 23
Sprinkler 10, 18, 21, 36, 93, 94, 159
Sunrise 11, 17, 41, 42, 134
Sunset 11, 17, 41, 42, 134, 135, 136, 137, 138, 143, 144
Surge protector 31, 135, 162, 163, 165, 168
Switch box 68, 69, 72, 82
Switch leg 9, 68, 72, 75, 81, 82, 83, 84
Switch module 8, 19, 31, 55, 61, 62, 63, 64, 67, 70, 74, 75, 77, 85, 87, 93, 140, 169, 172
Switch-leg 9, 75

T

Telephone 12, 18, 89, 94, 107, 114, 115, 128, 140, 151, 152, 153, 154, 156

Telephone controller 151, 153, 154

Thief 97, 103, 115

Thermostat 6, 10, 90, 94, 95, 120, 139, 152, 155

Three-way switch 9, 66, 74, 78, 83

Timed events 11, 39, 134, 137, 138, 154, 157

Touch-tone 12, 135, 151, 152, 153, 154, 156

Transceiver 8, 43, 44, 45, 46, 47, 48, 49, 107, 129, 172

Transmitter 109, 110, 111, 112, 178

Traveler 75, 76, 84, 85, 86

Triggers 11, 114, 143, 144, 149

U

Universal relay module 10, 90, 91, 92, 94, 95, 96, 97, 98, 99, 100, 120, 128

Universal remote 8, 43, 46, 48, 49, 119, 129, 172

USB 132, 133, 135, 171, 172

V

Vacation 16, 103, 117, 132, 138, 152

Voice announcement 12, 157

Voice control 12, 132, 133, 156, 158, 159

Voice control module 12, 159

Voice mail 153

Voice message 114, 139

Voice recognition 12, 139, 156, 158, 159, 171, 172

Volume 14, 49, 100, 101, 122, 124, 128, 129, 166

W

Wall controller 9, 67, 69, 146, 148

Wall Switch 8, 19, 27, 30, 31, 32, 49, 50, 51, 52, 53, 55, 61, 62, 67, 69, 71, 78, 131, 142, 146, 169, 171

Water heater 12, 152, 156

Window sensor 10, 103, 104, 105, 106, 108, 109, 110, 111, 115

Wiring device 56, 57

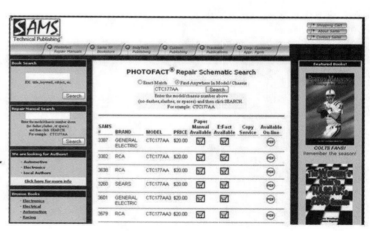